Approaches to Social Inequality and Difference

Series Editors
Edvard Hviding
University of Bergen
Bergen, Norway

Synnøve Bendixsen
University of Bergen
Bergen, Norway

The book series contributes a wealth of new perspectives aiming to denaturalize ongoing social, economic and cultural trends such as the processes of 'crimigration' and racialization, fast-growing social-economic inequalities, depoliticization or technologization of policy, and simultaneously a politicization of difference. By treating naturalization simultaneously as a phenomenon in the world, and as a rudimentary analytical concept for further development and theoretical diversification, we identify a shared point of departure for all volumes in this series, in a search to analyze how difference is produced, governed and reconfigured in a rapidly changing world. By theorizing rich, globally comparative ethnographic materials on how racial/cultural/civilization differences are currently specified and naturalized, the series will throw new light on crucial links between differences, whether biologized and culturalized, and various forms of 'social inequality' that are produced in contemporary global social and political formations.

More information about this series at
http://www.springer.com/series/14775

Margit Ystanes • Iselin Åsedotter Strønen
Editors

The Social Life of Economic Inequalities in Contemporary Latin America

Decades of Change

palgrave
macmillan

Editors
Margit Ystanes
University of Bergen
Bergen, Norway

Iselin Åsedotter Strønen
University of Bergen and the Chr.
Michelsen Institute (CMI)
Bergen, Norway

Approaches to Social Inequality and Difference
ISBN 978-3-319-61535-6   ISBN 978-3-319-61536-3   (eBook)
DOI 10.1007/978-3-319-61536-3

Library of Congress Control Number: 2017955007

© The Editor(s) (if applicable) and The Author(s) 2018. This book is an open access publication.
Open Access This book is licensed under the terms of the Creative Commons Attribution 4.0 International License (http://creativecommons.org/licenses/by/4.0/), which permits use, sharing, adaptation, distribution and reproduction in any medium or format, as long as you give appropriate credit to the original author(s) and the source, provide a link to the Creative Commons license and indicate if changes were made.
The images or other third party material in this book are included in the book's Creative Commons license, unless indicated otherwise in a credit line to the material. If material is not included in the book's Creative Commons license and your intended use is not permitted by statutory regulation or exceeds the permitted use, you will need to obtain permission directly from the copyright holder.
The use of general descriptive names, registered names, trademarks, service marks, etc. in this publication does not imply, even in the absence of a specific statement, that such names are exempt from the relevant protective laws and regulations and therefore free for general use.
The publisher, the authors and the editors are safe to assume that the advice and information in this book are believed to be true and accurate at the date of publication. Neither the publisher nor the authors or the editors give a warranty, express or implied, with respect to the material contained herein or for any errors or omissions that may have been made. The publisher remains neutral with regard to jurisdictional claims in published maps and institutional affiliations.

Cover photo © peeterv / iStock. All rights reserved.

Printed on acid-free paper

This Palgrave Macmillan imprint is published by Springer Nature
The registered company is Springer International Publishing AG
The registered company address is: Gewerbestrasse 11, 6330 Cham, Switzerland

This book is dedicated to the numerous people across Latin America who resist and struggle against social inequalities every day.

Acknowledgements

This volume grew out of a workshop on inequality in Latin America, organised by the editors in Bergen, in March 2015. We would like to extend our most heartfelt gratitude to everyone who was somehow involved in this event and made possible the stimulating discussions and friendly atmosphere that characterised it. Sarah A. Radcliffe and Cristiano de Moraes both participated in the workshop, and while unfortunately other commitments hindered their inclusion in this book project, we are deeply grateful for their contributions at the event.

We would also like to thank Christian Michelsen Institute (CMI) for hosting the workshop. To Inge Erling Tesdal at CROP/UiB Global, we could not possibly thank you enough for all the administrative work and support you provided and for making sure every detail of the event ran smoothly. Charlotte Lillefjære-Tertnæs and the rest of the staff at CROP and UiB Global also contributed in various ways and provided a supportive milieu for the event.

Funding for the workshop was generously provided by NorLARNet (Norwegian Latin America Research Network) and the Research Council of Norway's SAMKUL programme (Cultural conditions underlying social change).

At the Department of Social Anthropology, University of Bergen, we would like to thank our colleagues for support and stimulating conversations. In particular, we extend our gratitude to Palgrave Macmillan's series editors, Synnøve Bendixsen and Edvard Hviding, for taking an interest in this project and for their assistance along the way.

The contributions in this volume have been developed further since the original workshop. Some of the authors have come to the project at later stages, but have also participated in various rounds of revision. We thank you all for being so willing to rework and revise your contributions according to our suggestions and thus making this a genuinely collaborative effort.

On a more personal note, the editors would also like to thank our families and friends for their support and patience throughout the period we have been working on this volume.

Margit extends her most heartfelt gratitude to her parents, Sunneva and Per Ystanes, for their unwavering emotional support and practical assistance with all kinds of things. I am also deeply thankful to friends for still being there despite my prolonged absences, whether spent in my office or doing fieldwork. Finally, I would like to express my deep gratitude to Alejandro Huidobro Goya for sharing both life and work with me. Thank you for inspiring me every day, for making me grow in ways I never imagined and for keeping everything together while the finalising of this book absorbed me. Most importantly, thank you for filling my life with love and laughter.

Iselin is deeply grateful to her parents, Frode and Åse KarinStrønen, who as always have provided vital emotional and practical support in the process of finishing this book. I don't know how I would have done it without you. Thank you. My heartfelt gratitude is also extended to Marieke Mulders Steine for moral support during the last-minute frenzies, and to Siv Mælen for always being there. Thank you also to Nefissa Naguib and Maria Victoria Canino, both of whom provided important and wise words of advice in the process of finalising the book. As always, my deepest gratitude goes to my daughter, Cecilia, who stoically has waited out hours and hours of mummy being lost behind a computer screen in the final phase of this process. You must be the most patient five-year-old in the world. Thank you for reminding me every day that there are more important things to life than writing books, the importance of the topic notwithstanding.

Rio de Janeiro and Bergen,   Iselin Åsedotter Strønen and Margit Ystanes
April 19, 2017

Contents

Part I Social Lives, Economic Ideas   1

1 Introduction   3
   Iselin Åsedotter Strønen and Margit Ystanes

2 Reformism, Class Conciliation and the Pink Tide:
   Material Gains and Their Limits   35
   Pedro Mendes Loureiro

Part II The Case of Brazil   57

3 Entangled Inequalities, State, and Social Policies
   in Contemporary Brazil   59
   Sérgio Costa

4 #sosfavelas: Digital Representations of Violence
   and Inequality in Rio de Janeiro   81
   Margit Ystanes

5 Urban Development in Rio de Janeiro During
   the 'Pink Tide': Bridging Socio-Spatial Divides
   Between the Formal and Informal City?   107
   Celina Myrann Sørbøe

6 Meanings of Poverty: An Ethnography of Bolsa
   Familia Beneficiaries in Rio de Janeiro/Brazil   129
   Michele de Lavra Pinto

Part III Subjectivities and Structures   151

7 Political Polarisation, Colonial Inequalities
   and the Crisis of Modernity in Venezuela   153
   Iselin Åsedotter Strønen

8 Market Liberalisation and the (Un-)making
   of the 'Perfect Neoliberal Citizen': Enactments
   of Gendered and Racialised Inequalities Among
   Peruvian Vendors   183
   Cecilie Vindal Ødegaard

9 Coming of Age in the Penal System: Neoliberalism,
   'Mano Dura' and the Reproduction of 'Racialised'
   Inequality in Honduras   205
   Lirio Gutiérrez Rivera, Iselin Åsedotter Strønen,
   and Margit Ystanes

Part IV Land, the Eternal Legacy of Inequality   229

10 Settlers and Squatters: The Production of Social
   Inequalities in the Peruvian Desert   231
   Astrid B. Stensrud

11 Latin American Inequalities and Reparations   253
   Marvin T. Brown

Part V   Postscript   273

12   Postscript   275
       Sian Lazar

Index   283

Contributing Authors

Marvin T. Brown teaches ethics in the Philosophy Department at the University of San Francisco. As a teacher, consultant, and writer, he has written about processes of dealing with disagreement, the ethics of organisations, and more recently alternative economics. Brown's books have been translated into Spanish, Portuguese, German, Polish, Italian, Korean, and Chinese. His last book, *Civilizing the Economy* (2010), describes how a civic approach to the economy allows us to design just and sustainable systems of provision. Brown has given presentations and workshops on dialogical decision-making and related topics in Argentina, Venezuela, and Brazil. His current work aims to demonstrate the connections between violations of our common humanity and the challenge of climate change.

Sérgio Costa is Professor of Sociology at the Institute for Latin American Studies and Institute of Sociology at Freie Universität Berlin. He is a cospokesperson of desiguALdades.net, Research Network on Interdependent Inequalities in Latin America, and spokesperson of the Merian International Centre Conviviality in Unequal Societies. His disciplinary interests are political sociology, comparative sociology and contemporary social theory. He has specialised in democracy and cultural difference, racism and antiracism, as well as social inequalities and transnational politics. His most recent book publication is *Global Entangled Inequalities: Conceptual Debates and Evidence from Latin America* (co-editor). For more details, see: http://www.lai.fu-berlin.de/en/homepages/costa/index.html

Michele de Lavra Pinto has a PhD in History and Politics from CPDOC/ FundaçãoGetúlio Vargas (FGV/RJ), a Master's in Social Anthropology and licentiate degree in Social Science from the Federal University of Rio Grande do Sul (UFRGS) in Brazil. She has edited the books *Youth, Consumption and Education 1,2,3 and 4* and the book *Consumption and Sociabilities: Spaces, Meanings and Reflections*. Her research centres mainly on the areas of consumption anthropology and economic anthropology.

Sian Lazar is a Senior Lecturer in Social Anthropology at the University of Cambridge, UK. Her research focuses on citizenship, social movements and collective politics more broadly in Latin America, especially Argentina and Bolivia. She is the author of El Alto, Rebel City. Self and Citizenship in Andean Bolivia (2008), and The Social Life of Politics. Ethics, Kinship and Union Activism in Argentina (2017), among other publications.

Pedro Mendes Loureiro holds a BA in Economics from the Federal University of Minas Gerais (UFMG, Brazil) and an MSc in Economics from the University of Campinas (Unicamp, Brazil). He is an Economics PhD candidate at SOAS, University of London, researching the left-of-centre governments in Latin America (the "Pink Tide"). This research project seeks to unpack the advances and limitations of their economic and social policies, focusing on the politicisation of shifts in class inequality and capital accumulation. His other research interests include heterodox theoretical frameworks (Marxist, post-Keynesian, institutionalist), state theory, interdisciplinary and pluralist approaches, mixed methods, financialisation and Latin American economic history.

Cecilie Vindal Ødegaard is an associate professor at the University of Bergen, Department of Social Anthropology. Her research focuses on informal economies under neoliberal regimes, gender, inequalities, cosmologies and Andean conceptualisations of nature. Based on research in Peru since the 1990s, articles of Ødegaard have appeared in journals such as *Journal of the Royal Anthropological Institute, Ethnos Journal of Anthropology, Journal of Development Studies, Journal of Borderlands Studies* and *Journal of Ethnobiology and Ethnomedicine*, among others. She is the author of *Mobility, Markets and Indigenous Socialities: Contemporary Migration in the Peruvian Andes* and has contributed with research-based chapters in the volumes *Contested Powers: The Politics of Energy and Development in Latin America* (University of Chicago Press 2015) and

Critical Anthropological Engagements in Human Alterity and Difference (Palgrave Macmillan 2016).

Lirio Gutiérrez Rivera studied anthropology (Universidad de los Andes—Colombia) and political science (FreieUniversität Berlin). Currently, she is an assistant professor at the Department of Political Science, Universidad Nacional de Colombia—Medellin Campus. Prior to relocating to Colombia, Lirio was a postdoc researcher at the desigualdades.net Research Network at the Freie Universität Berlin. She researches urban violence, marginality, contemporary prison and incarceration, and Central America migration. In the latter, she has researched Palestinian migration to Honduras and their emergence as an economic elite, as well as Honduran women fleeing gender violence and crime in their home country. She has carried out fieldwork in Honduras and Colombia. Her current research focuses on urban politics, planning, and gender in Medellin, Colombia.

Celina Myrann Sørbøe has a Master's degree in Latin American studies from the University of Oslo. She is currently a PhD candidate at the Norwegian Institute for Urban and Regional Research, Oslo, and Akershus University College of Applied Sciences. Sørbøe has lived and conducted fieldwork in Rio de Janeiro for two years between 2012 and 2016, eight months of which she lived in Rocinha (four months in 2012 and four months in 2016).

Astrid B. Stensrud holds a PhD in social anthropology from the University of Oslo. She currently has a postdoctoral position at the Department of Social Anthropology, University of Oslo, as part of the project "Overheating: The Three Crises of Globalization". Having done ethnographic research in the Peruvian Andes since 2001, her current research interests include political practices, difference and inequality, environment-human relations, climate change, water management, globalisation and the state. The PhD dissertation focused on entrepreneurial activities and animistic practices in a working-class neighbourhood in Cusco, Peru. Stensrud's current postdoctoral project examines responses to climate change, water politics and identity politics in the Majes-Colca watershed in Arequipa, Peru.

Iselin Åsedotter Strønen is Associate Professor of Social Anthropology at the University of Bergen, Norway, and affiliated researcher at the Christian Michelsen Institute (CMI), Norway. She has done extensive field research in Venezuela since 2005, focusing on the relationship between the urban popular sectors and the Venezuelan state in the context of the Bolivarian process. Thematically, she has explored issues such as participatory politics, gender, state transformations, oil culture, consumption, corruption, poverty and inequality. Her latest publications include *Grassroots Politics and Oil Culture in Venezuela: The Revolutionary Petro-State* (Palgrave, 2017), and Everyday Crafting of the Bolivarian State: Lower-Level Public Officials and Grass Root Activism in Venezuela, which appeared in *Latin American Perspectives*. Strønen is also involved in ethnographic research in Angola and Brazil.

Margit Ystanes is postdoctoral fellow at the Department of Social Anthropology, University of Bergen. She obtained her PhD from the University of Bergen in 2011, with the dissertation *Precarious Trust: Problems of Managing Self and Sociality in Guatemala*. Ystanes' current work investigates the use of sporting mega-events as a tool for urban and economic development in Rio de Janeiro. In particular, she focuses on the use of forced evictions, and the resistance against them, as well as their impact upon social relationships and stated aims of poverty reduction and urban integration. Ystanes' work includes the co-edited volume (with Vigdis Broch-Due) *Trusting and Its Tribulations: Interdisciplinary Engagements with Intimacy, Sociality and Trust* and the documentary *Dirty Games: Olympic Evictions in Rio de Janeiro* (co-directed with José Alejandro Huidobro Goya, 2017).

List of Photos

Photo 4.1 Interconnected worlds: as Rio prepared to host the 2016 Olympics, the hashtag #cidadeolympica, used by the city administration for propaganda purposes, was inscribed onto the urban landscape as a physical manifestation of the interconnection between the virtual and "real life" (Photo: Margit Ystanes) — 88

Photo 4.2 Graffiti in Vila Autódromo shows that the residents consider the confiscation of their neighbourhood as a transfer of public land to private actors: "When there are no more public areas to sell, they will sell the favelas. Who will protest?" (Photo: Margit Ystanes) — 97

Photo 7.1 Statue of Simón Bolívar in Paseo de los Próceres in Caracas. Note the wall carvings behind him. Bolívar liberated Venezuela and several of the surrounding countries from the Spanish Crown. He was from a wealthy creole family, and driven by his political ambitions and his (for the time) progressive, egalitarian views, he split off from his class background. This is also what has given him such mythical qualities in the context of the Bolivarian process (Photo by the author) — 165

Photo 7.2 Typical *barrio* homes (Photo by the author) — 173

Photo 7.3 Gated mansions in an affluent neighbourhood in the east of Caracas (Photo by the author) — 174

Photo 7.4 Labour Day in Western Caracas, May 1, 2011 (Photo by the author) — 176

Photo 10.1 'New Hope' (*Nueva Esperanza*) is the name of one the marketplaces in Villa El Pedregal and the name of the association of vendors and merchants (asociación de comerciantes) who work there (Photo by the author)   241

Photo 10.2 Day labourers (*peones*) harvesting potatoes on the land of a settler farmer (*colono*) (Photo by the author)   247

List of Figure

Fig 3.1　Average monthly earnings in Brazil, 2012 (average earnings from the main occupation of the population over 16 years old) calculated for the intersection of inequality factors: sex, race, and region (figures in Brazilian Reais as of September 2012) NE Northeast, CW Center West　　67

PART I

Social Lives, Economic Ideas

CHAPTER 1

Introduction

Iselin Åsedotter Strønen and Margit Ystanes

Latin America has for long been the most unequal continent in the world. At the turn of the millennium, voters rebelled against this situation by ushering left-wing and centre-left political candidates into power in country after country. The so-called Pink Tide emerged, and hopes of more equal, economically self-supported societies sprung up all over the continent. After decades of neoliberal policies, increasing inequality and escalating protest, questions of redistribution and social and economic rights were now finally central to the political agenda. In that process, socio-cultural hierarchies and their interconnections with economic inequalities were also forcefully contested and challenged.

Ever since the colonial encounter between pre-Hispanic peoples and European conquistadors, Latin American social orders have been built on a foundation of inequality. This foundation is the outcome of a complex interplay between economic and political relations, social imaginaries and notions of "otherness", kinship and morality—usually conceptualised as class, ethnicity, "race" and gender. Thus, both historically and today,

---

I.Å. Strønen
University of Bergen and the Chr. Michelsen Institute (CMI), Bergen, Norway

M. Ystanes (✉)
University of Bergen, Bergen, Norway

© The Author(s) 2018
M. Ystanes, I.Å. Strønen (eds.), *The Social Life of Economic Inequalities in Contemporary Latin America*, Approaches to Social Inequality and Difference, DOI 10.1007/978-3-319-61536-3_1

inequality in Latin America has never been a question of economic relations alone, but an outcome of their entanglements with social relations, value systems, ideals and notions of morality and of human difference (see, e.g. Casaús Arzú 2007; Edmonds 2010; Hale 2006; Larkins 2015; Martinez-Alier 1989; Milton 2007; Nelson 1999; Scheper-Hughes 1993; Stepan 1991; Streicker 1995; Ystanes 2016). Latin American social orders are therefore complex and hierarchical, based on a multifaceted set of principles, and have been so since their inception.

This edited volume explores how attempts to change historically constituted inequalities rubbed against their foundation during the Pink Tide. The two decades that have passed since the election of Hugo Chávez in 1998, representing the beginning of a new era, have indeed been marked by change. However, those pushing for change also found that their scope of possibility was far from unlimited. Furthermore, many key issues, such as security politics, land distribution and taxation, neoliberal policies, modes of governance and so on, have frequently not been genuinely re-thought or questioned, even by Pink Tide governments. The neoliberal strategies for addressing these issues are indeed part of a deeply integrated *doxa* for large segments of society. They also dovetail with ideas and approaches that have long historical roots in Latin America. Hence, the purpose of this volume is to deepen existing understandings of what was achieved during the Pink Tide era in Latin America and of what was outside the scope of possibility.

Among the unquestionable achievements are the formation of new political and social subjectivities and the advancement of political and socio-cultural agendas from below. Concurrently, many people experienced significant improvements in their material well-being. Even so, as many of the chapters in this book point to, gains in the social and economic domain were and are fragile. They have proved highly susceptible to reversal in the face of a return to right-wing politics, falling commodity prices and economic austerity. An important conclusion emerging from this edited volume is thus that the achievements towards greater equality during the Pink Tide were important and substantial, yet the basic tenets of hierarchical social models remain.

This conclusion is not only supported by what took place in Pink Tide countries, but also by a comparison with processes unfolding in countries that only flirted superficially with the turn to the left, such as Peru and Honduras. For example, Ystanes' chapter (Chap. 4, this volume) shows that the militarisation of urban spaces in Rio de Janeiro has common features with the criminalisation of male, dark-skinned, poor youth in Honduras, as explored in the chapter by Gutierrez Rivera, Strønen and Ystanes (Chap. 9). Furthermore, unequal access to land and the legacy of slavery are both fundamental causes of contemporary inequality in Latin America. Nevertheless, as Brown discusses (Chap. 11), a genuine redistribution of land or reparations for slavery to Afro-descendants have not been prioritised on the political agenda anywhere on the continent, Pink Tide countries or elsewhere. The comparative approach of this volume thus presents us with a sobering reminder of the ruptures produced by the Pink Tide as well as the continuities. As the Pink Tide ebbs, much has changed, yet Latin America remains marked by economic models interwoven in global capitalism, disproportionally benefiting local and global elites, and social models continuously reproducing hierarchical lifeworlds and social orders.

Several of the chapters in this book deal with Brazil, and we have organised them together as a separate section. Our justification for paying such keen attention to the Brazilian case, and in particular how it unfolded in Rio de Janeiro, at the expense of a more diverse selection of case studies, is threefold. Firstly, Brazil has overwhelmingly been considered one of the most successful instances of Pink Tide politics. This makes taking a closer look at the contradictions of this case worthwhile. Secondly, by exploring both the successes of the Pink Tide, such as the Bolsa Familia programme, and parallel processes based on neoliberal thinking, such as the militarisation of urban spaces, this helps us understand the complexity of Pink Tide contexts. Thirdly, by contrasting limitations in the macro-political scope of possibility with social and political struggles as they unfold locally, we gain a better insight into how these two levels shape and inform each other. With regard to the latter two points, Rio de Janeiro constitutes a particularly interesting location. During the Pink Tide years, this city hosted four sporting mega-events.[1] Such events are known to accelerate urban development processes (Gaffney 2010), yet also create considerable resistance (Cornelissen 2012), and indeed, intense contestations between political, social and economic aspirations from above and below played out in Rio during the Pink Tide years. This makes Rio de Janeiro an interesting location for exploring the gains and limitations of official policies and social movements alike. Underlying all of these efforts is an attention to the historically constituted values and ideas contributing to shaping economic processes in Brazil and beyond.

Disentangling "the Economy"

The title of this book, *The Social Life of Economic Inequalities in Contemporary Latin America: Decades of Change*, points to the importance of grasping the complex interplay between multifaceted and historically constituted configurations of inequality, economic processes and social life. The temporal-analytical axis guiding our analysis has three elements. The starting point is historically constituted forms of inequality on the Latin American continent, and their contemporary configuration. The second element is the accentuation of inequalities during the neoliberal turn. The third analytical frame is how different forms of inequalities have been contested, challenged as well as reproduced during the so-called Pink Tide. The majority of the chapters are qualitative in their approach, allowing us to draw upon the capacity of ethnography to engage with human existence as it unfolds within "thickly" conceived lifeworlds. This approach challenges us to think through the complex entanglements between economic processes and socio-cultural hierarchies.

Given that economic inequality is a constituent and defining feature of Latin American societies, we pose that this feature has to be an integral part of any meaningful analysis of how the Pink Tide era unfolded. The economic domain, in a reductionist sense, may be understood as monetary policies, economic reforms, macroeconomic structures and fluctuations, budgetary allocations and so on. However, as anthropologists, we are trained to think about the economic domain in a much wider sense. Indeed, the economic life of any society is firmly tied in with its social life and notions of morality and value. This insight was firmly established by Polyani (1944), who argued that the ascendancy of market rationality and its accompanying economistic reductionism was not only incompatible with, but also ultimately experienced as, an assault on social life and social processes. Nevertheless, just like the Kula exchange of bracelets and necklaces that Bronislaw Malinowski (2014) famously studied in the Trobriand Islands during World War I (and which inspired Polyani's work), contemporary capitalist exchange is not an outcome of "natural economic laws", but of the actions, beliefs and values of those involved in it. These processes are always historically contingent, and always affecting, shaping, experienced and conceptualised incongruously by unequally positioned groups and persons. Different socio-economic groups, in turn, are configured by complex cultural, social and moral hierarchical schemes.

As the Pink Tide is now ebbing, the critique of its shortcomings often centres on the choice of economic policies of the governments in question. Our contribution to this debate is to firmly state that economic processes cannot be understood through assessing economic policy choices or models alone, because social imaginaries and economic ideas are embedded in one another. Together they contribute to shaping and moulding human communities and economic conditions (Brown 2010). Indeed, while often perceived as neutral and objective, our ideas, models and scientific concepts grow out of culturally and historically specific contexts (see, e.g. Buck-Morss 2009; Daston and Galison 1992; Martin 1990; Ortner 2016; Stepan 1991). The work they do in the world is discursive in the Foucaultian (1981) sense—they do not only represent attempts to describe and analyse reality, they also reflect ideological currents and contribute to shaping the world. Within the economic discipline, this problematic rose to the surface after the financial crisis in 2007, when the orthodoxy that undergirded the crisis was critiqued by students and academics alike (see, e.g. Inman 2013). Indeed, critical economists suggest the discipline has privileged tools that are incompatible with the analysis of the real world (Reinert et al. 2017:10).

Here, our ambition is to explore the encounter with the "real world" of some of the economic policies shaping and moulding Latin American societies at this historical moment. We do this through ethnographic explorations of social life as it unfolds in contexts marked by these policies, and through discussions of the contexts and principles framing contemporary inequalities. The volume is multidisciplinary, bringing together scholars from different fields. What unites us all is the critical lens through which we approach economic policies and the historically and socially constituted ideas that undergird them.

Fragile Changes

As mentioned above, the most central argument presented in this volume is that in spite of the advances made during the Pink Tide, deep-seated aspects of Latin American lifeworlds upholding hierarchal social orders remain largely intact. This, in turn, makes for an unstable foundation for advancing equality, in both its material and socio-cultural dimensions. As the chapters from Brazil and Venezuela show, popular movements, taking advantage of the political space opened up by socially progressive governments, challenged historical discrimination based on class, ethnicity, "race" and gender. Yet, this also produced a counter-reaction amongst traditional power holders—that is, the lighter skinned and socio-economically more privileged parts of society—who fiercely contested claims to socio-economic redistribution and socio-cultural recognition emerging from below. In Brazil, the traditional, right-wing elites have regained power, and there are very real possibilities that Venezuela, in deep crisis as we finalise this work, will soon find itself in the same position. What the outcomes of these processes will be remains to be seen.

Another important dimension of the Pink Tide era is the absence of a fundamental restructuring of "trickle-up" economic models. As Costa (Chap. 3, this volume) shows, the tax systems of Latin American countries remain skewed towards upholding rather than mitigating inequalities produced by capitalist markets. Income and consumption are taxed highly, while taxation on capital, profit and high income is low or non-existent. This means that lower-income families and individuals, who spend a much larger chunk of their income on consumption, carry the tax burden disproportionately. At the same time, the concentration of wealth on a few hands remains largely unchallenged, even under Pink Tide governments. Why, when as Costa (Chap. 3) demonstrates, tax reform would be the most efficient way to reduce inequality, has this not been done? In answering this question, as Costa points to, one has to take into consideration that traditional political and economic elites continue to define the scope of possibility in Latin America—also in the Pink Tide countries. One of the consequences of this limited scope for de facto redistribution is, as Loureiro (Chap. 2, this volume) shows, that Pink Tide governments relied on increased state spending in order to strengthen socio-economic vulnerable groups, rather than progressive redistribution. Significantly, the increased state spending was made possible by the favourable boom in global commodity prices—not least oil and gas—occurring in parallel with the Pink Tide era. The fragility of this model is highly evident now, after the economic downturn starting in 2013—above all in oil-reliant Venezuela. Whilst it is very easy to criticise various Pink Tide governments for pursuing such a model, it is analytically unsatisfactory if we do not simultaneously consider their actual scope of possibility in the economic and political domain. As Lazar emphasises in the postscript (Chap. 12), this space has been quite limited during the Pink Tide. This concerns both Latin American nations' unequal integration into global commodity and financial markets, and the limited room for bargaining vis-à-vis domestic and foreign powerholders.

Colonial Inequality: Conquest, Slavery and the Invention of "Race"

Before we continue to analyse the economic dimensions of Latin American societal developments, it is useful to go back to the early formations of Latin American societies. It is important to remember that they have been highly complex, yet essentially unequal social orders since their inception. This can be illustrated by Martinez-Alier's (1989) comparison of nineteenth-century Cuba to Dumont's (1980) analysis of the Indian caste system. While Dumont considers hierarchy in India to be governed by a single principle that encompasses all others—the ritual opposition between purity and impurity—Cuba prior to the abolishment of slavery in 1886 was more complicated. Here, people were positioned in a hierarchical social order according to numerous principles that were often expressed in contradictory ways in a single person. The opposition between slaves and free persons, illegitimate and legitimate birth, dark skinned and light skinned persons, African and European origin, poor and rich, infamous and honourable, mixed and unmixed, plebeians and nobles, and so on, were all operative principles in the Cuban slave society (Martinez-Alier 1989:131). People did not always fall neatly into one side of these oppositions; a light skinned person was not necessarily wealthy, honourable and of legitimate birth, just like a dark-skinned person was not necessarily poor, of illegitimate birth or a slave. As such, Latin American colonial hierarchies were multifaceted sites of contestation rather than fixed entities.

The origins of this situation can be traced back to how the Europeans' encounter in 1492 with what they coined the "New World" profoundly shaped their ideas of human difference. Earlier, notions of European superiority rested partly on medieval theology, in which blackness was often linked to the devil and sin. Africans were considered inferior because Europeans associated their appearance with this colour. There was thus a focus on differences in physical appearance, but this was not yet thought about as biological "race". Instead, the word "race" was understood as "lineage" in European languages at the time—that is, it referred to a notion of kinship rather than fundamentally different kinds of human beings (Wade 1997). However, as Europe embarked on the era of discovery and colonialism, a multitude of concerns—economical, practical, philosophical and theological—merged in a single conception—that of human "races" (see Ystanes 2011:92–108 for a discussion of this process). DaMatta points out that "'contact situations' tend to create an ideology to explain the relationship of domination or subordination among social systems" (1991:13). In the European subordination of what eventually came to be known as Latin America, the concept of human "races" played an important role in legitimising it. This concept was used not only to gain acceptance for various aspects of the colonial project, but also to structure the colonies into exceedingly complex hierarchies, as illustrated by Martinez-Alier's (1989) study of nineteenth-century Cuba (see also Casaús Arzú 2007).

In Spanish America, "race" was first and foremost conceptualised as *pureza de sangre* (blood purity); a concept derived from a Catholic doctrine dating back to the thirteenth century (Stolcke 1993). Up until this point, Christians, Muslims and Jews were presented as living harmoniously together on the Iberian Peninsula. However, during the thirteenth century, this situation changed. The segregation of Christians from non-Christians was done with reference to the doctrine of *pureza de sangre*. Originally, this idea was derived from medieval physiological theories and the belief that a child's substance was provided by the mother's blood. Purity of blood in this context meant descent from Christian women. During the sixteenth century, however, the doctrine of blood purity acquired new meaning. From being considered a religious/cultural discrimination that could be overcome through conversion to Christianity, it was now transformed into a racist doctrine of original sin. Descent from Jews or Muslims was now regarded as a permanent and indelible stain. When these ideas were later applied in the colonial setting, the doctrine of blood purity led to a heightened concern among Europeans and their descendants over endogamous marriage and legitimate birth (Stolcke 1993:31–32).

Legitimate birth was used as a means to ensure and attest racial purity, which were prerequisites for inclusion into the upper echelons of colonial society. When a child was born, his or her birth certificate would state whether or not the child had purity of blood. Essentially, purity of blood in this context meant that the child was born from European born or "white" parents who were married to each other. This status would determine the child's position in the social system; any kind of higher-status occupations or positions could be held only by people who were of pure blood. People of mixed blood or Africans and indigenous people were assigned to different positions of slavery, servitude or lower-paid jobs. By now, blood purity had come to be understood as "racial" purity (see, e.g. Casaús Arzú 2007; Martinez-Allier 1989; Wade 1997 for more on these processes).

The Creole elites—people of Spanish origin born in the Americas—who became the new power holders after independence, were inspired by ideas from the Enlightenment in Europe. However, they were highly selective in how they interpreted and absorbed them. Whilst they eagerly fought for national sovereignty and free trade, "modern ideas about individual freedom, right of man, and equality" (Grosfoguel 2000:349) were underplayed. Rather, the Creole elites continued formerly colonial practices of coerced labour carried out by those on the bottom of the racial hierarchies, as well as maintaining the hierarchies themselves (Grosfoguel 2000:349). This is of course not very different from how Europeans and North Americans approached the ideas of the Enlightenment, for this was indeed a period filled with contradiction and ambiguity:

> The Age of the Enlightenment was an age in which the slave drivers of Nantes bought titles of nobility to better parade with philosophers, an age in which a freedom fighter such as Thomas Jefferson owned slaves without bursting under the weight of his intellectual and moral contradictions. (Trouillot 1995:78)

In similar ways, "white" Creole elites carved out the structural features of the nascent Latin American nation states in such a way that it continued to reproduce and legitimise their dominance, and colonial subjects were never really fully extended complete citizenship in the new sociopolitical order (Grosfoguel 2000:368). Quijano has termed this situation "Coloniality of Power" (2000), and its implication is that "the first decolonization was incomplete" (Grosfoguel 2000:368). Hence, as the chapters in this volume show, the ideas undergirding these hierarchies continue to mark Latin American societies today. This is an important reminder that poverty or economic disparity is never just about money, but is constituted in the encounter between economic processes, moral concerns and political ambitions. Before we start addressing these issues in their contemporary configuration, we will make an interlude of recent Latin American economic history.

STRUCTURALISM AND DEPENDENCY THEORY

In the 1950s and 1960s, attempts to build up national industry through Import Substitution Industrialisation (ISI) were at the centrepiece of Latin American economic development theories and practices. The *cepalistas*, spearheading what came to be known as (Latin American) structuralism, were working through the UN Economic Commission for Latin America (CELAC) under its influential director Raúl Prebisch. The core of structuralist theory was that countries that produced manufactured goods would always have better terms of trade at international markets than countries exporting primary products. Hence, if Latin American countries were to be able to compete with the industrialised world, they had to build up their own industrial and manufacturing sectors through protective policies. Industrialisation policies, pursued to counter the effects of the Great Depression on Latin American economies, had been well under way at the continent also well before CELAC was established in 1948 (Love 2005:103). Indeed, many Latin American regimes pursued developmentalist agendas during the first half of the century. The focus was on infrastructural, agricultural and industrial development, as well as some degree of social development. Notable examples here are Juan Domingo Perón in Argentina, Marcos Pérez Jiménez in Venezuela, Getúlio Vargas in Brazil, Víctor Raúl Haya de la Torre in Peru and Lázaro Cárdenas in Mexico.

However, CELAC, with its vast networks of intellectuals and policy analysts, systematically assessed regional economic development trajectories into a broader theoretical and empirical framework, and had great success in making contacts with governments, industrialists and international organisations (Love 2005:117). The structuralist school also fostered the emergence of dependency theorists. Whilst a central feature of the *dependentistas'* intellectual positioning was criticism of CEPAL's ideological affiliation with developmentalism and modernisation theories (Grosfoguel 2000:358), many of the most notable dependency theorists were also direct offshoots of the Prebisch-school, including Prebisch himself (Love 2005:119).

Dependency theory's criticism of developmentalism and modernisation theory was focused on debunking the notion that underdeveloped countries would, through applying the right policies, follow the same development trajectories as the Western world and eventually reach the stage of industrialised modernity. Rather, they maintained that development and underdevelopment were mutually constitutive features, because "the underdeveloped" world (i.e. the former colonial regions) is continuously politically, economically, technologically, culturally and epistemologically subordinated by the capitalist (previously colonialising/imperial) centres. In contrast to the original *cepalistas*, who maintained that underdeveloped countries could industrialise and develop within the capitalist system, many dependency theorists maintained that underdeveloped nations had to separate themselves from it, with revolution if necessary, in order to gain independence and prosper.

Developmentalism and the "Discovery" of the Third World

Intellectually, developmentalism and modernisation theories were principally emerging from Western academic institutions. However, as Arturo Escobar argues, a "hegemonic worldview of development" (Escobar 1995:19) was crafted through deeply interlinked political, economic and discursive rearrangement of large parts of the globe. Following the "discovery" of mass poverty in countries outside European, North-American and communist-controlled territories after the World War II, the so-called Third World regions in the world were constituted as a site of intervention and "development." Scientists, technocrats and "experts", sent out by Western institutions, universities and governments, descended upon Third World countries and populations with the aim of propelling them into taking the great leap from their underdeveloped state of being into modern, progressive peoples and places. In the words of June Nash: "The discourse of modernization presumed that Third World countries (those not aligned with the superpowers in the 'Cold War'), would, with the right combination of investment and disengagement from traditional pursuits, evolve in the same way as 'advanced' capitalist countries" (Nash 2003:60).

However, as Escobar has shown, the development agenda was also as much about domestic economic concerns in the West, particularly the USA, as it was about benevolent enlightenment of underdeveloped regions. Following the economic downturn after World War II, the USA was in dire need to open up new markets for capitalist expansion and to put US dollars into circulation at the global market. Third World countries were endowed with generous loans to pursue large-scale development projects and national development agendas. When the world economy started to slump in the late 1970s and eventually turned into crisis in the 1980s, these debt burdens would be the principal means of coercion for forcing countries across the continent into pursuing structural adjustment policies and the neoliberalisation of Latin American societies and economies.

The Rise of Neoliberalism in Latin America

As Love (2005) indicates, there was a range of structural, political and economic factors that contributed to the ISI strategy's eventual demise, an issue that is far beyond the scope of this chapter to address. However, what is important to assess in depth is the broader context in which the neoliberal era was ushered in.

Before proceeding, we will briefly state what we mean by neoliberalism in response to Laidlaw's polemic, but not entirely unjust, claim that neoliberalism often appears in anthropological texts as a designation for "everything the author doesn't like" rather than for a specific set of ideas or policies (2016:20). Indeed, the economic policies, modes of governance and techniques of the self that are at times included under the label "neoliberalism" are numerous and fragmented (see, e.g. Cook 2016; Coombe 2016; Gershon 2016; Hale 2006). Here, we take neoliberalism to be a particular set of economic policies and modes of governance as well as an ideological template. As we will expand upon below, these two dimensions are inseparable.

The neoliberal "policy package" was implemented unevenly across the Latin American continent. At first, as we will discuss further below, it was implemented by authoritarian governments. Later, this process was deepened and expanded following the transition to electoral democracy. Yet, in general terms, the neoliberal recipe consisted of fiscal discipline, privatisation, restructuring of labour markets, trade and financial markets, as well as the re-organisation (and reduction) of the public sector and public services (Gwynne and Kay 2000:144; Margheritis and Pereira 2007:34). Illustrating the dominant role of US-based institutions in spearheading this shift, its implementation across the globe became known as the Washington Consensus.

In Latin America, the neoliberal consensus was by and large crafted within a limited, yet transnational sphere consisting of domestic economic and political elites, and foreign policy makers, politicians, intellectuals, academics and business interests. In essence, it represented the ideas and interests of transnational capitalist sectors within and beyond Latin America's borders (Margheritis and Pereira 2007:42). Local opposition and subaltern critique was excluded, conditioned and muted. Within this echo chamber, social concerns were extraneous to the ideological and political premise of the model, namely macroeconomic stability. At the time, it was pursued with near-religious fervour. Complex economic, socio and political realities were ignored at the expense of a "one-size fits all blueprint model". As Arturo Escobar has polemically worded it, "'the essential is to press on with structural reforms', or so the litany goes. People's welfare can be bracketed for a while, even if hundreds of thousands might die. Hail the market" (Escobar 1995:58). Or, as Immanuel Wallenstein equally polemically worded it, invoking Margaret Thatcher's dogmatic statement: "(…) let us face Mecca five times a day and intone Allahu Akhbar TINA—There is No Alternative" (Wallenstein 2005:1265).

As the social consequences of the first round of neoliberal reforms became too evident in the course of the so-called lost decade in the 1980s, policy makers and academics sought to come up with suggestions as how to mitigate these through some formula for "neoliberalism with a human face". Yet, these suggestions were highly patchy and underdeveloped, and the basic premises of a neoliberal model as such were never challenged (Margheritis and Pereira 2007:37–39).

"Trickle-Up" Effects and Mounting Opposition

In order to understand both the temporal heterogeneity of the neoliberal expansion and its continuous universality for nearly two decades, it is important to note that in the short term, neoliberal policies frequently produced some immediate stabilising macroeconomic results. It reduced inflation, brought in new capital and fomented economic growth (Margheritis and Pereira 2007:26). However, it also created new cycles of boom and bust. Economic growth tended to slow down, new rounds of financial volatility set in and a host of social problems deepened as poverty, unemployment and socio-economic inequality grew. In reality, privatisation processes often consisted of transferring state monopolies into private hands, and became associated with massive corruption scandals. In country after country, social protests against not only neoliberal policies per se, but also the political classes that implemented them, gained pace.

In sum, a political crisis was under way, whereby the legitimacy of the political system at large was gravely undermined. In the years leading up to the end of the millennium, country after country saw political protests and uprisings directed against politicians associated with neoliberal policies. In Bolivia this led to the resignation of Gonzalo Sánchez de Lozada in 2002, in Ecuador it led to the resignation of Jorge Jamil Mahuad in 2000 and in Argentina it led to the resignation of Fernando de La Rua in 2001.

The popular Argentine slogan *que se vayan todos* (everyone must go), meaning that everyone associated with the political establishment had to be replaced, expressed the sentiment that swept across the continent. When Lula won the presidency in Brazil in 2002, social protests against the neoliberal prescription of Fernando Henrique Cardoso had marked the country for several years. In Venezuela, Chavez's ascendance to power in 1998 marked the end of a decade of intense political conflict and increasing resistance against neoliberal policies and the political system associated with them. Emblematic in this respect is the bloody popular uprising in 1989, the so-called *Caracazo*. Erupting as a spontaneous response to a new package of structural adjustments, and resulting in an unofficial death toll of somewhere between 1000 and 3000 casualties, el Caracazo has been characterised as "the largest and most violently repressed revolt against austerity measures in Latin American history" (Coronil 1997:376). In hindsight, it remains clear that the memories of el Caracazo and the years preceding it provided a powerful contrasting backdrop and incitement to the explicit anti-neoliberal ideology and sentiments characterising the Chávez years in Venezuela (see Strønen, Chap. 7, this volume, for more on the Caracazo).

Before we turn to the culmination of these processes in the Pink Tide, we will expand upon the implementation and outcomes of neoliberalism in Latin America.

Authoritarian Experiments in Neoliberalism

In ideological terms, neoliberalism can be understood as a utopian project with freedom as its highest purpose (Harvey 2007; Klein 2007). It is based on the theory that human well-being can best be achieved with the maximisation of "entrepreneurial freedoms within an institutional framework characterised by private property rights, individual liberty, unencumbered markets, and free trade" (Harvey 2007:22). Ironically, perhaps, given the emphasis of freedom in the neoliberal project, its initial introduction in Latin America was enforced by an authoritarian regime. In fact, Chile became a virtual laboratory for neoliberal experimentation after the democratically elected president Salvador Allende was ousted in a CIA-backed coup on 11 September 1973 and replaced by General Augusto Pinochet (Klein 2007). At the time, the Chilean economy suffered from hyperinflation, and Milton Friedman and a group of Chilean economists educated under him known as the "Chicago boys" were enlisted to counsel the new regime on how to address this situation.

Soon, other authoritarian regimes such as Argentina and Brazil followed Friedman's prescription for their troubled economies. The wider context for this development was the "dirty wars" unfolding in Latin America during the Cold War era, where the USA involved themselves on the side of right-wing military dictatorships as a means of curbing socialism. During the early neoliberal experiments in authoritarian Chile, Argentina and Brazil, resistance was met with violence: torture, massacres, disappearances, assassinations and concentration-camp-style prisons (see, e.g. Feitlowitz 1998; Klein 2007).

While the marriage between authoritarian regimes and projects of policy reform oriented towards freedom may appear contradictory, this was not so for Milton Friedman. He believed that for neoliberalism to be fully implemented, a degree of shock, a clearing out of the old, a blank slate, was required. After the 1973 coup in Chile, Friedman advised Pinochet "to impose a rapid-fire transformation of the economy—tax cuts, free trade, privatized services, cuts to social spending and deregulation" (Klein 2007:8). He theorised that the speed, suddenness and scope of these economic shifts would provoke psychological reactions in the population that would "facilitate the adjustment" (Milton and Rose D. Friedman cited in Klein 2007:8). The term Friedman coined for this tactic was "economic shock treatment".

Harvey characterises the brutal experiments carried out in the Latin American "laboratories" of the 1970s and 1980s as creative destruction carried out in the periphery, only to later become a model for the formulation of policies in the centre (Harvey 2007). In other words, Latin America became a testing ground for neoliberalism before it was later introduced in the USA and the UK under Reagan and Thatcher.

One of the defining features of neoliberalism, even as it was lopsidedly implemented across the globe, was that it contributed to eroding the metaphorical social contracts that protected industrial labour and the citizenry alike from the worst excesses of capitalism (Ortner 2011). The unwillingness of the citizenry to give up these social contracts was what motivated the Latin American authoritarian experiments in neoliberalism during the 1970s and 80s. Klein notes that "while Friedman's economic model is capable of being partially imposed under democracy, authoritarian conditions are required for the implementation of its true vision" (2007:12). The main reasons for this can be found in one of the conclusions from the Chilean experiment; the outcome of neoliberal economic policies is deepened inequality. Its initial introduction culminated in a new economic crisis, as Chile's economy crashed in 1982. Debt exploded, hyperinflation returned and unemployment hit 30 per cent—ten times higher than under Allende (Klein 2007:104). By 1988, the economy had stabilised and was growing rapidly, yet 45 per cent of the population had fallen below the poverty line. In contrast, the richest 10 per cent had increased their income by 83 per cent, and even in the mid-2000s, Chile remained one of the most unequal societies in the world (Klein 2007:105). The outcome of neoliberal economic policies, then, was not a stable economy and steady growth, but rather, increased inequality and volatility.

CLASS STRUGGLE FROM ABOVE

One might ask why an economic model that has produced such staggering inequality and repeated financial crises could become hegemonic. As the uneven geographical distribution of neoliberalism and its partial and lopsided application from one country to another shows; it was by far the only imaginable solution to the recession of the early 1970s (Harvey 2007:27). It was, however, a solution that successfully restored the economic and political power of elites, who found their position threatened by the conjoining of labour and social movements throughout much of the advanced capitalist world. Harvey therefore suggests that we should regard neoliberalism not as the utopian project of freedom it is often presented as, but rather, as a project to re-establish conditions for capital accumulation and to restore class power. Indeed, its primary achievement has been precisely the restoration of class power, and its principles are quickly abandoned whenever they conflict with this particular project (Harvey 2007:27–29).

Despite the rhetoric about curing sick economies, Harvey notes that the record of neoliberalism in stimulating economic growth is poor; between 2000 and 2007, global growth rates barely touched 1 per cent. In contrast, in the 1960s, before the introduction of neoliberal economic policies, aggregate growth rates were around 3.5 per cent. Episodes of periodic growth have nevertheless served to obscure the reality that, generally, neoliberalism was producing low growth and numerous financial crises. However, neoliberalism has worked very well to restore class position to ruling elites in countries such as the USA and the UK, or create conditions for capitalist class formation in countries such as China, India and Russia. Thus, the effect of neoliberalism has been redistributive rather than generative, transferring wealth from the masses towards the upper classes, and from vulnerable to wealthier countries (Harvey 2007:33–34). Another outcome of neoliberalism has been continued destruction of the natural environment, which together with the numerous economic crises has produced an all-encompassing existential precariousness for humans and non-humans alike (Tsing 2015).

In Latin American lifeworlds, the consequences of this class struggle from above were acutely felt by the lower classes. Eduardo Silva (2012), for example, argues with reference to Argentina, Bolivia and Ecuador that neoliberalism was perceived of as an assault on life itself. Not only did it subject people to hunger, misery and unemployment, but it also denied them the possibility to live a life with dignity, and to "affirm the value in the rituals of living (birth, puberty, marriage, childrearing, anniversaries, public festivals, close friendship and death)" (Silva 2012:23). Likewise, in Venezuela, neoliberalism created a perfect storm of unemployment, declining wages, harsher working conditions and an increasingly commodified "welfare marked" in which the poor were unable to participate. For the popular classes, this left them in a state of permanent scarcity and insecurity, fomenting social violence and personal tragedies, and excluding people from aspirations of a life project (Strønen 2017). In short, the consequences of neoliberal politics not only affected the structural conditions for social life and social reproduction (i.e. school, employment, welfare), but it also reached into the deepest sentiments of personal and collective human existence.

NEOLIBERALISM AND CONFINED POSSIBILITIES

While increased inequality has undoubtedly become the main narrative about neoliberalism, Tsing urges us to study capitalism without the crippling assumption that there can be only one powerful current at a time (2015:4). And indeed, there are some currents diverging from the main narrative in the events we are exploring here. For example, neoliberalism in Latin America has to some extent implied the transfer of power away from central governments and towards other entities. Municipal government has been strengthened, as has community organisations, collective institutions and links with transnational fields of networked power (Coombe 2016:251). However, such formal decentralisation of power has not necessarily empowered local actors as it has often been accompanied by de facto transfers of power away from the local level (Hale cited in Coombe 2016:251). New spaces of contestation and struggle have nevertheless been created as the neoliberal project worked to expand marked relations into culturally defined zones of life. These processes have been embraced by a variety of actors[2], and have tended "to incite new forms of struggle, knowledge mobilization and identity formation" (Coombe 2016:251). Hale (2006:75) argues that from the early 1990s, two strands of state ideology—orthodox neoliberal economic policies and a progressive stand on cultural rights—merged to yield a new mode of governance throughout Latin America. The reasons why these apparently contradictory principles could coexist so successfully, according to Hale, are that:

> […] if civil society organizations opt for development models that reinforce the ideology of capitalist productive relations, they can embody and advance the neoliberal projects as collectives not individuals. As long as cultural rights remain within these basic parameters, they contribute directly to the goal of neoliberal self-governance; they reinforce its ideological tenets while meeting deeply felt needs; they register dissent, while directing these collective political energies toward unthreatening ends. (Hale 2006:75)

In the case of Guatemala, these developments created conditions that made it possible for the pan-Mayan movement to make considerable advances in challenging racism and discrimination. However, these advances are not without ambivalence and hindrances. As the biological racism that previously undergirded the Guatemalan social hierarchy became increasingly untenable, other ideas supporting "racialised" hierarchisation have moved to the foreground. Thus, many *ladino*[3] Guatemalans now consider indigenous people to be inferior, not because of their "race", but because of their culture, or because they are poor (Hale 2006; see also Nelson 1999; Ystanes 2016).

Furthermore, while neoliberalism has contributed to the conditions that made it possible for the indigenous population to advance their claims for equal rights, it has also led to a deepening of gendered forms of labour exploitation (Nelson 1999). The introduction of *maquila* work and the Guatemalan standards for the minimum wage reflect this. Previously, a distinction was made between agricultural labour and other kinds of work. Agricultural work was mostly performed by indigenous people, and had a lower minimum wage. In recent years, however, the distinction is made between work in the *maquila* industry and other kinds of work, where the former is mostly performed by women and has a lower minimum wage. To some extent, poor women have come to occupy a stigmatised position that was previously associated with indigenous people. Hence, since the nature of hierarchising notions of difference in Latin America is fluid and interconnected, wage discrimination can shift from "racial" to gendered justification and has done so within the neoliberal context (Ystanes 2011:149).

Another example of the lopsided potential offered to marginalised groups in the neoliberal economy is offered by Ødegaard (Chap. 8). Neoliberal expansion in Peru has in some respects opened up an economic space for indigenous women to manoeuvre, the *chola*, as largely informal vendors of diverse commodity products. Through navigating back and forth between the formal and informal economy:

> the chola may appear as the 'perfect neoliberal citizen'; as hard-working and self-made, and accommodating her own quest for social mobility to growing demands of growth, flow and consumption. (Ødegaard, Chap. 8, this volume)

Yet, the *chola's* position in the socio-economic domains is continuously fragile, and frequently considered illicit or illegitimate by the authorities and the dominant classes.

Likewise, as Stensrud (Chap. 10, this volume) asserts, the neoliberalisation of the agricultural economy in Peru has provided peasants with a partial integration into domestic and global markets. Nevertheless, this market insertion is characterised by highly insecure access to water, land and capital, as well as frenzied attempts to interpret and navigate in fluctuating market demands. Seen together, these two chapters from Peru perfectly illustrate how the neoliberalisation of Latin American economies has facilitated certain spaces for economic survival for those on the lower societal ladder; yet these spaces are highly circumscribed by, as well as accentuate, historically constituted modes of inequality. Whilst capital under neoliberalism is allowed to thrive, those on the bottom are often left to "creatively" scramble for existence within a socio-cultural and economic matrix where the cards are stacked against them.

THE PINK TIDE

The Pink Tide, post-neoliberalism, the turn to the left, the neoliberal backlash: these are some of the terms and concepts that have been used to describe the political shifts taking place on the Latin American continent at the turn of the millennium. Garavito, Barrett and Chavez date the emergence of "the new left" to the Zapatista uprising on 1 January 1994 in protest of the free trade NAFTA-agreement between Mexico, the United States and Canada (Garavito et al. 2004:27). As their edited volume shows, leftist candidates' success at the ballot box a few years later has to be intrinsically understood in relation to social mobilisations from below that had been taking place for a long time (Garavito et al. 2004).

However, at the level of government, the Pink Tide can be dated to Hugo Chávez's election victory in Venezuela in 1998, followed by Lula's electoral victory in Brazil in 2002, Néstor Kirchner's election victory in Argentina in 2003, Evo Morales' electoral victory in Bolivia in 2006, Rafael Correa's election victory in Ecuador in 2006, Manuel Zelaya's election victory in Honduras in 2006, Michelle Bachelet's election victory in Chile in 2006, Daniel Ortega's electoral victory in Nicaragua in 2007, Álvaro Colom's electoral victory in Guatemala in 2007, Fernando Lugo's electoral victory in Paraguay in 2008, José "Pepe" Mujica electoral victory in Uruguay in 2010 and Ollanta Humala in Peru in 2011.

As Ruckert et al.'s (2017) review of scholarly approaches to "post-neoliberal" governments in Latin America reveals, these governments, as well as the analytical and classificatory characterisations of them, were extremely heterogeneous. Academic debates, and not to speak of media reports, have been circumscribed and coloured by the highly politically contentious context in which the turn to the left unfolded. As Escobar noted, "how one thinks about these processes is itself an object of struggle and debate" (Escobar 2010:2).

Echoing Castañeda's much-discussed categorisation of the "good" and the "bad" left (Castañeda 2006), divisions were often made by scholars, journalist and other observers between "moderate", "centre-left", "pragmatic", "reformist" or "good" governments on the one hand, and "populist", "radical" and "bad" governments on the other hand. Venezuela, Ecuador and Bolivia, and sometimes also Argentina, were commonly lumped together as the prime examples in the "bad" populist leftist category, whilst Brazil and Chile were taken to be the lead examples of moderate "good leftists". The remaining governments were placed at the different points of this sliding matrix, depending on context and the eye of the observer.

Indeed, there were enormous differences between both the ideological focus and the actual policies of these governments. As Escobar (2010) commented, the State projects instigated by formal political power were "not panaceas of any sort, on the contrary, they are seen as fragile and full of contradictions" (Escobar 2010:2). This observation is even more evident today. However, at the time and in the big picture, the turn to the left in the formal political landscape were interpreted as a broad backlash against the neoliberal hegemony, right-wing politics and traditional political elites. It was the fruit of a long struggle, made possible by long-term social mobilisation from below. This backdrop eventually provided a broad spectrum of popular movements with considerably more space and leverage as political and social actors, crafting a new (though highly heterogeneous and contradictory) nexus between formal power and non-elitist actors.

Indeed, as Moraña (2008) argues, the political experiences of the "institutionalised left" in Latin America in the course of the Pink Tide "cannot be understood except as the counterpart of social movements that exists outside the limits of traditional politics (...)" (Moraña 2008:34). Even though the genesis, strength and form of social movements and popular mobilisation varied considerably from one country to another, a wave of popular empowerment, optimism and solidarity swept across national borders. This was accompanied by a prevailing sense that the time had come to truly challenge the complex hierarchies that left so many Latin Americans in positions of social, cultural and economic "otherness". The World Social Forum, first organised in Porto Alegre in 2001, is a case in point. It managed to bring together tens of thousands of heterogeneous groups of activist under the slogan "Another World is Possible", making visible and asserting "the existence of alternatives to neoliberal globalization" (de Sousa Santos 2008:253). In the years after the millennium, the multiplicity of cultural-political projects, cosmologies, ideologies and utopias crafted and imagined as alternatives to neoliberalism and liberal democracy gained visibility. The coining of projects such as *"socialismo del Siglo XXI*, plurinationality, interculturality, direct and substantive democracy, *revolución ciudadana*, endogenous development centered on the *buen vivir* of the people, territorial and cultural autonomy, and decolonial projects" (Escobar 2010:2) were not only discursive novelties, but they also denoted the emergence of multiple counter-hegemonic visions of ways to organise human society.

Re-inserting the Social

It is essential to recognise that the Pink Tide was far more than an orientation to "classical" left-wing postures such as increased social welfare, state involvement in the economy and increased articulation between the state and non-elite sectors. Rather, echoing Polyani's thesis of capitalism's double movement, it was a popular reaction against the expanding commodification of ambits that are essentially part of social life and survival such as labour, land and money (Silva 2009; Margheritis and Pereira 2007:28). In contesting the increasing gap between human needs and economic realities, it was a call for a re-articulation between the social and the political; "a call for a new kind of politics, rooted in and responsive to local traditions and communities, and an attempt to forge a new pact between society and the state" (Grugel and Riggirozzi 2012:3).

During the Pink Tide, attempts to reverse neoliberalism's socially destructive legacy was characterised by the merging of claims for the recognition of cultural and social diversity with claims for socio-economic redistribution and poverty reduction. In Venezuela, the Bolivarian discourse stressed popular identities and practices as the basis for crafting new social and political models, at the same time as diverse experiments with popular participatory democracy was directly contraposed to liberal democracy's elitist nature. "Bolivarianism" offered previously marginalised sectors a new historical narrative and new moral grounding for asserting themselves as a historical subject, *el pueblo,* whose time had come to claim rectification for accumulated injustice (Strønen, Chap. 7 this volume).

In Bolivia, the country's indigenous majority was for the first time in history represented by "one of their own", and indigenous cosmologies and socialities became part of the official story about the nation's collective foundation and heritage. In no way were the relationships between these governments and their constituencies peaceful and streamlined. Rather, they were fraught by contradictions, complex political manoeuvring, or what is perhaps best captured by the Aymaran scholar Pablo Mamani's concept "strategic ambiguity" (Fernandes 2010:28). It is nevertheless important to recognise that the new relationship between formal powerholders and popular subjects opened up a space where claims for recognition, social and economic rights, and a seat at the political table could be legitimately articulated and negotiated. Generally speaking, the coming-to-power of new political actors from non-elitists background is highly important for understanding the qualitative shift in the texture of relations between formal political power and socioculturally marginalised groups. As de Sousa Santos notes, "absent from the minds [of the dominant classes] has always been their own inexperience of the suffering, death, pillage, imposed as experience upon the oppressed classes, groups or peoples" (de Sousa Santos 2001:191). What the Pink Tide did, was to recognise these life experiences sustained by large parts of Latin American peoples, and to name it by its rightful name: inequality and injustice.

As part of this process, efforts to address socio-economic inequalities in more comprehensive ways were introduced at the state level. According to Costas and de Lavra Pinto (Chaps. 3 and 6, this volume), the Lula and Rousseff governments in Brazil managed to significantly improve key indicators of poverty, unemployment and access to social welfare. Likewise, as Strønen (Chap. 7) indicates, the Chávez government quickly reduced the country's poverty rates as well as the Gini-indicator between 2004 and 2012, before the economic crisis struck. In that period, Venezuela's poor and marginalised enjoyed an unprecedented access to healthcare, education and pensions, as well as significant improvements in housing and infrastructure. Bolivia, Ecuador and Argentina also introduced or expanded targeted welfare programmes, leading to notable reductions in poverty levels (Grugel and Riggirozzi 2012:9–10).

Lavra Pinto (Chap. 6) brings our attention to interesting aspects of these processes, which is indicative of how they differ from neoliberal conceptions of welfare based on strict evaluations of economic need (see, e.g. Haney 2000). She found that social workers tasked with the implementation of the Bolsa Familia programme in Rio de Janeiro, employed a wider conceptualisation of "poverty" than economic scarcity alone. Often, they showed solidarity with beneficiaries based on knowledge of their whole life situation, and helped them navigate the system accordingly. This exemplifies how policies introduced by Pink Tide governments often allowed for an enhanced attention to people's whole lives, and a recognition of the social aspects of inequality.

THE (PARTIAL) RETURN OF THE RIGHT

During the Pink Tide era, successive attempts were made to halt the turn to the left and to restore traditional right-wing power. Lugo's presidency in Paraguay was aborted by a parliamentary coup in 2012, and Zelaya was effectively shut out from power through a parliamentary/military coup in 2009. In Venezuela, the aborted coup against Chávez in 2002 and the oil strike/sabotage in 2002/2003 were effectively attempts to restore class power, and both Bolivia and Ecuador have been through episodes of tense conflict, including an alleged attempted coup against Correa in 2010. In Brazil, the country's ruling elites managed to put an end to the Lula-Rousseff era in 2016, through a process that is difficult to assess as anything else than a parliamentary coup.

Current experiences from Paraguay, Brazil and Honduras, as well as from Argentina where the business mogul Mauricio Macri won the presidential elections in 2016, indicates that when the traditional elites return to power, they are eager to curb social mobilisation from below and pursue classic right-wing politics. In Brazil, for example, the Michel Temer government has already passed legislation that will deepen and reinforce inequalities, rather than working to undo them. The official reason for this is to reduce government spending as a way of tackling the unfolding financial crisis. However, such austerity measures have been discredited as they deepened the depression and delayed recovery after they were implemented in European countries after the 2007–2008 financial crisis (Krugman 2015). It is also well known that large-scale cuts in public spending combined with privatisation reinforce economic inequality, as they redistribute resources away from the wider public and into the hands of elites (Klein 2007). Despite all this, in Brazil, austerity measures are now being introduced against the backdrop of elite and upper-middle class anxieties about "poor" people gaining access to more and more distinguishing forms of consumption (Ystanes 2015:230), education, positions and gains in identity politics. As a result, those Brazilians who rose to the lower rungs of the middle class during the last couple of decades may now find their new class position to be quite insecure.

The Social Life of Economic Inequality

As the chapters in this volume show, neoliberalism and neoliberal rationality continue to imbue Latin American societies, in spite of the counter currents produced by the Pink Tide. Indeed, much of the increased participation in consumption for Latin America's "poor" is achieved through access to credit, granted by stores and other entities eager to capture this segment of society as consumers (see, e.g. Han 2012). An intervention that illustrates this well is the "pacification" of Rio's favelas prior to the 2014 FIFA World Cup and the 2016 Olympics (see, e.g. Larkins 2015; Salem 2016; Savell 2014; Sørbøe 2013). The rhetoric employed to legitimise this grand-scale militarisation of urban neighbourhoods is to force out drug traffickers who are operating from these areas, and to "reconquer" the territories for the Brazilian state. This would allow favela residents to be finally included in the formal city as full members of society. The army is enlisted in this effort; on preannounced dates they arrive with tanks and soldiers, and once the area is secured, the military police set up permanent presence. However, the full inclusion of favela residents as citizens has not been achieved through this project, which has been tarnished by police violence, an inability to contain drug trafficking and lack of social programmes. What has been achieved, however, has been the penetration of the formal economy into favela territories that were previously off limits because of the dominance of organised crime. Those who observed the "pacification" of Rio's favelas say that the cable TV companies literally entered just behind the invading army. Chain stores and other formal businesses soon followed. When the Special Forces (BOPE) advanced into the Rocinha favela, corporate representatives eager to tap the lucrative favela market outnumbered the invading police threefold. Salespeople distributed flyers for bundled service packages even before victory had been declared (Larkins 2015:139). While previously favela residents had affordable access to the Internet, cable TV and various other services via a black market controlled by traffickers, "pacification" captured them as consumers for the formal economy. In true neoliberal spirit, the markets were significantly expanded; by 2014, 264 favelas housing 1.5 million residents were included in this project (Salem 2016:4).

In tandem with Pink Tide policies, then, neoliberal approaches to governance, where one of the main purposes of the state is to create markets (Harvey 2007:22–23), have been continued. The pacification of Rio's favelas exemplifies how the efforts to secure the city before the recent mega-events simultaneously constituted the creation of new formal markets. The chapters by Lavra Pinto, Sørbøe and Ystanes (Chaps. 6, 5 and 4) explore some of the lives lived within these ambiguous contexts. As they show, residents in "pacified" favelas found both empowerment and improved economic situations, as well as the continuation of structural and physical violence, exclusion forced evictions, and new forms of economic marginalisation. This ambiguity is illustrative of processes explored also in other chapters.

For example, Brown (Chap. 11) makes an important point about the contradictions involved in some of the gains in identity politics. Brazilian Quilombo communities, that is, descendants of communities founded by runaway slaves during the colonial era, have been recognised as ethnic groups with collective rights to their own culture and ways of life. However, recognition has not included the means whereby these rights could be meaningfully exercised, such as land. In fact, more than 2400 communities are recognised as Quilombo, yet only 220 have received land titles. Although social rights and the right to exercise them in particular places are intimately connected, as the chapters by Stensrud, Sørbøe and Ystanes

(Chaps. 10, 5 and 4) also show, the distribution and occupation of land remain firmly governed by market concerns (see also Rolnik 2015). The valuation of land in the market, however, is in turn governed by social structures imbuing different locations with dissimilar values, as Brown (Chap. 11) emphasises. The role of land in the reproduction of inequality is therefore created by a circular movement between social and financial processes. On the one hand, spatial politics produce a geography of inequality which informs markets of the value of a piece of land. On the other hand, this precise quantification of inequality through the valuation of land reinforces its inscription in the physical landscape.

The question of land goes to the core of why the scope for challenging inequality has been circumscribed in Pink Tide countries. A legacy of inequality, established through conquest, colonialism, slavery and forced labour, racism, gender discrimination, authoritarian regimes and neoliberal policies, is inscribed in Latin American social landscapes through unequal access to, ownership over, life conditions in and the right to exist in, particular places.

The ethnographic chapters in this volume all explore different configurations of this problematic. Sørbøe (Chap. 5), for example, shows that the "pacification" of Rocinha and its accompanying urban upgrade programme centred on the notion of the favela as a particular kind of place; one that could simultaneously be opened up for the formal economy and for tourists, be the location of spectacular infrastructure projects aimed to promote Rio as a "global city", and one where criminals could be contained in order to make the formal city more secure. The life conditions of those who already had their lives and relationships embedded in this place were of less concern. The ideological foundation for such an approach rests upon the inscription of inequality in the physical landscape, as described above. In similar ways, Ødegaard (Chap. 8) argues that the production of a particular kind of "governable spaces" in Peru may serve to exclude some actors and forms of economic activities from these spaces, and therefore, reinforce existing inequalities. De Lavra Pinto (Chap. 6) shows how inequality is also inscribed into the landscape within Rio's favelas; the closer a person lives to the edge of the favela, near the "asphalt", the wealthier they are perceived to be. Strønen (Chap. 7) describes the division over Chávez's Bolivarian process as one where the different opinions are more or less located on separate sides of the Caracas valley. Stensrud (Chap. 10) analyses how the Majes Irrigation Project in southern Peru has turned a desert into fertile land and a place of opportunity, yet also a place where inequality is reproduced. Gutiérrez Rivera, Strønen and Ystanes (Chap. 9) discuss how the War on Drugs has contributed to reproducing and reinforcing the marginalisation of young, "racially othered" men living in poor neighbourhoods in Honduras, Venezuela and Brazil. Finally, Ystanes (Chap. 4) analyses the social media-based activism-as-journalism that has arisen in favelas that were adversely affected by mega-event preparations in Rio, and how it thematises the inscription of inequality in the city's urban landscape.

In discussing how reparations associated with land can play a role in challenging entrenched inequalities, Brown (Chap. 11) emphasises that this is not a question of eliminating private property, but of changing the distribution of the values produced by and attributed to land. This could happen through economic tools like taxation, through a deeper recognition of the social role of land and the idea of land as commons, rather than merely a financial asset. Most fundamentally, though, Brown argues that reparations are not just about acknowledging past injustices through payments or land title, but of repairing human relationships. In order to achieve such a thing, close attention must be paid to the social life of economic inequality: the worldviews that uphold it, their historical legacies and how they are embedded in contemporary relationships. Indeed, inequality in Latin America is an outcome of a complex interweaving of the ambitions, beliefs, actions and worldviews of past and present persons and institutions. Inequality is a feature of a relationship between different social groups, and this relationship is continuously both reproduced and challenged by contemporary Latin Americans. The struggle for more egalitarian societies has therefore been fought on several fronts during the Pink Tide; in the field of economic policies, as well as social rights and identity politics. As the chapters in this volume show, for those advocating or supporting this process from below, it is essentially about repairing human relationships; about working towards social worlds where their common humanity is fully recognised, and their life projects, dreams and ambitions can be valued the same as others'.

Notes

1. The 2007 Pan-American Games, the 2013 FIFA Confederations Cup, the 2014 FIFA World Cup and the 2016 Olympics.
2. See also Comaroff and Comaroff (2009) for a comparative discussion of such processes beyond Latin America.

3. *Ladinos* are Guatemalans of mixed origin who foreground the European part of their heritage and identify with national culture, while shoving the indigenous part into the background.

References

Brown, Marvin. 2010. Free Enterprise and the Economics of Slavery. *Real-World Economics Review* 52: 28–39.
Buck-Morss, Susan. 2009. *Hegel, Haiti, and Universal History*. Pittsburgh: University of Pittsburgh Press.
Casaús Arzú, Marta Elena. 2007. *Guatemala: Linaje y Racismo*. Ciudad de Guatemala: F & G Editores.
Castañeda, Jorge. 2006. Latin America's Left Turn. *Foreign Policy*, May/June. Available at https://www.foreignaffairs.com/articles/southamerica/2006-05-01/latin-americas-left-turn. Accessed 17 Apr 2017.
Comaroff, John L., and Jean Comaroff. 2009. *Ethnicity, Inc*. Chicago/London: University of Chicago Press.
Cook, Joanna. 2016. Mindful in Westminster: The Politics of Meditation and the Limits of Neoliberal Critique. *HAU: Journal of Ethnographic Theory* 6 (1): 141–161.
Coombe, Rosemary J. 2016. The Knowledge Economy and Its Cultures: Neoliberal Technologies and Latin American Reterritorializations. *HAU: Journal of Ethnographic Theory* 6 (3): 247–275.
Cornelissen, Scarlett. 2012. 'Our Struggles Are Bigger than the World Cup': Civic Activism, State-Society Relations and the Socio-Political Legacies of the 2010 World Cup. *British Journal of Sociology* 63 (2): 328–248.
Coronil, Fernando. 1997. *The Magical State: Nature, Money, and Modernity in Venezuela*. Chicago: University of Chicago Press.
DaMatta, Roberto. 1991. *Carnivals, Rogues, and Heroes. An Interpretation of the Brazilian Dilemma*. Notre Dame: University of Notre Dame Press.
Daston, Lorraine, and Peter Galison. 1992. The Image of Objectivity. *Representations* 40: 81–128.
Dumont, Louis. 1980. *Homo Hierarchicus. The Caste System and Its Implications*. Chicago/London: University of Chicago Press.
Edmonds, Alexander. 2010. *Pretty Modern. Beauty, Sex and Plastic Surgery in Brazil*. Durham/London: Duke University Press.
Escobar, Arturo. 1995. *Encountering Development. The Making and the Unmaking of the Third World*. Princeton: Princeton University Press.
———. 2010. Latin America at a Crossroads. *Cultural Studies* 24 (1): 1–65.
Feitlowitz, Marguerite. 1998. *A Lexicon of Terror. Argentina and the Legacies of Torture*. Oxford/New York: Oxford University Press.

Fernandes, Sujatha. 2010. *Who Can Stop the Drums? Urban Social Movements in Chávez' Venezuela*. Durham/London: Duke University Press.
Foucault, Michel. 1981. The Order of Discourse. In *Untying the Text: A Post-Structuralist Reader*, ed. Robert Young, 51–78. Boston/London/Henley: Routledge & Kegan Paul.
Gaffney, Christopher. 2010. Mega-Events and Socio-Spatial Dynamics in Rio de Janeiro, 1919–2016. *Journal of Latin American Geography* 9 (1): 7–29.
Garavito, César A. Rodríguez, Patrick S. Barrett, and Daniel Chavez. 2004. *La nueva izquierda en América Latina. Sus orígenes y trayectoria futuros*. Grupo Editorial Norma
Gershon, Ilana. 2016. 'I'm Not a Businessman, I'm a Business, Man': Typing the Neoliberal Self unto a Branded Existence. *HAU: Journal of Ethnographic Theory* 6 (3): 223–246.
Grosfoguel, Ramon. 2000. Developmentalism, Modernity, and Dependency Theory in Latin America. *Neplanta: Views from the South* 1 (2): 347–374.
Grugel, Jean, and Pía Riggirozzi. 2012. Post-neoliberalism in Latin America: Rebuilding and Reclaiming the State after Crisis. *Development and Change* 43 (1): 1–21.
Gwynne, Robert N., and Cristobal Kay. 2000. Views from the Periphery: Futures of Neoliberalism in Latin America. *Third World Quarterly* 21 (1): 141–156.
Hale, Charles R. 2006. *Más Que Un Indio (More than an Indian). Racial Ambivalence and Neoliberal Multiculturalism in Guatemala*. Santa Fe: School of American Research Press.
Han, Clara. 2012. *Life in Debt. Times of Care and Violence in Neoliberal Chile*. Berkeley: University of California Press.
Haney, Lynne. 2000. Global Discourses of Need: Mythologizing and Pathologizing Welfare in Hungary. In *Global Ethnography: Forces, Connections, and Imaginations in a Postmodern World*, ed. Michael Burawoy, Joseph A. Blum, Sheba George, Millie Thayer, Zsuzsa Gille, Theresa Gowan, Lynne Haney, Maren Klawiter, Steve H. Lopez, and Sean Riain, 48–73. Berkeley/Los Angeles/London: University of California Press.
Harvey, David. 2007. Neoliberalism as Creative Destruction. *The Annals of the American Academy of Political and Social Science* 610: 22–44.
Inman, Phillip. 2013. Academics Back Students in Protests Against Economics Teaching. *The Guardian*, November 18. Available at http://tinyurl.com/kn9ledb
Klein, Naomi. 2007. *The Shock Doctrine: The Rise of Disaster Capitalism*. London/New York: Penguin.
Krugman, Paul. 2015. The Austerity Delusion. *The Guardian*, April 29. Retrieved https://www.theguardian.com/business/ng-interactive/2015/apr/29/the-austerity-delusion

Laidlaw, James. 2016. Through a Glass, Darkly. *HAU: Journal of Ethnographic Theory* 6 (2): 17–24.
Larkins, Erika Mary Robb. 2015. *The Spectacular Favela: Violence in Modern Brazil*. Oakland: University of California Press.
Love, Joseph Leroy. 2005. There Rise and Decline of Economic Structuralism in Latin America. New Dimensions. *Latin American Research Review* 40 (3): 100–125.
Malinowski, Bronislaw. 2014. *Argonauts of the Western Pacific*. New York: Routledge.
Margheritis, Ana, and Anthony W. Pereira. 2007. The Neoliberal Turn in Latin America: The Cycle of Ideas and the Search for an Alternative. *Latin American Perspectives* 34 (3): 25–48.
Martin, Emily. 1990. Toward an Anthropology of Immunology: The Body as Nation State. *Medical Anthropology Quarterly, New Series* 4 (4): 410–426.
Martinez-Alier, V. 1989. *Marriage, Class and Colour in Nineteenth-Century Cuba. A Study of Racial Attitudes and Sexual Values in a Slave Society*. Ann Arbor: The University of Michigan Press.
Milton, Cynthia E. 2007. *The Many Meanings of Poverty. Colonialism, Social Compacts, and Assistance in Eighteenth-Century Ecuador*. Stanford: Stanford University Press.
Moraña, Mabel. 2008. Negotiating the Local: The Latin American "Pink Tide" or What's Left for the Left. *Canadian Journal of Latin American and Caribbean Studies* 33 (66): 31–41.
Nash, June. 2003. Indigenous Development Alternatives. *Urban Anthropology and Studies of Cultural Systems and World Economic Development* 32 (1): 57–98.
Nelson, Diane M. 1999. *A Finger in the Wound. Body Politics in Quincentennial Guatemala*. Berkeley/Los Angeles/London: University of California Press.
Ortner, Sherry B. 2011. On Neoliberalism. *Anthropology of This Century* (1). Retrieved http://aotcpress.com/articles/neoliberalism/
———. 2016. Dark Anthropology and Its Others. *HAU: Journal of Ethnographic Theory* 6 (1): 47–73.
Polyani, Karl. 1944. *The Great Transformation*. New York: Farrar & Rinehart.
Quijano, Anibal. 2000. Coloniality of Power, Eurocentrism, and Latin America. *Nepentla: Views From the South* 1 (3): 533–580.
Reinert, Erik, Jayati Ghosh, and Rainer Kattel. 2017. Understanding Economic Development and Demolishing Neoliberal Development Myths. *WEA Commentaries* 7 (1): 10–12.
Rolnik, Raquel. 2015. *Guerra Dos Lugares: A Colonização Da Terra E Da Moradia Na Era Das Finanças*. São Paulo: Boitempo Editorial.
Ruckert, Arne, Laura Macdonald, and Kristina R. Proulx. 2017. Postneoliberalism in Latin America: A Conceptual Review. *Third World Quarterly* 38 (7): 1583–1602. https://doi.org/10.1080/01436597.2016.1259558.

Salem, Tomas. 2016. *Taming the War Machine: Police, Pacification and Power in Rio de Janeiro.* Thesis Submitted for the MA Degree at Department of Social Anthropology, University of Bergen.

Santos, Boaventura de Sousa. 2001. Nuestra America: Reinventing a Subaltern Paradigm of Recognition and Redistribution. *Theory, Culture and Society* 18 (2–3): 185–217.

———. 2008. The World Social Forum and the Global Left. *Politics & Society* 36 (2): 247–270.

Savell, Stephanie. 2014. *The Brazilian Military, Public Security, and Rio de Janeiro's 'Pacification.'* Anthropoliteia.net.

Scheper-Hughes, Nancy. 1993. *Death Without Weeping: The Violence of Everyday Life in Brazil.* Berkeley/Los Angeles: University of California Press.

Silva, Eduardo. 2009. *Challenging Neoliberalism in Latin America.* Cambridge: Cambridge University Press.

———. 2012. Exchange Rising? Karl Polyani and Contentious Politics in Contemporary Latin America. *Latin American Politics and Society* 54 (3): 1–32.

Sørbøe, Celina Myrann. 2013. *Security and Inclusive Citizenship in the Mega-City. The Pacification of Rocinha, Rio de Janeiro.* Thesis Submitted for the MA Degree at Department of Literature, Area Studies and European Languages, University of Oslo.

Stepan, Nancy Leys. 1991. *"The Hour of Eugenics". Race, Gender, and Nation in Latin America.* Ithaca/London: Cornell University Press.

Stolcke, V. 1993. Is Sex to Gender as Race Is to Ethnicity? In *Gendered Anthropology*, ed. T. del Valle, 17–37. London/New York: Routledge.

Streicker, Joel. 1995. Policing Boundaries: Race, Class, and Gender in Cartagena, Colombia. *American Ethnologist* 22 (1): 54–74.

Strønen, Iselin. 2017. *Grassroots Politics and Oil Culture in Venezuela. The Revolutionary Petro-State.* New York: Palgrave Macmillan.

Trouillot, M.-R. 1995. *Silencing the Past. Power and the Production of History.* Boston: Beacon Press.

Tsing, Anna Lowenhaupt. 2015. *The Mushroom at the End of the World: On the Possibility of Life in Capitalist Ruins.* Princeton/Oxford: Princeton University Press.

Wade, Peter. 1997. *Race and Ethnicity in Latin America.* London: Pluto Press.

Wallerstein, Immanuel. 2005. After Developmentalism and Globalization, What? *Social Forces* 83 (3): 1263–1278.

Ystanes, Margit. 2011. *Precarious Trust. Problems of Managing Self and Sociality in Guatemala.* Dissertation Submitted for the Degree of Philosophiae Doctor (PhD) at the University of Bergen.

———. 2015. 'Problemet Er at vi Ikke Aner Hvor Dette Bærer': Dystopiske Fremtidsforestillinger i Sportsarrangementenes Tid. *Norsk Antropologisk Tidsskrift* 26 (3/4): 221–239.

———. 2016. Unfixed Trust: Intimacy, Blood Symbolism, and Porous Boundaries in Guatemala. In *Trusting and Its Tribulations: Interdisciplinary Engagements with Intimacy, Sociality and Trust*, ed. V. Broch-Due and M. Ystanes, 37–59. London/New York: Berghahn.

Open Access This chapter is licensed under the terms of the Creative Commons Attribution 4.0 International License (http://creativecommons.org/licenses/by/4.0/), which permits use, sharing, adaptation, distribution and reproduction in any medium or format, as long as you give appropriate credit to the original author(s) and the source, provide a link to the Creative Commons license and indicate if changes were made.

The images or other third party material in this chapter are included in the chapter's Creative Commons license, unless indicated otherwise in a credit line to the material. If material is not included in the chapter's Creative Commons license and your intended use is not permitted by statutory regulation or exceeds the permitted use, you will need to obtain permission directly from the copyright holder.

CHAPTER 2

Reformism, Class Conciliation and the Pink Tide: Material Gains and Their Limits

Pedro Mendes Loureiro

INTRODUCTION

Towards the end of a long period of developmental regimes, from roughly 1930 to 1980, Latin America became the world's laboratory for neoliberalism, pioneering transitions in Chile and Argentina in the early and mid-1970s. This soon spread to most of the continent, and, alongside a crisis-ridden decade of the 1980s, Latin America underwent the most thorough neoliberal transformation in the world (Sader 2011). Countries across the region promoted trade and financial liberalisation, cut the already small welfare entitlements and privatised state assets, whilst firms integrated themselves into low-value-added sections of global value chains (Medeiros 2011). What resulted was an unstable, low-growth model dependent on foreign direct investment, as well as rising unemployment, labour market informality, poverty and inequality.

Towards the end of the 1990s, popular approval of neoliberal governments consequently fell and, starting with Venezuela in 1998, many

---

The author would like to thank Alfredo Saad-Filho, Ben Fine and Leandro Vergara-Camus for the invaluable discussions that helped shape this chapter, as well as Coordenação de Aperfeiçoamento de Pessoal de Nível Superior (Capes) for the grant [BEX 1669/14-1] that made this research possible.

P.M. Loureiro (✉)
SOAS, University of London, London, UK

© The Author(s) 2018
M. Ystanes, I.Å. Strønen (eds.), *The Social Life of Economic Inequalities in Contemporary Latin America*, Approaches to Social Inequality and Difference, DOI 10.1007/978-3-319-61536-3_2

countries elected presidents running on platforms allegedly antithetical to neoliberalism. This continental movement, known as the 'Pink Tide', made use of particularly positive global conditions to deliver material gains. Relatively fast growth rates in central countries, the strong Chinese demand for commodities underpinning its breakneck development and abundant international liquidity combined to benefit low- and middle-income economies (Saad-Filho 2013). Left-leaning Latin American governments capitalised on this moment to implement economic planning initiatives and novel welfare policies, such as conditional cash transfers (CCTs). These latter policies were financed mostly through higher taxation of soaring commodity exports. Under a changed economic and social policy mix, growth rates picked up and social conditions improved, partially reverting the negative consequences of neoliberalism and cementing popular support.

The Pink Tide would soon ebb, however, in a spiral of economic and political crises. Governments could not continue to deliver social improvements when, under deteriorating international conditions, tougher distributional choices had to be made. Combined with allegations of corruption and the repression of worker and indigenous struggles, important constituencies were alienated and a growing sense of disillusionment took hold. Traditional right-wing parties furthermore took hold of these scenarios to reorganise themselves and regain power. Several left-of-centre governments have thus been, legally or not, ousted from power since the 2009 Honduran military coup against Manuel Zelaya. This picked up speed with the 2015 right-wing victory of Mauricio Macri in Argentina and the 2016 parliamentary coup against Dilma Rousseff in Brazil.

In light of the Pink Tide's unravelling, the moment thus seems ripe for an appreciation of the significance of this historical moment and what it entailed. This chapter attempts to offer such a contribution: understanding to which extent have the Pink Tide governments implemented or not a clear break with neoliberalism and contributed to launching a sustained process of material gains for the working classes in Latin America. In order to do so, it discusses the economic and political trends prevailing in the continent as a whole, focusing on changes to the productive structure of the economies, the new matrix of social policies and the political strategies carried out to keep these governments in power. These three dimensions can be respectively synthesised in a shift towards neo-extractivism, or the renewed dependence on the export of primary commodities; the rise of conditional cash transfer policies (CCTs) as the main form of social safety nets; and the establishment of broad electoral fronts and a neo-corporatist pattern of class relations, which is to say, a state-centred mediation of capital-labour-social movements relations.

The main argument of this chapter is that the Pink Tide governments have indeed *promoted* changes that economically benefitted the working classes, but they could not secure the *sustainability* of this process. As explored below, the very processes that led to better standards of living reinforced a precarious international insertion of the countries, as they stimulated a neo-extractivist pattern of accumulation. Politically, the governments' strategies disorganised the working classes and social movements, as they depended on class conciliation measures and the repression of independent struggles. Without, furthermore, a clear battle for ideas and a vision of the future, the terrain on which the struggle was to be fought became shallow, limited to defending material gains. Therefore, these improvements were not accompanied by self-reinforcing economic and political conditions, but rather by an increased likelihood of any situation of crisis being 'solved' via an exclusionary shift in policies or government. In broad terms, the forces behind these governments have advanced an 'inconsequential' attempt at counter-hegemony, which relied too much on short-term factors and did not transform the state, the economy and prevalent ideas in ways that would progressively establish structural conditions compatible with popular goals.

The argument can be divided into four elements. First, there were substantial material gains for the working classes not entirely ascribable to positive international economic conditions, but partially due to active government policies, especially minimum wage hikes and CCTs.

Second, to bring about these improvements, the governments (i) relied on and promoted a neo-extractivist pattern of accumulation; (ii) reproduced themselves politically via broad fronts, centrally relying on neo-corporatist class conciliation measures, cash transfers to the most destitute groups and the repression of struggles by groups not aligned to the government, and (iii) did not promote far-reaching transformations of the state institutionality, of class relations or of visions about the trajectories development should assume.

Third, neo-extractivism and neo-corporatist class conciliation eroded the sustainability of this process, as they respectively (i) cemented a peripheral insertion in the world market and a class structure with a sizeable amount of precarious employment and (ii) disorganised the working classes and social movements, which were then incapable of mounting (extra-institutional) pressure. Finally, it therefore became increasingly likely that, when these social formations faced a crisis, it would not be the progressive elements in these hybrid state forms to be deepened. On the contrary, a transformation of state power in an exclusionary direction was to be expected, as indeed has been happening throughout the region.

The remainder of the chapter is structured as follows. The second section reviews the changing productive structure and international insertion of Latin American economies, differentiating between national experiences where possible. This comprised the rising importance of extractive activities and deindustrialisation, leading to a re-primarisation of exports—that is, the decrease of manufactured goods and the rise of low-value-added, unprocessed commodities in total exports. The third brings forth the class structures associated to this pattern of accumulation and changes to the standards of living. It is shown that the latter improved and there was reduced labour informality, but also structural precariousness in face of the poor quality of the jobs created.

The text then covers the changes to the state form, in two steps. The section 'The Changing Character of State Power: A Neo-corporatist Mediation of Class Relations' shows how the Pink Tide governments were neo-corporatist, as they attempted to directly mediate class relations by bringing them into the state apparatus. The support for domestic capitalists and the dissemination CCTs, which reduced poverty and inequality, are highlighted. The section 'Class Conciliation, Demobilisation and Repression' then explores the political underpinnings of this class conciliation process, namely, the incorporation *cum* co-option of social movements and class entities into the state and the repression of independent struggles. The section 'Final Remarks' summarises and concludes the chapter, underscoring the inherent limits to the non-confrontational strategy advanced by the Pink Tide.

THE PRODUCTIVE STRUCTURE: NEO-EXTRACTIVISM AND DEINDUSTRIALISATION

Neoliberalism and the debt crisis of the 1980s promoted deep transformations to the economy of Latin America. The continent's growth rate, on average 5.8 and never below 3.0 per cent between 1961 and 1980, dropped to 2.3 per cent between 1981 and 2000, with several years of negative or near-zero growth (World Bank 2015). At the same time, the region's insertion in the world market was made more precarious, with manufacturing decreasing substantially (see below). The abandonment of active industrial policies and the trade and financial opening were the main factors behind this (Bogliaccini 2013), leading to greater vulnerability and the recurrent crises of the 1990s.

Since the 2000s, however, the renewed dependence on the extraction and export of primary commodities has been the central feature of the Latin American economy. This has been variously described as a neo-extractivist pattern of accumulation (Veltmeyer 2013; Webber 2014), a re-primarisation of the structure of exports (Gonçalves et al. 2009) or, indeed, a commodities consensus (Svampa 2013). The central feature this characterisation conveys is that the extraction and export of primary goods has become the driving element of capital accumulation in Latin America. This does not imply such activities are the largest element of GDP, but rather that they are the main dynamic force in the economic cycle.

Estimations show how the foreign sector drove the growth of Latin American economies during the 2000s, led by commodity exports (Caldentey and Vernengo 2010).[1] Accordingly, agricultural and extractive commodities have risen from 41 to 53 per cent of total Latin American exports between 1999 and 2013, whilst manufacturing decreased from 58 to 44 per cent (Ray et al. 2015, 5). If the centrality of unprocessed commodity exports is similar to 'old' extractivism, what qualifies it as *neo*-extractivism is, in turn, the greater participation of the state in these activities, essentially via taxation on which social policies are funded (Arsel and Angel 2012; Arsel 2012; Gudynas 2012).

The implications of this process can be felt at different levels. On a local scale, the communities directly affected by extractive projects are subjected to environmental degradation and a destabilisation of their social reproduction, given that very few benefits spill over (Veltmeyer 2013). This heightens the spatial inequality of accumulation and sponsors processes of accumulation by dispossession, in which transnational companies, guarded by state power, continuously advance over natural resources. This amounts to the expanded commodification of nature and the forced proletarianisation of small farmers and peasants (Webber 2014).

On a macro level, the results are more complex. The currency inflows obtained with commodity exports present both opportunities and risks, which can be analysed under the so-called Dutch disease and the possibilities of avoiding it. The risks exist insofar as a rapid inflow of money, generally due to higher export prices, might appreciate the domestic currency (i.e., make foreign currency, and thus also foreign-produced goods, cheaper) and thus decrease the international competitiveness of the manufacturing sector. As imports become cheaper, domestic manufacturers are forced out of business, which forestalls the diversification of the economy and decreases the quality of available jobs (Bresser-Pereira 2011; Frenkel and Rapetti 2012). Once this boom is over, the economy would find itself in a worse position, given that the production of commodities generates less and worse-quality jobs and does not promote technological upgrading. This is what is referred to as the Dutch disease, but it is not, it should be stressed, a necessary outcome of higher export prices. Given appropriate policies, the currency overvaluation can be checked and the resources directed to developmental objectives (Saad-Filho and Weeks 2013).

The actual results are mixed. On the one hand, higher commodity exports helped sustain growth (for a look into the different transmission mechanisms, see Ocampo 2009). Every single Latin American country accumulated a substantial amount of foreign reserves, and with the exception of Jamaica and Barbados the same happened for the Caribbean. Altogether, the region's gross international reserves increased from US$ 163 billion in 2001 (ECLAC 2010, 272) to US$ 830 billion in 2013 (ECLAC 2014, 191). Moreover, higher growth rates and taxation of exports provided resources for social policies.[2] On the other hand, except for Argentina, the region's exchange rates were overvalued during the 2000s (Frenkel and Rapetti 2012). Hence, the turn to neo-extractivism has contributed to an already existent and ongoing process of deindustrialisation (Bresser-Pereira 2011; Brady et al. 2011).

Following the initial dismantling of manufacturing under neoliberal governments, there thus was a 'standing still', defensive policy that perpetuated deindustrialisation. The region has, moreover, also been specialising in less competitive manufacturing sectors, which means that the manufacturing sectors and jobs that did manage to remain are lagging behind world competitors (CEPAL 2007; Cimoli et al. 2010). Consequently, whilst the Pink Tide governments cannot be held responsible for *initiating* deindustrialisation, their rule *deepened* it due to the reliance on a neo-extractivist pattern of accumulation.

Summing up, under the pressure of the commodities boom, virtually all Latin American countries shifted to neo-extractivism. If this allowed for financing social policies and alleviated the balance-of-payments constraint, it also entailed negative environmental consequences, spurred deindustrialisation and heightened mid-term external vulnerability. In other words, the Pink Tide marked an inflection with regard to the neoliberal governments insofar as they used a positive international scenario to finance social goals, but no greater breaks were to be found. Deindustrialisation was deepened, without any prospect for improving the region's peripheral position in the global market and the problems of its economic structure. The chapter now explores how this reflected on changing class structures, employment patterns and the standards of living of the population.

Class Structures and Standards of Living under the Pink Tide

During the neoliberal period, there was a general tendency towards greater inequality and labour precarisation in Latin America, with five major trends (Portes and Hoffman 2003; Robinson 2008; Cornia 2012). First, unemployment rose substantially and tended to remain high. Second, particularly for Central American and Caribbean countries, a migrant labour class grew and, with it, numerous households came to rely on remittances. Labour market informality was another main trend, which also took the form of precarious self-employment and micro-entrepreneurialism. This was associated to the fourth trend, widespread labour deregulation. Finally, the feminisation of labour was present throughout.

These processes had clear impacts in terms of inequality, poverty and wages. The Gini index of household per capita income, the most common measure of inequality, increased by 0.05 between the early 1980s and 2002 (Cornia 2012, 4). This represented an increase of approximately 10 per cent, starting from what was already a very high level. Poverty followed suit, as the proportion of the population below the poverty line increased from 40.5 to 44 per cent between 1980 and 2002 (Robinson 2008, 252). In absolute terms, this meant 84 million more people living in poverty. As for wages, the real minimum wage dropped on average 30 per cent between 1980 and 1990 and was mostly stagnant until 2000 (ILO 2002, 115).

In the beginning of the century, however, at least a partial reversal of these trends was underway, as poverty, income inequality and informality undoubtedly decreased (Cornia 2014; Lustig et al. 2013). During the 2000s, inequality decreased by almost the same amount it had increased in the previous two decades. Thus, the average Gini coefficient for Latin America fell by 0.04 between 2002 and 2010. Another way of looking at this is that the share of national income appropriated by the richest 10 per cent of the population decreased in almost all countries, whereas the bottom 50 per cent got more (Cornia 2012, 4).[3] The proportion of the urban population living in poverty decreased very substantially, more than reverting the neoliberal trend: poverty dropped 14 percentage points between 2002 and 2012 (ECLAC 2014, 137). There were also striking differences in terms of labour informality. If 80 per cent of the jobs created during the 1990s were in the informal sector, informality dropped by about 8 per cent during the 2000s (ILO 2013). Finally, real minimum wages increased, on average, by 54 per cent between 2000 and 2012 (ILO 2013, 127). This holds for all Latin American countries, with the exception of the Dominican Republic.

Importantly, there is strong evidence that these developments were in large measure due to government policies (Cornia 2012, 2014). In a study of 18 Latin American countries to explain what caused the changes to income inequality, Cornia (2012, 37) finds that external conditions and economic growth were of minor importance. The main factors responsible for the decrease of inequality were greater access to secondary education, higher minimum wages and lower labour informality, and greater government transfers. Government policies such as increasing the minimum wage and instituting conditional cash transfers were, therefore, central to the decrease of inequality.

Furthermore, the left-of-centre governments were seen to have reduced inequality considerably more than the rest. The broad left, including Bolivia under Evo Morales, Brazil under the *Partido dos Trabalhadores* (Brazilian Workers' Party, PT) and Venezuela, all decreased their levels of inequality during the 2000s. As for centre and centre-rights administrations, such as Uruguay in the first half of the 2000s and Mexico, there were mixed results and in some of them inequality rose. On average, the decrease was much slower for countries not under the Pink Tide governments (Cornia 2012).

In light of this, it is clear that the Pink Tide governments positively impacted the living standards of the working classes. These results discredit interpretations that ascribe to foreign conditions the direct determinant of improved living standards, such as considering that the commodities boom would have had positive results regardless of the orientation of the governments in power. As seen above, domestic political choices were key. That inequality and living standards improved more rapidly under the Pink Tide is also of central importance. The issue is then to explore the limits of this process.

The Changing Character of State Power: A Neo-corporatist Mediation of Class Relations

If the neoliberal state was mainly the enforcer of market discipline on capital and labour, under the Pink Tide it took on a more flexible character, which attempted to mediate (intra-)class relations via economic and social policies and negotiation procedures. A useful way of looking at this is through tripartite negotiation forums, or negotiation tables between state representatives, capital and labour to determine wages and working conditions. This meant, first, that capital-labour relations were explicitly brought into the state. This was predicated upon a more direct participation of state power in the relations between capitalists of different economics sectors, as well as in the reproduction of labour power. As regards the former, the main element was the attempt to steer accumulation towards a 'national development project', for which the governments had to prioritise the relevant sectors and companies. This was done, for example, by actively using procurement policies to stimulate domestic firms, offering tax subsidies for strategic sectors and the like. As for workers, a significant increase in social policies, however not universal, and rising minimum wages were key. Finally, as these processes of class conciliation reached their limits, the continued repression of 'hardliner' popular organisations ensued (see the examples of the TIPNIS march and the repression of *Piqueteros* below).

This state form, on the one hand, was capable of securing greater gains (as compared to the neoliberal state) for the working classes, as seen in the previous section. On the other hand, as its legitimacy was strictly associated to securing the profitability of various fractions of capital and certain gains for the working classes, it was largely dependent on maintaining high growth rates. It was thus inherently prone to destabilisation as growth faltered. Furthermore, this commitment to negotiation and the conciliatory dynamics it implied made it incapable of promoting wide-ranging transformations. In short, it secured certain gains for the working classes whilst preventing greater transformations: it could manage neoliberalism in a relatively progressive direction, but not break with it. These developments are reviewed in order.

In the transition to neoliberalism, state power was used to push the privatisation of state-owned enterprises (SOEs), market liberalisation and the rollback of sector-specific policies, such as discontinuing subsidies for strategic sectors or state-run research and development initiatives. Thereafter, it sought to advance the integration of national economies to the world market, privileging the interests of financial forms of capital and arbitrating less between other fractions. Likewise, the state did not participate directly in wage negotiations, but rather repressed workers' mobilisations. Therefore, competing in a globally integrated market became the central locus of class relations and the way to achieve wage gains or higher profitability, and state power actively enforced this (Bonnet and Piva 2012).

On the other hand, under the Pink Tide state power assumed more the role of an arbiter. Negotiation forums were central in this process. Through these, class representatives and social movements entered into negotiation processes with the government and capitalists, so that issues related to distributional conflicts, wage levels, investment priorities and so on were addressed in an explicitly politicised and state-centred manner (Bonnet and Piva 2012; Piva 2011).[4]

There are three main results that came from this neo-corporatist pattern of organising class relations. First, to a certain extent it routinised social conflicts and directed capitalist accumulation strategies towards potentially developmental objectives (such as a pro-poor growth pattern, or growth with high wages). Second, it directly politicised accumulation, as state power came to be seen as responsible for the material outcomes of the various class fractions. Third, and as a consequence of this, the legitimacy of governments became increasingly attached to securing modest gains for the relevant classes—bankruptcies of industrialists, for example, could no longer be 'explained away' as a result of inefficient competition (as in the 1990s), but become a directly political problem. As governments' legitimacy came to depend on securing—and being held responsible for—these material gains, the strategies below were put in place to tend to capitalists and the population at large.

With the Pink Tide, there was a recovery of state planning capacities and, in some cases, a partial re-nationalisation of formerly privatised SOEs. This is what many authors (Leiva 2008; Bresser-Pereira 2011; Féliz 2012) saw as a neodevelopmental state form, which actively intervened via subsidies and tax exemptions to stimulate particular economic sectors, used development banks to finance domestic firms, took on a greater role in providing infrastructure and other public goods and so on. In short, the neodevelopmental state attempted to steer accumulation towards a pattern compatible with a particular—and always selective—view of what national development would be (Boito Jr and Berringer 2014; Féliz 2012; Petras and Veltmeyer 2007). National development came to be associated, in particular, with the accumulation strategies of the internal bourgeoisie,[5] and this class fraction displaced the hegemonic position of transnationalised financial capital (Boito Jr and Berringer 2014).

Differently from the 'traditional' Latin American developmental state of the mid-twentieth century, however, the *neo*developmental state did not seek to overcome the countries' position in the world market; it was a watered-down version of its precursor (Leiva 2008). Thus, growth rates were lower, the structure of the economy (in terms of the predominant sectors) did not change substantially, and the local capitalists politically behind this state form were not interested in antagonising those of developed countries. In Boito Jr's and Berringer's words, 'neodevelopmentalism is *the developmentalism of the era of neoliberal capitalism*[…] the development policy that is possible within the limits of the neoliberal capitalist model' (2014, 97, emphasis in the original). In this sense, it was an inflection within neoliberalism, but not a break with the latter.

The neo-corporatist state also had to guarantee at least moderately rising living standards for the working classes, if some stability was to obtain. The main instruments employed were raising minimum wages and CCTs. The latter did increase profusely, whilst universal social safety nets and public services showed little improvement. In 2013, CCTs were present in 20 countries and reached approximately 120 million people, or 20 per cent of the region's population (Cecchini 2013). On the positive side, there is strong evidence that they were indeed able to reach the poor and very poor. There is also no evidence that if properly designed, they significantly stimulated labour market segmentation and informality, increased the fertility rate of beneficiaries (Stecklov et al. 2007) or reduced labour market participation (Alzúa et al. 2013). That they have lifted millions out of poverty at a very low cost of approximately 0.4 per cent of the region's GDP is no mean feat (Cecchini and Madariaga 2011).

In spite of this positive record for CCTs, the claims about their capacity of achieving longer-term goals—breaking the inter-generational transmission of poverty—are much harder to sustain, and as of yet there is no evidence in this regard (Valencia Lomelí 2008; Handa and Davis 2006). Moreover, given the small amount of the benefits provided, in most cases poverty *vulnerability* has not been adequately addressed, and improvements in the labour market were more important in reducing inequality. Finally, cheap though they might be, their cost-effectiveness is by no means demonstrated, given leakages and higher administrative costs as compared to universal programmes (Saad-Filho 2015). The extension of CCTs can thus be considered a welcome, if far from sufficient, development. Their widespread recommendation by the World Bank (Fiszbein et al. 2009) is a further indication that this form of social policy is safely within the realm of neoliberal policymaking.

Class Conciliation, Demobilisation and Repression

As regards the strictly political relation between the government and class entities, a two-sided process was in place. It comprehended, first, incorporating or co-opting the representatives of trade unions and social movements, who would participate in negotiation forums. As a corollary, it also involved isolating or repressing independent entities. The central element was thus 'convincing' labour and social movements to abandon extra-institutional mobilisation and direct action in favour of official channels. As part of this, many leaders of trade unions and social movements were incorporated into the state apparatus, assuming offices (Oliveira et al. 2010; Farthing and Kohl 2014). This amounted to a routinisation of social conflicts and the possibility of sharing, to an extent, in the gains capital enjoyed, albeit at the price of curtailing the tools popular sectors can use in their struggles (see examples below).

The second element was dividing class entities and social movements into 'good', negotiating ones, and 'bad', independent ones (Castorina 2013; Webber 2014; Galvão 2014). A line was thus drawn between the demands that could be processed and those that had to be ignored and repressed. This 'us versus them' approach created divisions within the popular sectors, and thus further restricted the horizons of what was at stake in official negotiations (Modenesi 2012). Combined as it was to actively repressing all forms of independent struggle, it led to demobilisation and less independent grassroots organising. Ironically, then, in the mid-term they hampered the continuity of reforms by hindering popular mobilisation from below, an important element in obtaining concessions from capital. This combination of improved material conditions without political empowerment, promoting instead class conciliation, is another illustration of the limits of the inflection under the Pink Tide.

All of these were widespread processes, of which three examples are offered. In Brazil, after the PT came to power, it appointed many union leaders to key positions in the state apparatus. The *Central Única dos Trabalhadores* (CUT), the main trade union federation, became organically linked to the routine management of the state. Once a combative and innovative organisation, it was already moderating itself throughout the 1990s; with the PT in power, however, it clearly opted for a negotiating strategy and abandoned tactics reliant on wide mobilisations of its base (Galvão 2014). As for the *Movimento dos Trabalhadores Rurais sem Terra* (MST), they did not establish organic links with the government, but likewise opted for a negotiating strategy in which the resort to direct action was strongly curtailed. As a militant put it, 'When government is ours, it's worse. The MST stops organizing protests' (Vergara-Camus 2009, 186). Finally, independent struggles were met with indifference to their demands, repression and police violence. The countrywide 2012 strike of federal university workers is a good example, but the response to the mobilisations of 2013 is the strongest. What came to be known as *Jornadas de Junho* were the first mass demonstrations in the country for decades, with millions of participants and outside the influence of government-aligned trade unions and social movements. Police violence caused them to grow and continued to be present throughout their whole unfolding, but was never condemned by president Dilma Rousseff, and their demands were not met (Moraes et al. 2014).

In Argentina, the introduction of *Plan Jefes y Jefas de Hogar* (PJyJH), a CCT programme, had important implications for the unemployed workers organisations known as *Piqueteros*, hitherto at the forefront of popular resistance to neoliberalism and the 2001–2002 crisis (Castorina 2013). The government selectively incorporated the leaders of certain organisations into the state apparatus to administer PJyJH benefits whilst repressing those that did not cooperate. 'Good *Piqueteros*' thus became government allies and received the power to administer cash transfers, and 'bad' ones were alienated and dwindled. This destroyed horizontal linkages between the various grassroots movements, but at the same time stabilised conflicts. As for labour struggles, the Labour and Social Development ministries were reinstated as the site of tripartite negotiations, with important implications for moderating workers' strategies. This state-sponsored negotiating strategy could bring important trade unions along, such as the *Confederación General del Trabajo de la República Argentina* (CGT) (Bonnet and Piva 2012; Bonnet 2012).

In the case of Bolivia a similar process of incorporation and repression took place. On the one hand, various organisations that formed the basis of the *Movimiento al Socialismo* (Movement Towards Socialism (MAS), the left governing party since 2006) have become part of the state apparatus and opted for institutional-based forms of struggle. The leaders of entities representing indigenous movements and trade unions, such as the *Confederación Sindical Única de Trabajadores Campesinos de Bolivia* (CSUTCB), have assumed several positions in office (Farthing and Kohl 2014). This 'de-colonisation' of the state, a central platform of the MAS government, has arguably led many marginalised groups to see themselves reflected in the state apparatus and allowed for real gains in negotiation processes (Ikemura Amaral 2014).

This incorporation of historically excluded groups in Bolivia comes with a caveat, nevertheless. When social movements understand the state is not acquiescing to their demands and go for direct action—which, it must be remembered, stands behind the insurrectionary movement that culminated in MAS's rise to power (Webber 2011)—they have been deemed 'imperialist conspiracies' or the agents of foreign NGOs, and are repressed. The clearest example of this process came in the wake of the conflicts around the TIPNIS national park (Territorio Indígena y Parque Nacional Isiboro Sécure), when mostly indigenous groups protested against government plans to build a motorway through it. As Sanchez-Lopez reports, 'the government disqualified the legitimacy of this civic action arguing that the indigenous organizations were manipulated by the "oligarchy elites, the green imperialism of Western NGOs and the US government"' and brutally repressed them (Sanchez-Lopez 2015, 24).

This whole process receives its perhaps clearest expression in the thought of Álvaro García Linera, Bolivia's vice-president and a prolific theoretician. As he puts it, 'the Bolivian people have consolidated their historical unity around a *single* project for the state, the economy and the society' (García Linera 2011, 7, our emphasis). In fact, since the consolidation of the revolutionary process we would be witnessing the dissolution of the state form into society, creating an 'integral state' (p. 10). The government and its allies would thus concentrate in themselves all the 'creative tensions' of the revolution, the only paths capable of further advancing popular goals (p. 28). The corollary is that every mobilisation not contained within these limits, such as those of communities that resist extractivism, must of necessity be denounced as particularistic, counterproductive or even imperialist (Webber 2014). The state form is thus the arbiter of all that is progressive, and there are only two positions: one is either for it, and (critically) supports it from within, or a right-wing agent of counter-revolution. No progressive stance outside of the state's realm is possible. Whilst García Linera restricts his analysis to Bolivia, it can arguably be extended to encompass the strategies and rhetoric of various other Pink Tide governments.[6]

Final Remarks

Latin America underwent a multifaceted process of social change that defies all summary interpretations. Neither a clear continuity with the immediately preceding neoliberal past nor a deep-rooted break with it, the

Pink Tide was a nuanced and internally differentiated inflection. There were undeniable material gains for the popular classes, as inequality, poverty and labour informality levels decreased, in large measure due to the political initiative of Pink Tide governments. This occurred, nevertheless, under very particular foreign conditions, given the coincidence of the high international commodity prices and capital flows to less-developed economies. Whilst the latter did not *determine* the processes indicated above, they do seem to have played a contradictory enabling role, and their overall impact is still far from clear. Additionally, the Pink Tide governments promoted problematic economic and political developments, which sapped the potential for a continued process of gains for the population.

The main inflections in the pattern of accumulation, social policies and the state form can be respectively described as the rise of neo-extractivism, the expansion of CCTs and minimum wage hikes and the transition to a neo-corporatist state. Neo-extractivism or the commodity consensus (Veltmeyer 2013; Svampa 2013) thus highlights the centrality of commodity exports, as well as the state's role in fostering them. This is linked to the idea of a compensatory state (Gudynas 2012), which taxed such activities to promote CCTs and minimum wage hikes. If this brought about material gains, it fell short, however, of instituting universal safety nets or de-commodifying basic needs, underscoring the limits of the transformations that took place. Finally, neo-corporatism suggests a state form that internalised class conflicts, circumscribing them to what was compatible with the then-prevailing pattern of accumulation. This is seen as an attempt to promote class conciliation by distributing material gains to various social movements and class fractions, whilst moderating their goals (Bonnet and Piva 2012).

A synthesis is proposed combining elements from these three dimensions—neo-extractivism, the expansion of CCTs and minimum wage hikes and the transition to a neo-corporatist state. This is intended both as a general interpretive framework of the Pink Tide governments and, more importantly, as a framework for comparing the different experiences within the continent. The main thread that runs through these dimensions is that, to different degrees, the Pink Tide governments chose the paths of least resistance in trying to advance a reformist project. They restricted their goals, adopted tactics consistent with this and delivered what was possible under these circumstances: some gains to the working classes when compared to the neoliberal past, but without promoting structural changes and at the cost of preventing popular empowering. Lower informality combined to precarious employment, reducing inequality but only to the levels of the 1980s, and achieving higher growth rates whilst cementing a peripheral insertion in the world market are illustrative. These were undoubtedly important inflections, but not strong enough breaks to institute self-sustaining processes that would endure.[7]

In this vein, there was a strategic complementarity between neo-extractivism, a CCT-based social policy mix and neo-corporatism. These were all mechanisms for social compromise that, compared to the preceding phase of strict neoliberalism, allowed for relatively greater gains for the working classes. The inherent downside, however, was that they prevented popular empowering, contentious politics and a clearer break with the prevailing productive and class structure. Whilst it is beyond the scope of this chapter to try to discern the precedence or causation of each of these elements, it is argued that over time, through a trial-and-error process, they reinforced and supported each other. As neo-extractivism offered funding for CCTs, there was interest in stimulating commodity exports; CCTs together with rising real minimum wages sustained popular approval of the governments; and faster growth with lower inequality legitimated neo-corporatist, conciliatory class relations—which, in turn, helped guarantee the interests of local capitalists and so on.

This strategic complementary also explains the brittleness of the Pink Tide, as pursuing paths of least resistance eroded the political and economic resilience of these countries and hence made them vulnerable to destabilisation. The point is that there was a tendency for these forms (neo-extractivism, CCT-based social policies and neo-corporatism) to develop alongside each other and forestall alternatives in any single dimension. Why go for independent labour mobilisation when neo-corporatism was delivering wage gains? Why attempt a larger overhaul of macroeconomic policies if there had been growth and this would require confronting powerful interests? Fundamentally, how could any of these possibilities obtain without strong popular organisation? Attempting to change one dimension without supporting transformations in the others was hence extremely unlikely. The different elements were thus likely to stand and fall together, in the latter case particularly if subjected to foreign-determined shocks, of which the fall in commodity prices offers a prime example.

It is thus no surprise that, as foreign conditions worsened in the early and mid-2010s, the social formations found themselves in a debilitated position and the processes that sustained these governments in power were no longer operative. The predictable crisis that ensued thus did not lead to a deepening of the progressive elements in these hybrid state forms, particularly given the demobilisation of popular forces, but rather to exclusionary adjustments. Which is to say, instead of trying to solve the crises via public investment in infrastructure, tax reforms to redistribute money to the poor and so on, austerity measures were instead called for. This is diametrically opposed to the neoliberal crises of the late 1990s, which occurred in the wake of long-term processes of popular organisation and eventually led to the election of left-of-centre governments.

In the medium term, these paths of least resistance ironically went from being the most realistic options to utopic ones. They eroded their conditions of existence, without promoting structural economic and political transformations that could deepen their progressive impact. This underscores the dangers of broad political fronts and minimalist reformist programmes. Their very condition of success in the short term—appealing to a broad section of the population and avoiding overt conflict—prevents them from confronting established interests, particularly capitalist ones. On the contrary, the dynamics that unfold are all geared towards class conciliation and incremental reforms, thwarting more transformative actions and the very continuity of such already-diminished goals.

Notes

1. In Central America, remittances are the driving factor, which can be conceptualised as an export of labour (Robinson 2008; Caldentey and Vernengo 2010). Brazil is an outlier in terms of its drivers of growth, which were domestic after 2006 (Serrano and Summa 2015), but the commodities boom was still central as it provided reserves that displaced the balance-of-payments constraint to growth.
2. There is regional variation in the channels that connected higher exports to taxation and social policies. For example, Bolivia directly increased royalties and taxes on natural gas exports and earmarked some of these proceeds for social programmes. In Brazil, on the other hand, it was higher growth rates and labour formalisation that allowed the government to increase spending (Serrano and Summa 2015).
3. In Peru, for example, the 10 per cent richest got about 7 per cent less of national income between 2002 and 2009, whereas the bottom 50 per cent got about 3 per cent more. Costa Rica, Nicaragua and Colombia are the only exceptions to this trend (Cornia 2012).
4. Traditionally, corporatism refers to negotiation forums between organised labour, firm representatives and state managers. The distinction for Latin America, which merits the neo- qualifier, is the presence of social movements.

5. A Poulantzian concept, their interests are somewhat tied to accumulation in the domestic or regional market, as opposed to fully transnationalised class fractions, but not to the extent of the now-defunct national bourgeoisie (Boito Jr and Berringer 2014, 95).
6. As Sader (2013) put it for Brazil: 'This group, which allegedly took to the left of the PT to found PSOL [*Partido Socialismo e Liberdade*], quickly added itself, in a subordinate manner, to the right-wing attack on the government. […] The extreme left […] has, tacitly or explicitly, allied itself with the right against these [Pink Tide] governments.'
7. It is beyond the scope of this chapter to analyse the political alternatives and draft a different programme, which would in any case depend strongly on the conjuncture. Nevertheless, three general elements are central: timing, structural transformations and extra-institutional mobilisation. A pragmatic approach was arguably necessary in the initial moments of the Pink Tide governments, and the feasibility of openly class-confrontational programmes is indeed debatable. To overcome this, entrenching transformations of the economy and political institutions would be essential (such as universalising public services, preventing private financing of political campaigns and so on). When these governments enjoyed massive popular support, for example, towards the end of Lula's second term in Brazil (2010), these changes could be attempted. Popular mobilisation would be a means of pressuring for them, and this would in turn firmly cement the support basis of the parties. The precise changes and moments are sure to vary, but by merely managing the state without transforming, it the Pink Tide governments would increasingly trap themselves in a corner.

References

Alzúa, María Laura, Guillermo Cruces, and Laura Ripani. 2013. Welfare Programs and Labor Supply in Developing Countries: Experimental Evidence from Latin America. *Journal of Population Economics* 26 (4): 1255–1284.

Arsel, Murat. 2012. Between 'Marx and markets'? The State, the 'Left Turn' and Nature in Ecuador. *Tijdschrift voor economische en sociale geografie* 103 (2): 150–163.

Arsel, Murat, and Natalia Avila Angel. 2012. "Stating" Nature's Role in Ecuadorian Development: Civil Society and the Yasuní-ITT Initiative. *Journal of Developing Societies* 28 (2): 203–227.

Bogliaccini, Juan Ariel. 2013. Trade Liberalization, Deindustrialization, and Inequality: Evidence from Middle-Income Latin American Countries. *Latin American Research Review* 48 (2): 79–105.

Boito, Armando, Jr., and Tatiana Berringer. 2014. Social Classes, Neodevelopmentalism, and Brazilian Foreign Policy Under Presidents Lula and Dilma. *Latin American Perspectives* 41 (5): 94–109.

Bonnet, Alberto. 2012. La crisis del Estado neoliberal en la Argentina. In *El estado en América Latina: continuidades y rupturas*, ed. Mabel Thwaites Rey, 279–302. Santiago: Editorial ARCIS.

Bonnet, Alberto, and Adrián Piva. 2012. Un análisis de los cambios en la forma de estado en la posconvertibilidad. In *Argentina después de la convertibilidad (2002–2011)*, ed. Juan Grigera, 3–31. Buenos Aires: Imago Mundi.

Brady, David, Yunus Kaya, and Gary Gereffi. 2011. Stagnating Industrial Employment in Latin America. *Work and Occupations* 38 (2): 179–220.

Bresser-Pereira, Luiz Carlos. 2011. An Account of New Developmentalism and Its Structuralist Macroeconomics. *Revista de economia política* 31 (3): 493–502.

Caldentey, Esteban Pérez, and Matías Vernengo. 2010. Back to the Future: Latin America's Current Development Strategy. *Journal of Post Keynesian Economics* 32 (4): 623–644.

Castorina, Emilia. 2013. Crisis and Recomposition in Argentina. In *The New Latin American Left. Cracks in the Empire*, ed. Jeffery R. Webber and Barry Carr, 233–254. Plymouth: Rowman & Littlefield.

Cecchini, Simone. 2013. Transferências condicionadas na América Latina e Caribe: da inovação à consolidação. In *Programa Bolsa Família: uma década de inclusão e cidadania*, ed. Tereza Campello and Marcelo Cortês Neri, 367–396. Brasília: IPEA.

Cecchini, Simone, and Aldo Madariaga. 2011. *Conditional Cash Transfers Programmes: The Recent Experience in Latin America and the Caribbean*. Santiago: ECLAC.

CEPAL. 2007. *Progreso técnico y cambio estructural en América Latina*. Santiago: Naciones Unidas.

Cimoli, Mario, Gabriel Porcile, and Sebastián Rovira. 2010. Structural Change and the BOP-Constraint: Why Did Latin America Fail to Converge? *Cambridge Journal of Economics* 34 (2): 389–411.

Cornia, Giovanni Andrea. 2012. *Inequality Trends and Their Determinants: Latin America Over 1990–2010*, 1–46, WIDER Working Papers (2012/09).

———, ed. 2014. *Falling Inequality in Latin America: Policy Changes and Lessons*. Oxford: Oxford University Press.

ECLAC. 2010. *Economic Survey of Latin America and the Caribbean 2009–2010: The Distributive Impact of Public Policies*. Santiago: ECLAC.

———. 2014. *Economic Survey of Latin America and the Caribbean 2014: Challenges to Sustainable Growth in a New External Context*. Santiago: ECLAC.

Farthing, Linda C., and Benjamin Kohl. 2014. *Evo's Bolivia: Continuity and Change*. Austin: University of Texas Press.

Féliz, Mariano. 2012. Neo-developmentalism: Beyond Neoliberalism? Capitalist Crisis and Argentinas Development Since the 1990s. *Historical Materialism* 20 (2): 105–123.

Fiszbein, Ariel, Norbert Schady, Francisco H.G. Ferreira, Margaret Grosh, Niall Keleher, Pedro Olinto, and Emmanuel Skoufias. 2009. *Conditional Cash*

Transfers: Reducing Present and Future Poverty. World Bank Policy Research Report. Washington, DC: World Bank.
Frenkel, Roberto, and Martin Rapetti. 2012. External Fragility or Deindustrialization: What Is the Main Threat to Latin American Countries in the 2010s? World Economic Review 1: 37–57.
Galvão, Andréia. 2014. The Brazilian Labor Movement Under PT Governments. Latin American Perspectives 41 (5): 184–199.
García Linera, Alvaro. 2011. Las tensiones creativas de la revolución: la quinta fase del proceso de cambio. La Paz: Vicepresidencia del Estado Plurinacional de Bolivia.
Gonçalves, Reinaldo, Marcelo Dias Carcanholo, Luiz A.M. Filgueiras, and Eduardo Costa Pinto. 2009. Vulnerabilidad estructural externa en América Latina. In Los condicionantes de la crisis en América Latina: inserción internacional y modalidades de acumulación, ed. Enrique O. Arceo and Eduardo M. Basualdo, 119–138. Buenos Aires: CLACSO.
Gudynas, Eduardo. 2012. Estado compensador y nuevos extractivismos: las ambivalencias del progresismo sudamericano. Nueva Sociedad 237: 128–146.
Handa, Sudhanshu, and Benjamin Davis. 2006. The Experience of Conditional Cash Transfers in Latin America and the Caribbean. Development Policy Review 24 (5): 513–536.
Ikemura Amaral, Aiko. 2014. Os caminhos da politização da indigeneidade: um estudo sobre a identidade indígena na política boliviana pós-1985. Mestrado em Ciência Política Dissertação, Departamento de Ciência Política, Universidade de São Paulo.
ILO. 2002. 2002 Labour Overview Latin America and the Caribbean. Lima: ILO.
———. 2013. 2013 Labour Overview Latin America and the Caribbean. Lima: ILO.
Leiva, Fernando Ignacio. 2008. Latin American Neostructuralism: The Contradictions of Post-Neoliberal Development. Minneapolis/London: University of Minnesota Press.
Lustig, Nora, Luis F. Lopez-Calva, and Eduardo Ortiz-Juarez. 2013. Declining Inequality in Latin America in the 2000s: The Cases of Argentina, Brazil, and Mexico. World Development 44 (0): 129–141.
Medeiros, Carlos Aguiar. 2011. The Political Economy of Institutional Change and Economic Development in Latin American Economies. Journal of Economic Issues XLV (2): 289–300.
Modenesi, Massimo. 2012. Revoluciones pasivas en América Latina: una aproximación gramsciana a la caracterización de los gobiernos progresistas de inicio del siglo. In El estado en América Latina: continuidades y rupturas, ed. Mabel Thwaites Rey, 139–166. Santiago: Editorial ARCIS.
Moraes, Alana, Bernardo Gutiérrez, Henrique Parra, Hugo Albuquerque, Jean Tible, and Salvador Schavelzon, eds. 2014. Junho: potência das ruas e das redes. São Paulo: Friedrich Ebert Stiftung (FES) Brasil.

Ocampo, José Antonio. 2009. Latin America and the Global Financial Crisis. *Cambridge Journal of Economics* 33 (4): 703–724.
de Oliveira, Francisco, Ruy Braga, and Cibele Saliba Rizek, eds. 2010. *Hegemonia às avessas: economia, política e cultura na era da servidão financeira*. São Paulo: Boitempo.
Petras, James, and Henry Veltmeyer. 2007. The 'Development State' in Latin America: Whose Development, Whose State? *Journal of Peasant Studies* 34 (3): 371–407.
Piva, Adrián. 2011. Una aproximación a los cambios en la Forma de Estado en Argentina (2002–2009). *Theomai: estudios sobre sociedad, naturaleza y desarrollo* 23: 1–23.
Portes, Alejandro, and Kelly Hoffman. 2003. Latin American Class Structures: Their Composition and Change During the Neoliberal Era. *Latin American Research Review* 38 (1): 41–82.
Ray, Rebecca, Kevin P. Gallagher, Andres Lopez, and Cynthia Sanborn, eds. 2015. *China in Latin America: Lessons for South-South Cooperation and Sustainable Development*. Boston: Boston University's Global Economic Governance Initiative (GEGI).
Robinson, Wiiliam I. 2008. *Latin America and Global Capitalism. A Critical Globalization Perspective*. Baltimore: The John Hopkins University Press.
Saad-Filho, Alfredo. 2013. Mass Protests Under 'Left Neoliberalism': Brazil, June–July 2013. *Critical Sociology* 39 (5): 657–669.
———. 2015. Social Policy for Neoliberalism: The Bolsa Família Programme in Brazil. *Development and Change* 46 (6): 1227–1252.
Saad-Filho, Alfredo, and John Weeks. 2013. Curses, Diseases and Other Resource Confusions. *Third World Quarterly* 34 (1): 1–21.
Sader, Emir. 2011. *The New Mole: Paths of the Latin American Left*. London: Verso.
———. 2013. Por que a extrema esquerda fracassou. *Blog do Emir*. Accessed 5 Feb 2015.
Sanchez-Lopez, Daniela. 2015. Reshaping Notions of Citizenship: The TIPNIS Indigenous Movement in Bolivia. *Development Studies Research* 2 (1): 20–32.
Serrano, Franklin, and Ricardo Summa. 2015. Aggregate Demand and the Slowdown of Brazilian Economic Growth in 2011–2014. *Nova Economia* 25 (especial): 803–833.
Stecklov, Guy, Paul Winters, Jessica Todd, and Ferdinando Regalia. 2007. Unintended Effects of Poverty Programmes on Childbearing in Less Developed Countries: Experimental Evidence from Latin America. *Population Studies* 61 (2): 125–140.
Svampa, Maristella. 2013. Consenso de "commodities" y lenguajes de valoración en América Latina. *Nueva Sociedad* 244: 30–46.

Valencia Lomelí, Enrique. 2008. Conditional Cash Transfers as Social Policy in Latin America: An Assessment of Their Contributions and Limitations. *Annual Review of Sociology* 34 (1): 475–499.

Veltmeyer, Henry. 2013. The Political Economy of Natural Resource Extraction: A New Model or Extractive Imperialism? *Canadian Journal of Development Studies/Revue canadienne d'études du développement* 34 (1): 79–95.

Vergara-Camus, Leandro. 2009. The Politics of the MST: Autonomous Rural Communities, the State, and Electoral Politics. *Latin American Perspectives* 36 (4): 178–191.

Webber, Jeffery R. 2011. *Red October: Left-Indigenous Struggles in Modern Bolivia*. Leiden: Brill.

———. 2014. Revolution Against 'Progress': Neo-extractivism, the Compensatory State, and the TIPNIS Conflict in Bolivia. In *Crisis and Contradiction: Marxist Perspectives on Latin America in the Global Political Economy*, ed. Susan Spronk and Jeffery R. Webber, 302–333. Leiden: Brill.

World Bank. 2015. *World Bank Open Data*. Accessed 4 May 2015.

Open Access This chapter is licensed under the terms of the Creative Commons Attribution 4.0 International License (http://creativecommons.org/licenses/by/4.0/), which permits use, sharing, adaptation, distribution and reproduction in any medium or format, as long as you give appropriate credit to the original author(s) and the source, provide a link to the Creative Commons license and indicate if changes were made.

The images or other third party material in this chapter are included in the chapter's Creative Commons license, unless indicated otherwise in a credit line to the material. If material is not included in the chapter's Creative Commons license and your intended use is not permitted by statutory regulation or exceeds the permitted use, you will need to obtain permission directly from the copyright holder.

PART II

The Case of Brazil

CHAPTER 3

Entangled Inequalities, State, and Social Policies in Contemporary Brazil

Sérgio Costa

INTRODUCTION: ENTANGLED INEQUALITIES

As a topic dating back to the very beginnings of sociology and economics, social inequalities have been subject to a wide array of definitions backed for different analytical and political purposes. In the past decades, neoclassical approaches rose to prominence both within the disciplinary field of economics and leading international organisations such as UN development agencies and the World Bank. This, in turn, resulted in a specific definition of inequalities that is dominant in international academia and politics alike: according to this interpretation, social inequalities refer to asymmetric individual chances to access socially valuable goods. Consequently, individual income differences within national borders as measured by the Gini index have become the central instrument to measure inequalities.

A first draft of this paper was delivered at the Workshop Rethinking Inequalities in Latin America, Bergen, and Norway, 5–6 March 2015, and at the University Aarhus, Denmark, on 7 October 2015. I thank the participants of these events as well as Luiz Carlos Bresser-Pereira and the editors of the present volume for valuable comments. I am alone responsible for eventually remaining imprecisions.

S. Costa (✉)
Freie Universität Berlin, Berlin, Germany

© The Author(s) 2018
M. Ystanes, I.Å. Strønen (eds.), *The Social Life of Economic Inequalities in Contemporary Latin America*, Approaches to Social Inequality and Difference, DOI 10.1007/978-3-319-61536-3_3

This narrow definition of inequalities presents practical advantages insofar as it offers a measurable basis for comparisons between individuals and national societies. However, it does not adequately take into account other crucial dimensions of inequalities as captured by more complex conceptualisations. Recent objections to this narrow definition can be classified into four groups related to the interest in researching inequalities: inequalities (1) of what, (2) between whom, (3) when, and (4) where. In the following, I will discuss these objections with regard to recent developments in Brazil. In particular, I will show how a more complex conceptualisation of inequality is necessary to adequately assess the gains in inequality reduction achieved during Brazil's engagement with the Pink Tide.

Inequalities of What?

A focus on inequalities of chances implicitly or explicitly rests on a liberal assumption according to which social positions in modern societies are solely or mainly determined by individual achievements. Therefore, if individuals have similar social opportunities, disparities in their life conditions allegedly reflect differences in terms of their individual effort. This supposition has been largely criticised by authors demonstrating that ascriptions concerning gender, race, ethnicity, and social prejudices remain relevant for individual opportunities of social mobility—also in contemporary societies (for an encompassing critique: Boatcă and Roth 2016). In Latin American societies, the role of ascriptions in shaping social inequalities is especially relevant due to the fact that being identified with categories coined to describe subordinated groups during the colonial period such as "black", "mestiza/mestizo", and "india/indio" still determines, to a large extent, the position occupied by individuals in current socio-economic hierarchies. In most cases, these colonial categories have been removed from the legal or policy framework, and, in cases where they do still appear, they are used not for discriminating against groups but rather for naming target groups of affirmative action policies in favour of blacks, women, indigenous peoples, and so on. However, as outlined in the introduction of this volume, these categories operate as ascriptive filters in everyday life, hindering the correspondent groups from accessing higher social positions, even in those cases for which formal equality of opportunities do exist. Because of this ascriptive bias, it seems analytically more accurate to shift the focus from inequality of opportunities in formal terms to inequality of results, understood as the final positions which individuals or groups of individuals achieve in the socio-economic structure.

Of course, socio-economic inequalities in terms of income and wealth are crucial for determining differences in concrete living conditions—after all, the wealthiest groups have better housing, better medical assistance, more and better leisure as well as longer life expectancies than groups which occupy a lower position in the social-economic structure. Nevertheless, two other dimensions of social inequalities, mostly faded out in conventional inequality research, are also decisive in determining distances between living conditions faced by different social groups: *power asymmetries* and *socio-ecological inequalities*. *Power inequalities* refers to both unequal capabilities to exert influence in decisions which affect one's personal trajectory and the asymmetric distribution of political and social rights and entitlements. Power asymmetries are obviously connected with socio-economic inequalities; however, they also encompass inequalities related to the level of enforcement of citizenship rights and welfare schemes. Accordingly, welfare states able to offer good public educational, health or transportation services enormously contribute to reducing the impact of (existing) socio-economic inequalities on (existing) living conditions (Kreckel 2004; Therborn 2013). In contrast, states which concentrate their social policies on cash transfers to the poor make only a small contribution to the reduction of disparities in living conditions (Lavinas 2013).

Socio-ecological inequalities, for their part, refers to both the unequal access to environmental goods such as fresh water, clean air, parks, and so on and the unevenly distributed capacity to obtain protection against ecological risks, including natural disasters and also manufactured jeopardies (pollution, irradiation, etc.). Provided that environmental goods are vastly commodified in contemporary societies and ecological risks can be outsourced and even exported, socio-ecological inequalities are not a lineal product of the "natural" geography of environmental goods and "bads". On the contrary, recent scholarship in this field defends the idea of a "constitutive interconnectedness" of nature and society inasmuch as:

> Social relations of power and domination are constitutive for environmental problems; and vice versa that the way in which nature is appropriated, transformed and represented is constitutive for the (re-)production of social relations of power, domination and inequality. (Dietz 2014, 16)

To sum up the arguments developed up to this point, researching inequalities from an encompassing perspective firstly requires a change of perspective, moving from inequalities of opportunities to inequalities of positions. Secondly, it implies a multidimensional concept of inequality able to consistently connect socio-economic, socio-ecological, and power inequalities.

Inequalities Between Whom?

Using concepts and references such as horizontal inequalities (in contrast to vertical inequalities; Stewart 2010), categorical inequalities (Tilly 1999), and intersectional inequalities (Anthias 2013, 2016), various authors stress the importance of researching inequalities not only between individuals but also between groups defined by social ascriptions. As summarised by Tilly,

> [l]arge, significant inequalities in advantages among human beings correspond mainly to categorical differences such as black/white, male/female, citizen/foreigner, or Muslim/Jew rather than to individual differences in attributes, propensities, or performances. (Tilly 1999, 7)

Today, more than 15 years after the publication of Tilly's seminal book on durable inequalities, several studies in a variety of fields have demonstrated the importance of intermediate categories, between and within the seemingly binary constructions Tilly used, in determining social inequalities. For example, it has been shown that within the categorical pair citizen/foreigner, one can identify key series of gradations such as the legal status of immigrants, their country of origin, and so on that determine their rights and possibilities, varying significantly among "foreigners" (see, e.g. Góngora-Mera et al. 2014). Similarly, as Lavra Pinto shows (this volume), there are significant inequalities within Rio de Janeiro's favelas—not just between favela residents and those of formal neighbourhoods. Moreover, the temporal aspect is often neglected: positions and labels adopted by individuals or groups may vary considerably over time, with groups who defined themselves as peasants later identifying themselves as indigenous or of African origin. That is to say that persistent inequality affecting similar demographic groups may be expressed by different categories (e.g. peasant, indigenous, indigenous women, etc.) in different historical circumstances (see Gonçalves and Costa 2016). Aside from that, definitions such as categorical inequalities or horizontal inequalities remain analytically useful because they reinforce the importance of social ascriptions in stabilising inequality patterns. In particular, *intersectional approaches*, for their part, have convincingly shown that positions in social structures always derive from complex interplays of categorisations of race, gender, class, and so on.

Inequalities When?

Economists usually study inequalities from a synchronic, contemporary perspective paying no attention to the fact that existing social structures reflect necessarily long-time historical processes (e.g. López-Calva and Lustig 2010).

Since the paradigmatic contribution of Tilly (1999), different studies have sought to enlarge their temporal perspective in order to unpack the historical formations of inequality structures. In the case of Latin America, several historiographic studies have reconstructed the nexus between contemporary inequalities and the history of this region shaped by colonialism, slavery, as well as by the reception of scientific racism after national independence (e.g. Stepan 1991; Andrews 2004). Conceptually, linking past and contemporary inequalities found in Latin America remains a challenge. This is because historically "persistent inequalities" have assumed new faces through history based on internal or external factors such as the enforcement of citizenship rights or the integration of local and global economies. Baquero (2015) draws on the geological metaphor "layered inequalities" to respond to this conceptual gap. According to this concept, inequalities which emerged in a certain historical epoch are superposed (but not substituted) by more recent structures of inequalities.

Other authors have also tried to solve this conceptual temporal problem by drawing on the idea of inequality regimes (Costa 2011; Góngora-Mera 2018). At the theoretical level, "inequality regimes" combines the idea of regime as a relational unity of analysis as found in concepts such as the human rights regime or the global climate regime with a more critical Foucauldian perspective, according to which a regime always implies power asymmetries and social control. A regime of inequality encompasses at least four dimensions: (i) logics of stratification/redistribution defined as static (caste societies), dynamic (class societies) or combined (class with racial/ethnic/gender ascription); (ii) political, scientific, and popular discourses according to which individuals or groups interpret and construct their own positions and that of others in society; (iii) legal and institutional frameworks (e.g. apartheid law, multicultural or antidiscrimination laws, policies); and (iv) models of conviviality in everyday life (segregating or integrating convivial forms). Empirically, this approach has been applied to the study of inequalities which affect Afro-descendants in Latin America. In this case, we could identify four regimes of inequalities: slavery (until the nineteenth century), racist nationalism (from the end of the nineteenth century to the first decades of the twentieth century), Mestizo nationalism (from the 1930s to the 1980s), and the compensatory regime (from the 1980s). The transition to the next historical regime of inequality does not imply a complete disappearance of inequalities created in a previous regime. Consequently, racist discourses which had appeared during slavery, for instance, were later reinforced during the prevalence of racist nationalism. Packed in new imageries (emphasis rather on cultural than on the biological inferiority of blacks), these racist discourses subsisted Mestizo nationalism and are still present in the current regime of inequality characterised by compensatory policies in favour of black populations.

Inequalities Where?

While conventional scholarship researches inequalities on a local or national scale, new approaches seek for understanding inequalities with a widened angle in order to capture transnational and global entanglements that shape local and national social structures. There are two main approaches which have recently dealt with inequalities from an amplified perspective: while transnationalism (see, e.g. the contributions assembled in Weiß and Berger 2008) is interested in understanding how different national social structures interact, for instance, in the case of social positions of migrants, world systems approaches are rather concerned with macro-structural persistent inequalities (see, for instance, Korzeniewicz and Moran 2009).

In accordance with these new developments in the field of inequality research, the network *desiguALdades.net*—a research network on interdependent inequalities in Latin America—coined the concept of *entangled inequalities*[1] understood as distances

> [...] between positions of certain individuals or groups of individuals in a relationally (not spatially) determined context. This concerns economic positions (defined by income, access to resources and so on) as well as

political and legal entitlements (rights, political power etc.). In order to understand the linkages from which unequal positions arise, it is necessary to have relational units of analysis that are dynamically defined in the process of inquiry itself. In a similar way, the interplay of social categorisations (gender, race, class, ethnicity etc.) cannot be articulated ex-ante in a formula. It can only be studied in the respective specific context. (Costa 2011, 21)

The approach "entangled inequalities" displays broad affinities with the interest of understanding inequalities in Latin America from an ethnographic perspective as outlined in the introduction of this book. Both the entangled inequalities and the ethnographic approach insist on the historical constitution and the intersectional character of social inequalities. Accordingly, both perspectives extend the scope of inequality research far beyond economic indicators in order to capture the impact of structural inequalities on lifeworlds. This does not imply a dichotomistic separation of social structures and everyday life, but just the opposite: by integrating the structural and life world dimensions of inequalities, these approaches shed light on the interconnections between these two dimensions to demonstrate that everyday interactions are both spaces of reproduction of social structures and also arenas in which social hierarchies are negotiated and transformed.

Recent changes promoted by Pink Tide governments in Latin America represent a privileged context to analyse the interplay between these two dimensions of inequalities. While cash transfer policies adopted by these governments have hugely reduced poverty, this kind of intervention has demonstrated a very limited power to transform "deep-seated aspects" of inequalities as described in the introduction of the present volume. Furthermore, if Pink Tide governments have tried to promote more emphatic shifts in existing social hierarchies, local elites have reacted by destabilising these governments. This happened in different terms but with a similar political plot in Argentina, Paraguay, and Brazil. The Brazilian case in particular is paradigmatic. Here, cash transfer policies have halved poverty rates in about 10 years. Real increases in the minimum wage and new economic opportunities created during the cycle of economic growth also started changing inequalities in everyday life, inasmuch as "newcomers" disputed spaces and goods of distinction reserved hitherto to the established middle classes. At this point oppositional forces became insurgent. Indeed, this dispute of previously reserved spaces and goods, in combination with the economic recession starting in 2015, led to the parliamentary coup d'état of 2016 (Costa 2018).

However, exploring the impact on everyday life produced by the policies adopted during the Pink Tide cycle in Brazil would go beyond the scope of this chapter. Therefore, I limit myself to analysing the redistributive shortcomings of these policies, and, in doing so, applying the framework of entangled inequalities.

Inequalities in Brazil: Recent Developments

After the Workers' Party (PT) came to power in 2003, remarkable economic and social improvements have been reached in Brazil. Thus, in line with developments observed in several Latin American countries, inequalities in Brazil have declined in this period. During the two administrations of former President Lula da Silva (2003–2006 and 2007–2010) and the first administration of President Dilma Rousseff (2010–2014), economic growth, improvements in the labour market, progress in deprived regions, and pro-poor policies interacted positively as drivers of inequality reduction. Accordingly, between 2002 and 2013, GDP per capita has increased by 64 per cent, poverty rates among Brazilians—including extreme poverty—declined from 48.4 to 23.9 per cent of the Brazilian population, and social policy expenditures rose from 12.7 to 16.8 per cent of the Brazilian GDP (Bielschowsky 2014; CEPAL 2014). In the same period, the Brazilian labour market underwent an auspicious change as unemployment rates declined from 11.7 to 5.4 per cent among the economically active population while the formal employment rate has impressively increased from 49.7 per cent in 2003 to 71.4 per cent in 2012.

It was also between 2002 and 2013 that income inequality as measured by the Gini coefficient decreased from 0.59 to 0.53. Yet despite this improvement, the Brazilian Gini coefficient for income is still above the Latin American average of 0.486. With the richest quintile possessing 53.6 per cent of all income, Brazil also remains the most unequal Latin American country when it comes to income concentration by upper classes (as a comparison, this rate amounts to 36.4 per cent in Latin America's least unequal country, i.e. Uruguay; see CEPAL 2014).

Concerning inequalities related to racial and gender categorisations, they remain at a high level, but there has been also an important reduction of income asymmetries during the administrations led by the Workers' Party. In 2002, women's total average income represented only half of the male average income, while in 2012 this proportion rose to 58 per cent. A similar change can be observed for racial income asymmetries:

In 2002, the average income among blacks corresponded to 47 per cent of whites' average income. Yet in 2012, this proportion amounted to 55 per cent. A similar tendency can also be observed in the case of regional inequalities since the Northeast, Brazil's poorest region, has recently experienced more development than other regions. But regional inequalities still matter, especially if combined with gender and race-related asymmetries, as the figure below illustrates quite well (Fig. 3.1).

Among analysts of Brazilian social structure, there is a broad consensus that the reduction in inequalities between 2003 and 2015 is rather a consequence of economic processes (such as increasing prices for commodities in international markets and moves in domestic labour markets) than of social policies. Accordingly, social policies based on cash transfers have a crucial impact on poverty reduction, but they are seen to be less effective for promoting redistribution (Gaulard 2011; Lavinas 2013; Lustig et al. 2013).

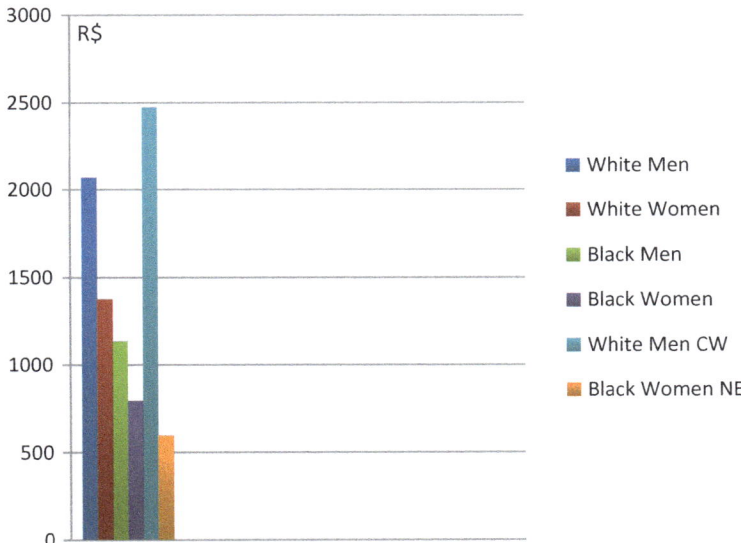

Fig. 3.1 Average monthly earnings in Brazil, 2012 (average earnings from the main occupation of the population over 16 years old) calculated for the intersection of inequality factors: sex, race, and region (figures in Brazilian Reais as of September 2012). *NE* Northeast, *CW* Center West
Source: Data from IBGE (2012) for selected groups

Analysts also question the sustainability of the decrease in inequalities in Brazil given the current adverse confluence of modest (or even negative) economic growth, "premature" deindustrialisation, a "reprimarisation" of exports, and falling commodity prices.[2]

Inequality analysts are also concerned about recent political developments. Due to the economic stagnation and political instability, former President Dilma Rousseff, in her second administration started in 2015, faced serious difficulties in sustaining the social gains obtained during the previous administrations. At the end of 2015, the Brazilian congress started an impeachment process against President Rousseff, who has allegedly violated Brazilian budgetary laws. The president was first suspended in April of 2016 and finally removed from office in August 2016. Vice-president Michel Temer assumed the government, promising to promote fiscal austerity and to cut social benefits introduced during the PT administrations. When he assumed the presidency, he first abolished the agency with ministerial status responsible for implementing policies meant to mitigate inequalities in terms of gender and race. In subsequent months, his administration has also adopted a series of unsocial and business-friendly measures, including but not limited to (i) a new programme of privatisation, ranging from oil exploration to public service, with the aim of boosting the economy; (ii) a constitutional amendment freezing social expenditures for 20 years which is expected to produce huge negative impacts for poor populations which are the most dependent on public services; and (iii) a plan to reform the pension system in a way which dramatically restricts benefits and increases contributions paid by employees (Fórum 21 et al. 2016).

The (Re)Distributive Impact of State Intervention

States remain key actors for promoting the mitigation of domestic inequalities created by economic interactions in capitalist societies—at least at the domestic level. Fiscal policies, including tax and social policies, and the offer of public and quasi-public goods represent classical instruments used by states to intervene in inequality structures. States can also intervene indirectly through measures—such as the introduction or increase of minimum wages—which lead to a redistribution in favour of low-paid workers.

Comparisons of the Gini coefficient before and after tax deductions and state transfers in different countries give a sense of how states use their redistributive power with very different intensities, as shown by data compiled by the World Bank (2014). Accordingly, the Gini coefficient before taxes and transfers in European OECD countries and in the Latin American countries is virtually identical. However, the final Gini coefficient, that is, after state's intervention through fiscal policy, is much higher in Latin American countries than in Europe. A comparison between two OECD countries, France and Mexico, makes this general tendency clear: the Gini coefficient in both countries before taxes and transfers is about 0.50. After fiscal policy, the French Gini coefficient decreases to 0.30; in Mexico it remains very high: 0.48.

Hence, Latin American states lack the power or the political will to strongly reduce market-produced income inequalities. In European countries, state interventions use to mitigate income inequalities by up to 50 per cent as, for instance, in the case of Slovenia and Norway (see World Bank 2014, 27). Although distinctive patterns of state transfers (comprehending how much and for whom the state invests its resources) partly explain these contrasting results of state intervention between Europe and Latin America, the pivotal difference lies in the tax structures which are much more progressive in Europe than in Latin America. Pink Tide governments in Latin America have not changed this tendency since tax reforms recently implemented in the different countries aimed to increment tax revenues following established patterns. That is, tax systems continue to be based on a high taxation of salaries and consumption and low or even inexistent taxation of capital gains and profits (Jiménez and López Azcúnaga 2012).

In the case of Brazil, overall tax collection did in fact increase from 31.8 per cent of the GDP in 2003 to 35.9 per cent in 2012, exceeding thus the average number of OECD states which is 34.6 per cent (Castro 2014). However, the composition of tax revenues in Brazil differs substantially from that of those countries which are more effective in diminishing inequalities. While indirect taxes, which are regressive,[3] represent 49.7 per cent of all collected taxes in Brazil, they held a much lower share of all collected taxes in European countries such as Germany (29.2 per cent) and Norway (27.3 per cent) (Castro 2014; data for 2012 from European Union 2014). In Brazil, the current composition of tax revenues has not varied substantively since the Workers' Party took office in 2003. This is also true for other regressive characteristics of the Brazilian tax system such as the lack of a tax on dividends (in Western European countries this taxation varies from 25 per cent in Belgium to 42 per cent in Denmark) and the low taxation of high incomes (in Brazil the highest income taxation is 27.5 per cent, whereas in Sweden, for instance, it amounts to 56.6 per cent).

This tax collection structure is also unable to change the concentration of wealth encompassing properties and entitlements. Based on the analysis of more than 25 million tax declarations, Castro (2014) concludes that only 406,064 tax payers (0.2 per cent of the Brazilian population) possess about 47 per cent of Brazil's wealth. Also, he calculates the Gini coefficient for wealth which has remained practically stable since 2006, namely, around the extraordinarily high value 0.85!

As far as income concentration is concerned, Castro simulates different changes in Brazilian taxation system and concludes that "merely" introducing a taxation of 15 per cent for capital and financial profits combined with tax rates of 35 and 40 per cent for high salaries could reduce the Gini coefficient by about 20 per cent. This would be more than what was achieved during the 12 years of PT administrations, the most successful period in terms of inequality reduction in Brazilian history. Before PT came to power, it was already aware of the impact of taxes on inequalities, as PT's electoral programme of 2002 unequivocally demonstrates:

> The first reform to be faced by the new administration, during its very first year, will be a tax reform whose aim is improving economic efficiency and reducing social inequalities. (PT 2002, 14, translated from Portuguese by the author)

Dilma Rousseff also largely emphasised, during the impeachment hearings in the Brazilian Federal Senate in August of 2016, how the Brazilian tax system prevents wealth redistribution. Now, if PT and even the former Brazilian president acknowledged the impact of taxes on redistribution, why did Rousseff and her predecessor Lula not conduct a single attempt to change—at least minimally—the regressive Brazilian tax structure? Although social scientists have not yet offered a definitive answer to this question, it seems reasonable that the explanation should be sought in power relations: because of its conservative allies in the Brazilian congress and the support it received from different sectors which profit from a regressive tax structure, such as agribusiness, big concerns from the mining, beverage and construction sectors, and banks, PT's administrations did not feel strong enough to pass a tax reform contrary to the interests of the rich.

All in all, social policies recently implemented in Brazil have had a low impact on inequalities compared with the redistributive potential of the tax reforms outlined above. In order to assess the impacts of diverse strategies adopted by PT administrations, three policies will be discussed below: (1) the cash transfer programme Bolsa Família, (2) quotas at federal universities, and (3) a minimum wage.

Cash Transfer Programme: Bolsa Família

As soon as the PT came into power, this programme of direct cash transfers to poor families with schoolchildren became the most outstanding feature of PT administrations. While a previous programme created during the former administration of Fernando Henrique Cardoso provided benefits for 3.6 million families in 2002, the Bolsa Família benefited 14.1 million families with about R$ 142 in 2013 (see Bielschowsky 2014). Bolsa Família's main recipients are women (93 per cent) and blacks (73 per cent).

Bolsa Família has played a pivotal role in reducing poverty in Brazil, although its costs are modest: Financed by public funding representing only 0.5 per cent of the Brazilian GDP, the programme reaches 25 per cent of the Brazilian population (see Pinto's Chap. 6 in this book). Nevertheless, Bolsa Família has a negligible relevance for mitigating income inequality: Bolsa Família and other cash transfer measures merely respond to 1 per cent of the Gini coefficient composition (according to Medeiros and de Souza 2013; see also Lavinas 2007, 2013).

The new administration led by Michel Temer first kept the programme. However, it has adopted several administrative measures to reduce the number of programme beneficiaries (Carta Capital 2016).

Quotas at Federal Universities

Although some policies had been already introduced by previous governments, the Workers' Party implemented a broad set of new policies to mitigate inequalities associated with gender and racial ascriptions. To accomplish this, two extraordinary agencies with ministerial status were also created in 2003: one for policies targeting women (SEPM) and another for policies promoting racial equality (SEPPIR). As shown elsewhere (Costa 2015), most of the measures implemented concentrate on combating discrimination which is only one among several mechanisms at work in the reproduction of racial and gender asymmetries. Additionally, the measures adopted reach only a small fragment of black or female Brazilians. The quota programme introduced in Brazilian federal universities in 2012 is one such case.

According to the programme, 50 per cent of all study placements at federal higher education institutions are to be reserved for students graduating from public schools and allocated according to the proportion of the black and indigenous populations living in the respective region. Yet, when taking into account that in 2013 only about 1.1 million of all

7.3 million undergraduate students in Brazil were enrolled at federal institutions (INEP 2014), and when also considering that blacks and indigenous represent about 51 and 0.5 per cent respectively of the whole Brazilian population, then it is clear that the federal quotas programme, if fully implemented, will only distribute approximately 283,000 university places according to racial/ethnic criteria. Therefore, the programme, because of its design, benefits a small group among the more than 100 million blacks und 800,000 indigenous living in Brazil, producing only minimal socio-economic aggregate effects. According to its opponents, the programme also contributes to racialising everyday relations since beneficiaries are forced to recognise themselves according to ethnoracial categories, this despite the fact that Brazilian society is characterised by the existence of a porous system of colour classification rather than a dichotomistic opposition between blacks and whites. Defenders of quota policies argue that, far beyond the still dominant self-representation of the Brazilian nation of a Mestizo country without sharp divisions between blacks and whites, lifeworlds of blacks and whites are to a large extent separated since they go to different schools, use different means of transport, and live in distinct residential areas. In this context, policies such as quotas rather promote interracial coexistence in a racially segregated society (for an overview of these arguments see Costa 2017).

That being said, critics do not delegitimise the programme because it has an obvious relevance for setting the imperative of overcoming racism in the core of Brazil's political agenda, even if its impact on promoting socio-economic redistribution in favour of the black or indigenous population as a whole is marginal.

Until February of 2017, when the present article was concluded, Temer's administration has not abolished the system of quotas at federal universities. However, federal universities suffered a cut of about 45 per cent in their budget with serious consequences for their quality and for their capacity to provide an adequate academic environment for students admitted through the quotas (Vieira 2016).

Minimum Wage

In response to consistent political pressure articulated by national associations of trade unions, the Brazilian government has readjusted the minimum wage in real terms consecutively since 2003. Since 2008, the adjustments have been coupled by law to inflation and the economic growth rate of 2 years prior to the increase. This policy has led to a real increase in the minimum wage by 75 per cent between 2002 and 2013 and is seen as the most important driver of the recent decline of inequalities in Brazil (Sabóia and Hallek Neto 2016; UNDP 2014). There are multiple factors explaining the redistributive effects of the minimum wage:

(1) Since about 70 per cent of Brazilian workers have an income of less than double the minimum wage per month, a real increment of minimum wage automatically leads to an improvement of well-being for a significant part of the population (DIEESE 2014).
(2) The rise in minimum wage reinforces the bargaining power of workers whose salaries are not coupled with the minimum wage and even for informal workers the minimum wage serves "as a benchmark for individual wage negotiations" (Berg 2012, 8).
(3) The automatic readjustment of lower pension values to the minimum wage results in real income improvements for the elderly and their families in the lower classes.
(4) Since women and blacks are overrepresented in low-wage labour sectors such as domestic work, which are directly governed by the minimum wage law, real increases of the minimum wage contribute to reduce inequalities in terms of gender and race (IPEA 2013).

This methodology for adjusting minimum wage had positive impacts for mitigating inequalities as long as the Brazilian economy presented high growth rates. However, since 2014, Brazilian GDP has dramatically contracted which will lead to a reduction of minimum wage in real terms with adverse consequences for redistribution in both terms: class, as well as gender, and race.

Conclusion: Entangled Inequalities and Recent Developments in Brazil

If the general framework of entangled inequalities is applied to assess the recent decline of inequality in Brazil, certain ambivalences in this process stand out. At the level of income differences, social distances were—at least until 2015—slightly reduced. However, this does not necessarily lead to a less unequal access to "socially-relevant goods" since wealth concentration remains virtually unaffected, and access to public and common goods such as a healthy environment and a well-functioning public transport system may have become even more unequal.[4] The missing sustainability of inequality reduction should be emphasised, too. As soon as the Brazilian economy started stagnating, less skilled workers were the first to lose their jobs, and with them, the better social position they had achieved during the Pink Tide cycle (Costa 2018).

The assessment of power asymmetries as a key aspect of the entangled inequalities approach is a complex endeavour since transparent indicators for measuring power asymmetries are not available. In general terms, it can be stated that the PT administrations have not represented a radical power shift in favour of the working and lower classes. Otherwise, these administrations would have reformed the regressive tax system targeting capital and financial profits. Notwithstanding, some particular groups—especially women and Afro-descendants—have been empowered insofar as their claims have been inserted on a large scale into the political agenda, being addressed by compensatory policies. However, these political gains are tenuous, since they were institutionalised not as rights granted by solid welfare institutions but as benefits within transitory social programmes (Lavinas 2013). Drawing on the vocabulary Chatterjee (2004) applies to analyse Indian politics, we can state that in the framework of the social programmes introduced by PT administrations, beneficiaries represent target populations, which have entitlements, but not full citizens with unnegotiable rights. With this distinction, I am not negating the huge relevance of these programmes for reducing poverty and temporarily empower minorities. My intention is to emphasise some insufficiencies of these policies to produce a power shift in favour of the poor and minorities in Brazil both in everyday life and at the level of political institutions. These policies, by establishing conditions of access (such as regular submission to certain medical exams, regular attendance of schools, etc.) and sanctions in the case that this conditionality is not observed represent rather a "dispositive to control the population" than an instrument to empower citizens (Bueno 2009, 44). Institutionally, most social policies adopted by PT administrations assumed the framework of social programmes and thus were not integrated into the Brazilian constitution as citizenship rights. As a consequence, there is only a very low institutional and political hurdle to abolish and remove them as witnessed in contemporary Brazilian politics. Indeed the fragility of gains for the poor and for less empowered groups such as the Afro-descendant population and women, obtained during the PT administrations, became evident when the former Vice President Temer assumed the government after Rousseff's impeachment. Using simple administrative measures, Temer's government could cut important social and political benefits these groups had obtained in recent years.

The dynamic of inequality reduction in Brazil speaks in favour of an intersectional approach able to integrate the complex entanglements between the varieties of inequalities concerning class, racial, gender, and regional ascriptions. It has been shown above that since class, gender, and racial disadvantages interact, policies aimed to reduce class inequalities such as Bolsa Família or a minimum wage bring more improvements for much more blacks and women at the level of income than policies exclusively designed to reduce gender and racial asymmetries accumulated throughout history. Nevertheless, affirmative action policies in favour of blacks, indigenous, or women remain crucial for reducing both power asymmetries as well as racism and sexism in everyday relations. Inasmuch as more blacks, women, and indigenous obtain an academic degree and occupy leading positions in hierarchically structured organisations and social spaces, they contribute to removing prejudices constructed over centuries of white and male supremacy and to transforming equality assured at the formal level into lived experience.

Notes

1. The use of the expression "entangled inequalities" is inspired by discussions on entangled modernity as developed by Conrad and Randeria (2002). A more detailed discussion on the concept entangled inequalities is developed in Costa (2011), Lillemets (2013), Braig et al. (2015) and Jelin et al. (2018).
2. Economists use the expression premature deindustrialisation (*desindustrialização precoce*) to refer to the current process of abrupt declining participation of industrial production in Brazilian GDP, a phenomenon that appears before the industrial sector is fully consolidated. Accordingly, deindustrialisation is motivated by a combination of a persistent overvalued currency (this situation has only changed within the economic and political crisis of 2015) leading to a stimulation of import of industrial products, high rates of interest which discourages industrial investments, and low level of foreign investment. "Reprimarisation" refers to an increasing participation of agrarian and mining products in exports (Cano 2012; Costa et al. 2015).
3. The regressive character of taxes associated with consumption derives from the fact that underprivileged classes spend a much greater proportion of their income on consumption than rich families do. Using data from 2008, IPEA (2009) calculated that while families with an income of up to twice

the minimum wage spent 53.9 per cent of their income paying taxes, those receiving more than thirty times the minimum wage spent 29 per cent on their taxes. The minimum wage corresponds to about US$ 297 per month (according to the exchange rate of 31 January 2017).
4. Although this paper does not address access to public and common goods, the topic is mentioned here in order to illustrate some implications of using the entangled inequalities approach. Moreover, several studies indicate that access to public and common goods has become increasingly unequal in contemporary Brazil. The case of access to transportation and a well-functioning traffic system is a striking example: Between 2003 and 2013, the number of registered vehicles in Brazil jumped from about 37 million to about 82 million (DENATRAN 2015). This has triggered a rise in traffic accidents with fatal victims especially among pedestrians and motorcyclists, those road users with lower incomes (Bacchieri and Barros 2011).

Bibliography

Andrews, George R. 2004. *Afro-Latin America, 1800–2000*. Oxford: Oxford University Press.
Anthias, Floya. 2013. Social Categories, Embodied Practices, Intersectionality: Towards a Translocational Approach. In *Interdependencies of Social Categorisations*, ed. Daniela Célleri, Tobias Schwarz, and Bea Wittger, 7–26. Madrid/Frankfurt: Iberoamericana/Vervuert.
———. 2016. Interconnecting Boundaries of Identity and Belonging and Hierarchy-Making Within Transnational Mobility Studies: Framing Inequalities. *Current Sociology* 64 (2): 172–190.
Bacchieri, Giancarlo, and Aluísio J.D. Barros. 2011. Traffic Accidents in Brazil from 1998 to 2010: Many Changes and Few Effects. *Revista Saúde Pública* 45 (5): 949–963.
Baquero, J. 2015. *Layered Inequalities. Land Grabbing, Collective Land Rights, and Afro-descendant Resistance in Colombia*. Berlin et al.: LIT Verlag.
Berg, Janine. 2012. *Labour Market Institutions for Just Societies*. Geneva: International Labour Office.
Bielschowsky, Ricardo. 2014. O modelo de desenvolvimento proposto por Lula e Dilma. In *Brasil em Debate*. http://brasildebate.com.br/o-modelo-de-dedesenvolvimento-proposto-por-lula-e-dilma/#sthash.WtLZN74s.dpuf. Accessed 2 Feb 2017.
Boatcă, Manuela, and Julia Roth. 2016. Unequal and Gendered: Notes on the Coloniality of Citizenship. *Current Sociology* 64 (2): 191–212.
Braig, Marianne, Sérgio Costa, and Barbara Göbel. 2015. Desigualdades sociales e interdependencias globales en América Latina. Una valoración provisional. *Revista Mexicana de Ciencias Políticas y Sociales* 40 (233): 209–236.

Bueno, Marina. 2009. As Condicionalidades do Programa Bolsa Família: O Avesso da Cidadania. *Lugar Comun* 29: 33–46.
Cano, Wilson. 2012. A desindustrialização no Brasil. *Economia & Sociedade* 21 (Special Issue): 831–851.
Carta Capital. 2016. Governo Temer suspende 1,1 milhão de benefícios do Bolsa Família. Carta Capital, November 07. http://www.cartacapital.com.br/politica/governo-temer-suspende-1-1-milhao-de-beneficios-do-bolsa-familia. Accessed 2 Feb 2017.
Castro, Fábio A. de. 2014. *Imposto de renda da pessoa física: comparações internacionais, medidas de progressividade e redistribuição*. Unpublished Master Thesis, Brasília, UnB.
Chatterjee, Partha. 2004. *The Politics of the Governed*. New York: Columbia University Press.
Comisión Económica para América Latina y el Caribe. CEPAL. 2014. *Panorama Social de América Latina 2014*. Santiago de Chile: CEPAL.
Conrad, Sebastian, and Shalini Randeria. 2002. Einleitung. Geteilte Geschichten – Europa in einer postkolonialen Welt. In *Jenseits des Eurozentrismus. Postkoloniale Perspektiven in den Geschichts- und Kulturwissenschaften*, ed. Sebastian Conrad and Shalini Randeria, 9–49. Frankfurt a.M.: Campus.
Costa, Sérgio. 2011. *Researching Entangled Inequalities in Latin America: The Role of Historical, Social, and Transregional Interdependencies*. desiguALdades. net Working Paper Series 9. Berlin: desiguALdades.net Research Network on Interdependent Inequalities in Latin America, 2015. http://www.desigualdades.net/Working_Papers/index.html
———. 2015. Protection Without Redistribution? Conceptual Limitations of Policies Meant to Reduce Inequalities Concerning Race and Gender in Brazil. In *A Moment of Equality for Latin America? Challenges for Redistribution*, ed. Barbara Fritz and Lena Lavinas, 235–252. Farnham: Ashgate.
———. 2017. Dilemmas of Inter-American Anti-Racism. Re-visiting 'On the Cunning of Imperialist Reason'. In *The Routledge Companion to Inter-American Studies*, ed. Willfried Raussert, 338–349. London: Routledge.
———. 2018. Millionaires, the Established, the Outsiders, and the Poor. Social Structure and Political Crisis in Brazil. In *Global Entangled Inequalities: Conceptual Debates and Evidence from Latin America*, ed. Elizabeth Jelin, Renata C. Motta, and Sérgio Costa, 178–195. London: Routledge.
Costa, Sérgio, Barbara Fritz, and Martina Sproll. 2015. Dilma 2: From Economic Growth with Distribution to Stagnation and Increasing Inequalities? *Latin American Studies Association Forum* XLVI (2): 21–24. https://lasa.international.pitt.edu/forum/past-issues/vol46-issue3.asp
Departamento Intersindical de Estatística e Estudos Socioeconômicos. DIEESE. 2014. A política de valorização do Salário Mínimo: persistir para melhorar. *Nota Técnica* No. 136.

Departamento Nacional de Trânsito. DENATRAN. 2015. Frota de veículos. http://www.denatran.gov.br/index.php/estatistica/237-frota-veiculos. Accessed 2 Feb 2017.

Dietz, Kristina. 2014. *Researching Inequalities from a Socio-ecological Perspective*, desiguALdades Working Paper Series 71. Berlin: desiguALdades.net Research Network on Interdependent Inequalities in Latin America. http://www.desigualdades.net/Resources/Working_Paper/74-WP-Dietz-Online.pdf

European Union. 2014. *Taxation Trends in the European Union: Data for the EU Member States, Iceland and Norway*. Luxembourg: Publications Office of the European Union.

Fórum, 21; Fundação Friedrich Ebert Stiftung (FES); GT de Macro da Sociedade Brasileira de Economia Política (SEP); and Plataforma Política Social. 2016. *Austeridade e Retrocesso*. São Paulo: Fórum 21, FES, SEP and Plataforma Política Social. http://brasildebate.com.br/wp-content/uploads/Austeridade-e-Retrocesso.pdf

Gaulard, Mylène. 2011. Balance sobre la cuestión de las desigualdades en Brasil. *Revista Problemas del Desarrollo* 166 (42): 111–134.

Gonçalves, Guilherme L., and Sérgio Costa. 2016. The Global Constitutionalization of Human Rights: Overcoming Contemporary Injustices or Juridifying Old Asymmetries? *Current Sociology* 64 (2): 311–331.

Góngora-Mera, Manuel. 2018. Transregional Articulations of Law and Race in Latin America: A Legal Genealogy of Inequality. In *Global Entangled Inequalities: Conceptual Debates and Evidence from Latin America*, ed. Elizabeth Jelin, Renata C. Motta, and Sérgio Costa, 43–58. London: Routledge.

Góngora-Mera, Manuel, Gioconda Herrera, and Conrad Müller. 2014. *The Frontiers of Universal Citizenship Transnational Social Spaces and the Legal Status of Migrants in Ecuador*, desiguALdades Working Paper Series 71. Berlin: desiguALdades.net Research Network on Interdependent Inequalities in Latin America. http://www.desigualdades.net/Working_Papers/index.html

Instituto Brasileiro de Geografia e Estatística. IBGE. 2012. *Pesquisa Nacional por Amostra de Domicílios*. Brasília: IBGE. http://www.ibge.gov.br/home/estatistica/populacao/trabalhoerendimento/pnad2012/default_sintese.shtm. Accessed 2 Feb 2017.

Instituto de Estudos e Pesquisas Educacionais Anísio Teixeira. INEP. 2014. *Censo da Educação Superior 2013*. Brasília: INEP.

Instituto de Pesquisa Econômica Aplicada. IPEA. 2009. *Receita pública: quem paga e como se gasta no Brasil*. Brasília: IPEA.

———. 2013. *Retrato das Desigualdades de Gênero e Raça*. 4th ed. Brasília: IPEA.

Jelin, Elizabeth, Renata C. Motta, and Sérgio Costa. 2018. *Global Entangled Inequalities: Conceptual Debates and Evidence from Latin America*. London: Routledge.

Jiménez, Juan P., and Isabel López Azcúnaga. 2012. ¿*Disminución de la desigualdad en América Latina? El rol de la política fiscal*, desiguALdades.net Working Paper Series 33. Berlin: desiguALdades.net Research Network on Interdependent Inequalities in Latin America. http://www.desigualdades.net/Working_Papers/index.html

Korzeniewicz, Roberto P., and Timothy P. Moran. 2009. *Unveiling Inequality: A World-Historical Perspective.* New York: The Russell Sage Foundation.

Kreckel, Reinhard. 2004. *Politische Soziologie der sozialen Ungleichheit.* Frankfurt: Campus.

Lavinas, Lena. 2007. Gasto social no Brasil: programas de transferência de renda versus investimento social. *Ciência & Saúde coletiva* 12 (6): 1463–1476.

———. 2013. 21st Century Welfare. *New Left Review* 84 (6): 5–40.

Lillemets, Krista. 2013. *Global Social Inequalities: Review Essay*, desiguALdades. net Working Paper Series 45. Berlin: desiguALdades.net Research Network on Interdependent Inequalities in Latin America. http://www.desigualdades.net/Working_Papers/index.html

López-Calva, Luis F., and Nora Lustig Lustig, eds. 2010. *Declining Inequality in Latin America: A Decade of Progress?* Baltimore: UNDP, Brookings Institution Press.

Lustig, Nora, Carola Pessino, and John Scott. 2013. The Impact of Taxes and Social Spending on Inequality and Poverty in Argentina, Bolivia, Brazil, Mexico, Peru and Uruguay: An Overview. *CEQ Working Paper* No. 13.

Medeiros, Marcelo, and Pedro H.G.F. de Souza. 2013. Estado e desigualdade de renda no Brasil: fluxos de rendimentos e estratificação social. *Revista Brasileira de Ciências Sociais* 28 (83): 141–150.

PT – Partido dos Trabalhadores. 2002. *Programa de Governo 2002.* São Paulo: Fundação Perseu Abramo.

Sabóia, João, and João Hallak Neto. 2016. *Minimum Wage and Income Distribution in Brazil from the 2000s*, Nopoors Working Paper 44. http://www.nopoor.eu/publication/minimum-wage-and-income-distribution-brazil-2000s. Accessed 2 Feb 2017.

Stepan, Nancy L. 1991. The hour of eugenics. In *Race, Gender, and Nation in Latin America.* Ithaca/London: Cornell University Press.

Stewart, Frances. 2010. Por qué persisten las desigualdades de grupo? Las trampas de la desigualdad horizontal. In *Teoría económica y desigualdad social. Exclusión, desigualdad y democracia. Homenaje a Adolfo Figueroa*, ed. Félix Jiménez, 269–298. Lima: Fondo Editorial de la PUC-Perú.

Therborn, Göran. 2013. *The Killing Field of Inequality.* Cambridge: Polity Press.

Tilly, Charles. 1999. *Durable Inequality.* Berkeley/Los Angeles/London: University of California Press.

United Nations Development Programme. UNDP. 2014. *Humanity Divided: Confronting Inequality in Developing Countries.* New York: UNDP.

Vieira, Victor. 2016. Universidades federais devem ter corte de até 45% nos investimentos. *O Estado de S. Paulo*, 11 August.

Weiß, Anja, and Peter A. Berger. 2008. *Transnationalisierung sozialer Ungleichheit*. Wiesbaden: VS.

World Bank. 2014. *Social Gains in the Balance: A Fiscal Police Challenge for Latin America and the Caribbean*. Washington, DC: World Bank.

Open Access This chapter is licensed under the terms of the Creative Commons Attribution 4.0 International License (http://creativecommons.org/licenses/by/4.0/), which permits use, sharing, adaptation, distribution and reproduction in any medium or format, as long as you give appropriate credit to the original author(s) and the source, provide a link to the Creative Commons license and indicate if changes were made.

The images or other third party material in this chapter are included in the chapter's Creative Commons license, unless indicated otherwise in a credit line to the material. If material is not included in the chapter's Creative Commons license and your intended use is not permitted by statutory regulation or exceeds the permitted use, you will need to obtain permission directly from the copyright holder.

CHAPTER 4

#sosfavelas: Digital Representations of Violence and Inequality in Rio de Janeiro

Margit Ystanes

Introduction

> …They said he was a criminal, but yet another innocent died, here we have workers and students, but for them, if you are up on the hill, you are a trafficker.[1]

The above quote was published on the Facebook page of *Coletivo Papo Reto* (the Straight Talk Collective), a Rio de Janeiro independent journalism collective in February 2015. A few days earlier, Diego Algavez, a 24-year-old motorbike taxi driver was killed by the military police in the Penha complex of favelas. The presence of the military police in Rio's favelas is part of the policy introduced to secure the city before the 2014 FIFA World Cup and the 2016 Olympics. The aftermath of Algavez' murder was covered in real time by Coletivo Papo Reto and Jornal a Nova Democracia, a Rio-based independent newspaper. One of the photos Jornal a Nova Democracia published on their Facebook site shows Algavez' dead body stretched out over his motorbike, on a busy street, in bright sunlight. He is face up, his hips and legs on top of his toppled motorbike.

M. Ystanes (✉)
University of Bergen, Bergen, Norway

© The Author(s) 2018
M. Ystanes, I.Å. Strønen (eds.), *The Social Life of Economic Inequalities in Contemporary Latin America*, Approaches to Social Inequality and Difference, DOI 10.1007/978-3-319-61536-3_4

His head and arms are extended behind him towards the ground, which is marked by the blood seeping from his mortal gun wound. Heavily armed policemen dressed in black guard the scene, while people crowd around.

Rio de Janeiro has a serious problem with police violence. In fact, the Rio de Janeiro Military Police has been identified as the force that most kill civilians worldwide (Gaffney 2014). The epigraph above refers to how victims of police violence are very often accused of being involved in drug trafficking—both by the police themselves and in media narratives. However, those killed by the police often turn out to be innocent bystanders, hit by stray bullets, or simply wrongfully targeted. There have even been incidents of small children killed by stray bullets while inside their homes. Therefore, the narrative often promoted by the police and mass media, speculating about victims' potential association with drug trafficking, in many cases both holds little credibility and is inflammatory.

This is especially the case for those who live in self-built neighbourhoods, or *favelas*, where police violence is mostly located. This situation is reflected in the above reference to being "up on the hill" (*no morro*, in Portuguese); *"for them, if you are up on the hill, you are a trafficker"*. In Rio de Janeiro, *morro*, or hill, is often used as a synonym for favela, as many of the city's numerous self-built neighbourhoods are established on the hillsides surrounding the centre and the famous beach areas. The idea that "if you are up on the hill, you are a trafficker" refers to the strong association between favela territories and organised crime in the social imaginary. The force of this imagery obscures the fact that most favela residents are ordinary citizens, workers and students.

The epigraph to this chapter appeared as a caption to a drawing by the artist Carlos Latuff, illustrating the experience of state violence amongst Rio's favela residents.[2] It depicts a young boy in front of a favela rising on the hill in the background. A wall and barbed wire separate the favela from the formal neighbourhoods outside it. There, a paraglider flies above the famous Sugar Loaf mountain cable car and the skyscrapers of Rio's financial centre—places of leisure and business where favela residents are "undesired". In the version of the drawing that appeared in the Facebook post, a graffiti painted on the wall had been added that read #soscomplexodoalemao. This refers to the origins of Coletivo Papo Reto in the Alemão complex of favelas, which is near the Penha complex where Diego Algavez was killed. The young boy in the foreground is depicted as a stereotypical favela kid: dark skinned, curly dark hair, shirtless and clutching a football under his arm. The football, of course, connotes both the Brazilian passion for the game, as well as the relationship between the FIFA World Cup and experience of state violence. A white-skinned man holding a gun to the boy's head from outside the wall has "state" written across the bottom of his suit's jacket. His head is cut off from the image, and as such he is anonymised. Yet, the depiction of a fair complexion on the hands pointing the gun, as well as the suit, gives some cues about his class and "racial" identity. In the background, a helicopter surveils the favela territory. The overall message of this post is that Rio's favelas and the people who live there are considered as external to the rest of Brazil, and a threat to, not included in, the narrative of Rio as an attractive "global city". Deep-seated inequalities are inscribed in the city's landscape, as illustrated by the physical barrier, the violent state and the surveillance helicopter. By incorporating all these elements, Coletivo Papo Reto's Facebook post illustrates various processes of violence and inequality being played out in Rio de Janeiro at the time: mega-event preparations, the militarisation of informal neighbourhoods, state violence, the "racial" component of class inequality, spatial separation, the vulnerability of unprotected bodies in the face of heavy weaponry and the protest against and documentation of these processes in social media.

Notably, these processes which reflect and grow out of deep-seated inequalities, happened at the height of Brazil's engagement with the Pink Tide. At the time, Brazil had received considerable praise for its ability to combine massive economic growth with reduction in poverty and inequality. In 2012, the country overtook the UK's former position as the world's sixth largest economy (Inman 2012), and 67 per cent of Brazilians considered themselves to be better off than their parents (Olsen 2012). When Brazil was awarded the 2016 Olympics in 2009, the country's middle class had grown by a population the size of California during the previous decade (Barbassa 2015, xiv). Awarding the games to Rio was considered "an unprecedented vote of confidence, a gold star to show that this forever-emerging nation had finally arrived" (Barbassa 2015, xv). However, the preparations for the Games, as well as the 2014 FIFA World Cup, would lay bare that inequality and old power structures continued to work in the Brazilian society (see also Costa (Chap. 3), Sørbøe (Chap. 5), this volume). In fact, the effort to use sporting mega-events to showcase the successes of the Pink Tide governments gave rise to numerous contradictions and an intensification of neoliberal approaches to securitisation as well as the access to urban land.

One of the traditional markers of inequality in Latin America is that of access to land. Struggles over different kinds of land, urban as well as rural, remain an aspect of contemporary struggles against inequality (Ystanes 2014; Ystanes 2016b; see Brown (Chap. 11), Sørbøe (Chap. 5), this volume, as well as Ng'weno 2007; Sawyer 2003; Rolnik 2015). Indeed, it is an aspect of inequality that Pink Tide economic policies did not significantly address. This chapter explores one particular configuration of this inequality; the struggle over access to, and militarisation of, urban spaces. In Rio de Janeiro, this struggle has profoundly marked its history. Urban development has to a large extent centred on removing the poor from attractive, centrally located areas, and making these areas available to the middle and upper classes (Pearlman 2010; de Magalhães 2013). After the introduction of democracy in Brazil in 1985, favela removals were rarer because of their association with military regimes of the past. However, policies intended to "reclaim" favela territories were reintroduced as the city prepared to host the recent mega-events (see e.g. Barbassa 2015; Larkins 2015; Ystanes 2016b; Rolnik 2015; Savell 2014; Salem 2016; de Magalhães 2013). This "reclaiming" consists of multifaceted processes involving mechanisms such as forced removals, rent inflation, gentrification and militarisation. The anti-mega event activism analysed in this chapter, speaks to these processes of exclusion and socio-spatial segregation. Inspired by Nancy Fraser (1990), I argue that such contestation constitutes a subaltern counterpublic. This counterpublic is born out of, challenges and testifies to the many shortcomings of the Pink Tide in terms of addressing entrenched inequalities in Brazil. In particular, it illustrates that such inequalities remain inscribed in Rio de Janeiro's urban landscape, despite the strides made towards reducing them in the last couple of decades.

Protesting the 2014 FIFA World Cup: Activism-as-Journalism Arises in Rio's Favelas

Many of the processes that reproduce inequality in Rio are tied in with a particular agenda for urban and economic development: the hosting of the 2014 FIFA World Cup and the 2016 Olympics. The preparations for these events complicated, and to some extent reversed, the overall project of reducing poverty and inequality. As this chapter illustrates, access to and the use of urban spaces became increasingly a privilege for better-off residents. Furthermore, the public provision of health and education went into crisis as funds were divested towards the events in the middle of a recession. This situation was the focus of critique and protests in the period between the FIFA Confederations Cup in 2013 and the 2016 Olympics. In Rio, *cariocas*, as locals call themselves, gathered regularly under the slogan *Não vai ter Copa!* (There will be no World Cup!) during the year leading up the 2014 event. These rallies were mostly made up by middle-class protesters who marched in the city centre and sometimes in the Copacabana beach neighbourhood, where the FIFA Fanfest was to be located.

At the same time, a number of alternative media outlets and activist collectives, such as the Coletivo Papo Reto, arose in Rio's favelas. Most of these are based in specific local communities. This sense of belonging is reflected in their names, such as *Ocupa Alemão, Jornal Alemão Noticias, Maré Vive, Rocinha em Foco* and *Voz da Comunidade*.[3] All of these collectives and news services use social media as their main platform of communication, primarily Facebook, Twitter, Instagram, Whatsapp, YouTube and blogs. The flow of communication goes both ways, with readers and followers alerting the collectives to news and sharing photos and updates that are distributed further. In addition, the activist collectives produce their own journalistic material, as well as short films that dramatise events and experiences. They also organise marches and events in their favela communities.

One of the main concerns of these activist collectives is to share information related to experiences of inequality and violence. In particular, they speak of racism and the new forms of violence and exclusion that have arisen from the mega-event security policies introduced in 2008 to subdue drug trafficking organisations in Rio's favelas. In an interview with one of the Coletivo Papo Reto members, he characterised the *Não vai ter Copa* approach as "a middle class discourse", too radical and with potential for provoking violent clashes. Instead, he explained, the Coletivo protested by emphasising that in its current form, the World Cup was "not for them". Facebook posts such as the one discussed above, and the coverage of events such as the murder of Diego Algavez by the military police, contain powerful, elaborate and painful messages about how, for favela residents, insecurity and exclusion is reinforced rather than reduced through the mega-event-related security policy.

This form of protest, which grows out of deep-felt experiences of exclusion and inequality, has made a far more durable impact on Rio's public spheres of deliberation than the street protest. Street protests are "one-off" events, and the messages protesters intend to communicate (e.g. "we want FIFA standard hospitals and schools") are often mixed up with facile slogans such as "Fuck FIFA" or interrupted by police violence against the demonstrators. Furthermore, after the surge during the 2013 Confederations Cup, the protests attracted relatively low numbers of people, thus leaving the impression that discontent with the mega-events is a rather marginal phenomenon. In addition, police violence against protesters and the pre-emptive arrest of several activists prior to a planned march on the day of the World Cup final in 2014 (Deak 2014; Nunes 2014; Brito 2014; Tsavkko Garcia 2014), did much to deter street rallies. In contrast, the messages produced by favela residents and posted on social media, are numerous, constant, concrete and rich in their detail about the problems they experience due to Rio's hosting of mega-events. Crucially, they cannot easily be stopped or censored by authorities. Of course, the long-term outcomes of these developments remain to be seen. Nevertheless, I argue that a methodology and an infrastructure for protest and activism based on social media and mobile technology is one of the most significant legacies of Rio's sporting mega-events. I will come back to this more in detail below.

Activism-as-Journalism and Subaltern Counterpublics

Most of the groups participating in this effort refer to themselves as community news services; they represent a form of alternative journalism. This conception of activism-as-journalism builds upon a long tradition in Latin America, where in particular the radio has been put to subversive use during times of oppression and civil wars, and as a corrective to mass media censorship. The Mexican *Canal Seis de Julio*, which started producing alternative video documentaries in 1989, first in VHS format and later digitally through their website and YouTube channel, is a case in point. Brazil may be a particularly fertile ground for the contemporary configurations of such activism, as its residents are amongst the world's most eager users of social media (Glenny 2016, 157).

The development of alternative, digital news services such as Coletivo Papo Reto contributes to diversifying the public sphere and challenging the state of affairs they critique. It is also testament to the persistent inequalities in Brazilian society. It is useful to explore the unfolding of these digital narratives in light of Nancy Fraser's critique of Jürgen

Habermas' notion of the bourgeois public sphere (Fraser 1990). While Habermas' classic text (1991) favours a single public sphere of deliberation,[4] Fraser argues that this is unrealistic, as numerous subtle mechanisms of exclusions exist, even when formal exclusions are eliminated. People do not leave behind their social positions as they enter the public sphere of deliberation, and their unequal statuses profoundly impact on what is supposed to be a debate between equals. This is of course particularly so in stratified societies. Fraser therefore argues that "in such societies, full parity of participation in public debate and deliberation is not within the reach of possibility" (1990, 66). This point is very much in line with the findings of anthropologists who have studied arenas of debate between unequally positioned participants (Caldeira 1988; Green 2003; Sawyer 2003; Ystanes 2011, 2014). Fraser maintains that "arrangements that accommodate contestation among a plurality of competing publics better promote the ideal of participatory parity than does a single, comprehensive, overarching public" (1990, 66).

The kind of digital community journalism Coletivo Papo Reto represents is a relatively new phenomenon and it is of course difficult to assess its significance with any kind of certainty as it unfolds. Indeed, Castells (2015, x) points out that networked social movements are often met with scepticism as to their tangible outcomes. Nevertheless, Castells goes on to suggest that the Internet is now such an integrated aspect of our existence that it does not make much sense to consider the virtual a segregated world. As such, it does not make sense either to distinguish between social media activism and real life activism. Activists I spoke to in Rio expressed similar views. Furthermore, social media activism has already contributed to producing tangible results with regards to forced evictions (Ystanes 2016a) and in the launching of the Nós por Nós phone app, specifically designed to help citizens report police violence without risks to their safety (Coelho 2016) (Photo 4.1).

Furthermore, using the Internet to widen the arenas for deliberation and the sharing of information holds value in and of itself. In Brazil, the relevance of this is heightened as the public sphere is infamously dominated by the Globo Media Group. It is of course difficult to quantify the influence held by this corporation in defining the terms of public debate. What is clear, however, is that the market position of their outlets is unique, both in terms of broadcast media and print media. Through their numerous entertainment shows, soap operas, debate programmes and news broadcasts, Globo has unmatched influence over what makes its way to the public

Photo 4.1 Interconnected worlds: as Rio prepared to host the 2016 Olympics, the hashtag #cidadeolympica, used by the city administration for propaganda purposes, was inscribed onto the urban landscape as a physical manifestation of the interconnection between the virtual and "real life" (Photo: Margit Ystanes)

via mass media outlets. Globo supported the military dictatorship from 1964 to 1985, something that continues to fuel suspicion among its critics. Today, the tendency for both news and entertainment to portray the perspectives of elites and authorities means that many favela residents perceive there to be no mass media outlet that represent their reality (see also Sørbøe's (Chap. 5), this volume). Social media based activism-as-journalism must be understood as a response to this situation, and as an attempt to create an alternative public sphere. As I will discuss below, the outcome of this effort is tangible, yet still not readily noticeable in the Brazilian mass media dominated public sphere.

Mega-Events, Security and Urban Development

As mentioned above, mega-events come with their own agenda for economic and social development. Indeed, hosting mega-events involve some of the most expensive, complex and transformative processes that cities and nations undertake (Gaffney 2010, 7–8). These events are so complex and large-scale, affecting so many aspects of social and political life, that they may provoke societal opposition on a broad range of issues (Cornelissen 2012, 333). It is expected that mega-events function as vehicles for "accelerated development". This generally involves making public money available for private profit creation, suspending a number of democratic processes, militarising public space and restructuring urban space in the image of global capital (Gaffney 2010, 8). These features of mega-event hosting are often thought of as recent developments, but in fact have been part and parcel of Olympic events since their reinvention in the late nineteenth century (Boykoff 2016).

The preparation for mega-events thus impacts on a number of societal processes, as has also been the case in Rio. The city has hosted numerous big events in recent years; the 2007 Pan American Games, 2013 FIFA Confederations Cup, the 2014 FIFA World Cup and the 2016 Olympics. This has led to further erosion of "already fragile democratic institutions, instituting a permanent state of exception" (Gaffney 2014). It is therefore not surprising that mega-events may become the focal points of struggles that extend far beyond the actual events themselves (Cornelissen 2012, 330). In Rio de Janeiro, the adaptation of the city for investments and tourism has been met with opposition from a number of social movements and activist networks (see also Sørbøe (Chap. 5), this volume). The protesters have criticised the insufficient investments in the public sector, the transfer of public funds towards event-related infrastructure, tax exemptions for event sponsors, as well as the racism and exclusionary thinking underlying certain event-related policies. As indicated above, the security policy introduced to make the city secure for tourists and investors has been highly controversial.

This relates to Rio de Janeiro's reputation for being a dangerous and violent city. An important aspect of Rio's preparations for the 2014 World Cup and the 2016 Olympics has therefore been to increase public security. This security problem is most strongly associated with the drug trafficking gangs operating out of many of the city's approximately 1000 favelas. According to the 2010 census, about 22 per cent of Rio's inhabitants live in favelas. These informal neighbourhoods have been developing since the nineteenth century as veteran soldiers, freed slaves and migrants settled in Rio's hillsides and outskirts. Today, favelas are expressions of continued socio-economic and "racial" inequality. The enduring impact of colonial slavery can be observed in the overrepresentation of Afro-Brazilians amongst the poor, most of whom live in favelas (although far from all favela residents are poor). Because of a historically constituted conceptual link between poverty, dark skin colour, stigma and criminality (Stepan 1991), these informal neighbourhoods have always been considered problematic by the city's political elite. Throughout Rio's history, urban development efforts have therefore often aimed to clear out favelas in the city centre and the famous beach neighbourhoods, and to move the poor to other, less attractive sites (Pearlman 2010; de Magalhães 2013).

Since the early 1980s, rivalling drug trafficking gangs have taken control over several favelas, thus reinforcing their association with danger and violence. Although most people living in favelas are ordinary workers, in the minds of many, they are intrinsically associated with the criminal activity going on there. This association is so strong that the words *pobre* (poor), *preto* (black), *favelado* (favela resident) and *bandido* (criminal) sometimes function as synonyms. A recent expression of this stigmatising association is a study in which 47 per cent of the interviewees, from 150 Brazilian cities, say they would not like to hire domestic workers who live in favelas. Sixty-nine per cent say they feel afraid when walking past a favela, and 51 per cent associate the word favela with drugs and violence (Brasil 2015). Hence, in the effort to enhance public security before the mega-events, expelling drug traffickers from favelas has been a priority. This is especially so in the favelas near the south zone beaches, near event infrastructure and near the airport. The policy, called *pacificação* (pacification), centres on the reconquering of favela territories on behalf of the Brazilian state. The army has moved into Rio's favelas one by one since 2008, on preannounced dates. With tanks and heavily armed soldiers, remaining traffickers are forced out or arrested, before permanent military police units called *Unidades de Polícia Pacificadora (UPPs)* are established.

Many non-favela residents consider the "pacification" policy a success and feel that Rio has become safer because of it. In their experience, the violence that used to spill over from the favelas and onto the "asphalt", as the formal neighbourhoods are nicknamed, has diminished. Nevertheless, the "pacification" policy is strongly contested by many favela residents who emphasise that it has not provided security for them, and that state presence in terms of public services and social programmes is still lacking. In some favelas in the south zone, "pacification" has opened up the area for the establishment of formal businesses and property speculation.

In other words, the residents of these territories have been "captured" as consumers in the formal economy (Larkins 2015), while gentrification processes have forced many of the original inhabitants to move to more affordable areas. The favelas have thus become increasingly available to non-residents of various kinds, yet "the asphalt" and the privileges it is associated with is not becoming equally available to favela residents. As the outcomes of gentrification processes are not being mitigated by social programmes or other state interventions, it has been suggested that the "pacification" policy is not so much about including favela residents into formal society, as about making these territories available for outside investments (Sørbøe 2013).

Another problem with the "pacification" policy from the point of view of favela residents is that drug trafficking continues despite police presence, and that confrontations between traffickers and police inside favelas remain a problem. There have been numerous reports of police violence and people being killed by the police. While the police usually claim that such incidents are the outcome of confrontations with criminals, video evidence provided by witnesses has shown that often, the versions of events provided by the police are very misleading (Timerman 2014). Indeed, many of those killed by the police turn out to be cases of police aggression, torture, mistaken identity, stray bullets or being caught in the crossfire, yet the responsible officers are rarely charged.

The number of deaths at police hands has remained high throughout the "pacification" process. In 2011, 524 people were killed by the police in Rio de Janeiro State (Prado 2014), and in 2012 the number was 415 (Duarte and Benevides 2013). In 2013, the police were considered responsible for 8.7 per cent of all murders (Benites 2014). Young, Afro-Brazilian men make up the majority of Brazilian murder victims (Puff 2014). The fact that a substantial number of them die at police hands in favelas has made critics—citizens, activists, academics and politicians— characterise this situation, and the public indifference to it, as a "genocide of the black youth" (Puff 2014; Ramos 2012; Duarte 2013) and as a "criminalisation of poverty" (Insurgencia 2014; Vaz 2014). Trust between favela residents and the police is thus frayed. So much so, that in the Alemão complex of favelas, many residents consider that the drug traffickers did a better job at providing security for the community than the police have been doing since "pacification" (Savell 2014).

Mega-Events and Access to Urban Spaces

The hosting of mega-events has laid bare that unequal access to urban spaces and territories has not been mitigated, but actually exacerbated during the Pink Tide-era in Rio de Janeiro. Evictions from poor neighbourhoods to make space for event infrastructure, gentrification and property speculation in favelas, the exclusion of street vendors from event venues and a security policy that leave many people feel targeted rather than protected in their own neighbourhoods, all contribute to making life more difficult for Rio's poor. The mega-events play a contradictory role in this scenario, with significant inconsistencies between discourse and reality, projected and actual outcomes. The awarding of the 2016 Olympics to Rio de Janeiro was widely considered a feather in the cap for the Pink Tide president Luiz Inácio Lula da Silva and a chance to showcase the successes of his governments. At the same time, Rio's Olympic bid document emphasised the adaption of the city for business and tourism as one of the main event legacies (Comité de Candidatura Rio 2016 2009). And indeed, the events were approached by local politicians and business owners as a chance to push through controversial decisions that were highly profitable for them, while funding for projected social legacy projects dwindled (Barbassa 2015).

As part of an event-related urban revitalisation, spectacular infrastructure projects were initiated. These include gondolas in the Providência and Complexo do Alemão favelas and the upgrading of Rio's historical port area (the Porto Maravilha project). The Maracanã stadium and the Galeão International Airport were reformed, and three bus rapid transit lines (BRT) connecting the Olympic Park, Deodoro (another Olympic venue) and the airport were constructed. All of these projects are critiqued for primarily adapting Rio for tourism and investment, and not alleviating problems of mobility for residents of the city. The projects are met with resistance from locals because people understand them to be realised at the expense of the provision of clean water, sewerage systems, waste disposal and electricity as well as quality education, health services and security for all residents in the city. The infrastructure projects have also brought with them a high number of forced evictions, and thus serve as an excuse for the city administration to clear attractive areas of poor residents. Indeed, while doing fieldwork in Vila Autódromo, a neighbourhood that was almost decimated during the construction of the Olympic Park (Ystanes 2016a, b), I was constantly reminded of this problematic. Here, there was no need for residents to leave the area in order for the Olympic Park project to be completed, yet, almost all of them were evicted with varying degree of force and pressure—most likely to make the area available for future property development. The people in Vila Autódromo considered the Transoeste BRT line, which connects the Olympic venues with Campo Grande, part of this plan. This new connection did little to improve their need for public transport in the area, yet made it more feasible to clear this attractive land of poor people without compromising the middle and upper classes' access to cheap service labour. Campo Grande is located almost 70 kilometres from the centre of Rio de Janeiro, and is a stronghold for paramilitary militias. Many of those forcibly evicted from central areas are re-located there. The new BRT line makes it easier to live in Campo Grande and retain work in the more centrally located areas they were forced to leave. At the same time, local bus lines that made movement within the area surrounding Vila Autódromo possible, were closed down as the BRT lines were introduced. This was phrased as an environmental measure, but the reality for people near the Olympic Park was that it first and foremost made it difficult to operate locally without private cars. The residents of Vila Autódromo therefore saw the BRT Olympic infrastructure project as yet another measure introduced by Rio's city administration to make it as difficult as possible for them to stay in the area.

This is part of a wider process of gentrification and exclusion in the city that was exacerbated by the sporting mega-events. As an Amnesty International representative put it:

> There is a process of gentrification taking place in the whole city that is connected to the sports events and how the government sees the city: it is no longer a place for residents, but as a business to sell to foreign investors. That's what the World Cup is about. (Gibson and Watts 2013)

In many ways, the developments brought about by hosting mega-events were counterproductive to the process of making Brazil a more equitable society, and harked back to an authoritarian past. Indeed, Marcelo Freixo (PSOL), state deputy and president of the Human Rights Commission of the Legislative Assembly of Rio de Janeiro sees the many deaths at police hands as a continuity with the military dictatorship:

> The enemy of the dictatorship was the communist, the academic, the journalist, who were imprisoned, tortured and killed. Today, there is still this logic of confronting the enemy. Only that today, the enemy is the poor, the one who is superfluous in the market society. We continue to have a security policy based in the idea of war. (Prado 2014)

Many Brazilians share this view, and are concerned about the direction their country has taken (see e.g. Ystanes 2015). As the digital representations of violence and inequality that arise out of the "pacification" policy illustrate, for many living in Rio's informal neighbourhoods, the situation is indeed experienced as critical. As regards the reproduction of inequality and exclusion through these policies, Gaffney (2010, 27) points out that there are significant similarities between how situations of crisis, war and disaster have been used to push through unpopular neoliberal policies (see Klein 2007), and the suspension of ordinary democratic processes to pave the way for mega-events as vehicles for "accelerated development". Spectacular displays of the security apparatus serve as powerful symbols of the degree to which militarisation of public space is integral to these processes (see also Larkins 2015). The high numbers of Military Police in riot-gear at demonstrations, at times appearing to outnumber the protesters, made it clear that opposition could be violently subdued at any moment—and at times it was. As the World Cup was under way, spectators entering and leaving the FIFA Fanfest metro station had to run the gauntlet of heavily armed soldiers and military vehicles, thus receiving a contradictory message of safety blended with mortal danger. The fact that on-going developments are understood by so many as criminalising social movements and poverty—and even as a genocide of the black youth (Duarte 2013; Puff 2014)—further emphasises that mega-events approached as "accelerated development" do not create a fertile ground for enhancing equality and social cohesion. Rather, this approach builds on and reinforces already existing inequalities. An arena where this effect can be clearly observed is the digital representations of it produced by those affected, across different favela communities.

Digital Representations of Violence and Inequality: Subaltern Counterpublics

Before, during and after the 2014 World Cup and the 2016 Olympics, activists and community journalists based in Rio's favelas have criticised the high levels of violence since "pacification" through social media. Here, they warn residents of on-going gunfights and document events and their experiences of living with this situation. Social media has also been used to rally people to participate in street marches and other events in affected areas. One such event was a peace march in protest of the "pacification" policy, where police violence was thematised and performatively re-enacted. Another was a march in favour of preserving the museum of the Maré complex of favelas, which was the outcome of a joint effort amongst collectives from several favelas as well as NGOs. Voz da Comunidade head a campaign distributing gifts and sweets to children in Complexo do Alemão for Christmas and Easter, and document its unfolding on social media. In November 2015, Coletivo Papo Reto organised a protest on the five-year anniversary for the "pacification" of Complexo do Alemão called *5 anos de paciFICÇÃO* (5 years of paciFIC-TION). These events were also documented on social media. For example, the *paciFICÇÃO* event produced numerous posts and photos in social media, and was also followed up with a long blog post on the Coletivo Papo Reto website explaining the reasoning behind the protest. In the main photo accompanying the blog post, one of the Coletivo members is seen holding up a banner in front of a UPP police that reads: *Pacificação sem oportunidade e educação é como apagar fogo com gasolina*. #soscpx – 1 (Pacification without opportunities and education is like putting out fire with gasoline). The hashtag #soscpx (SOS Complexo do Alemão) appearing on a banner in a street protest, which later makes its way onto social media and blogs, where it emerged in the first place, exemplifies Castells' (2015) point that social media activism and real life activism are inseparable. They feed each other rather than constitute different domains.

Running through the digital representations of violence and inequality are slogans and hashtags asking for peace and shouting SOS on behalf of their crisis-ridden communities (e.g #FavelaPedePaz (favela asks for peace), #sosfavela). The language applied in this activism emphasises the message that the pacification has thrown these communities into crisis rather than resolved their security problems. An example of this is the #100diasSEMpaz (#100daysWITHOUTpeace) hashtag that arose in the Alemão complex of favelas in the beginning of 2015 after 100 consecutive days of gunfire, in which residents, including a child, lost their lives.

Another social media campaign called *"Eu não mereço morrer assassinado"* (I do not deserve to be assassinated), got considerable attention in April 2014. It arose after Douglas Rafael da Silva Pereira, a 26-year-old dancer, was killed by the police in a "pacified" favela above Copacabana, and made explicit links between Afro-Brazilian ancestry and the risk of falling victim to police violence. The campaign thus denounced racism and the unequal value placed on human lives, both by the police and the wider public. It also emphasised their experience that the right to feel safe remains a privilege reserved for the generally lighter skinned inhabitants of middle-class neighbourhoods.

Shootouts taking place within the "pacified" favelas are often documented in videos uploaded to Facebook. Normally, these videos are filmed with mobile phone cameras through a window or from a rooftop. The visual contents serve to locate the event in a favela; what we see is usually a dark, empty alleyway with the typical several-storey brick houses. The soundtrack is the main feature of the videos and consists of the sound of intense gunfire. The captions accompanying such videos sometimes express rage at the situation in which the community finds itself and at the "pacification" policy. The disadvantaged position of favela residents in Rio's social landscape is sometimes also pointed out, either in the captions or in the comment sections. At other times, the caption simply warns: *Muitos tiros hoje!* (Much gunfire today!), and mentions the community or the specific location it takes place so that people can be informed and stay away.

The residents in Vila Autódromo, who fought forced evictions as the Olympic Park was built next to their neighbourhood, also used social media to organise events and protest, and to connect with an international public. Via Whatsapp groups for activists and journalists they swiftly managed to get the attention of supporters and international correspondents whenever a house was in risk of being demolished. They also organised cultural protest events, using social media tools to disseminate information about them both before and after. Showing a keen awareness of the power of image and alternative media, as they called it, the residents also wrote on the houses' outer walls to present their analysis of what was happening to their neighbourhood. *"Sometimes when journalists come here there is nobody available to talk to them, so we write on the walls so that they can do the talking"*, one of them explained (Photo 4.2).

Following Fraser (Fraser 1990), I take the social media representations of violence and inequality arising out of affected communities to constitute subaltern counterpublics. Subaltern counterpublics are defined as

> parallel discursive arenas where members of subordinated social groups invent and circulate counterdiscourses, which in turn permit them to formulate oppositional interpretations of their identities, interests, and needs. (Fraser 1990, 67)

Photo 4.2 Graffiti in Vila Autódromo shows that the residents consider the confiscation of their neighbourhood as a transfer of public land to private actors: "When there are no more public areas to sell, they will sell the favelas. Who will protest?" (Photo: Margit Ystanes)

An example of such a subaltern counterpublic, Fraser states, is the late-twentieth century US feminist discursive arena. Here, new terms for describing reality have been invented, such as "sexism", "double shift", "sexual harassment", "date rape" and so on. Gradually, these terms have made their way into debates beyond feminist circles, where they are both accepted and critiqued. This illustrates the potential of subaltern counterpublics to contribute to deliberations and contestations in other arenas. According to Fraser, subaltern counterpublics have a dual character in stratified societies. They function as spaces of withdrawal and regroupment, and simultaneously, as bases and training grounds for agitational activities directed towards wider publics. In this dialectic lies their emancipatory potential; the ability to somewhat offset the unjust participatory privileges enjoyed by the members of dominant social groups (Fraser 1990, 68).

It is of course an empirical question to be explored in each case to what extent subaltern counterpublics are separate from other publics. Fraser argues that insofar as these arenas are indeed publics, they are by definition not enclaves, although they can be involuntarily enclaved (Fraser 1990, 67). The online resources used to distribute the representations of violence and inequality discussed here arguably constitute a public. Facebook's "fan pages", Twitter accounts, YouTube, blogs and other websites are open and available to anyone with an Internet connection. Even personal Facebook pages are considered public, as many politicians and other public figures have learned upon posting controversial updates and being taken to task for it "in real life". Whatsapp, a messenger app that is hugely popular in Rio's favelas, constitutes a semi-public arena. The app allows for making large groups of users who can quickly disseminate information to one another through a single message, which may include photos, video or sound recordings. Because of this, activists I spoke to consider that Whatsapp plays a crucial role in creating consciousness and for mobilising around particular issues. For example, the establishment of a Whatsapp group including residents from all over Complexo do Alemão created awareness of the scale of shootouts in this vast area. As group members from different favelas within the complex shared information about their particular neighbourhood, this provided the impetus for the #100diasSEMpaz campaign discussed above.

A study from 2013 showed that 52 per cent of favela residents in Brazil has access to the Internet (Caldeiro 2013). A considerable number of those living in favelas, then, may potentially participate in the digital dissemination, consumption and debate about experiences of violence and inequality.

Perhaps because of the connection between the injustices they are protesting and the mega-events, the activities of Coletivo Papo Reto and others have caught the interest of international media. The Coletivo, for example, have been the subject of a New York Times article (Shaer 2015) and an Al Jazeera documentary. They cooperate with international activists, and in 2015 they received Brazil Foundation's annual International Philanthropy Award in New York. The tribulations of residents in Vila Autódromo have been documented by numerous international media outlets, e.g. The Guardian, Time, The Nation, USA Today, ESPN, New York Times, The Independent, LA Times, Al Jazeera, ROAR Magazine, to mention a few. The *"Eu não mereço morrer assassinado"* campaign was reported about on brasilpost.com.br, a Huffington Post site dedicated to news from Brazil in Portuguese (Thanyá 2014). Coletivo Papo Reto's Facebook page and others like it, are sometimes used as sources in the reporting of other alternative media, e.g. Jornal a Nova

Democracia, which exist both as a printed newspaper, a YouTube channel, a website and a Facebook site.

The digital representations of violence and inequality in question here are nevertheless quite excluded from Brazilian mass media narratives. As mentioned above, mass media in Brazil constitutes a relatively homogeneous sphere dominated by the Globo Media Group and the representation of middle- and upper-class worldviews. A member of the Coletivo Papo Reto told me, *"when the New York Times did a story on us, the Brazilian media did a story on the story, but not on us"*. Even so, some of these narratives do seep into other publics, and it is increasingly problematic to claim that they are completely enclaved. If we follow Fraser (1990), the work of these community activists can therefore be considered an important expansion of the public sphere of deliberation and contestation in Brazil. While their transformative potential with regards to influencing mainstream public debate and media remains to be seen, it is clear that a subaltern counterpublic has been established. At the moment, this counterpublic appears to function both as a community service providing crucial information, but also as a laboratory where approaches to representation and empowerment are being tested and refined. Increasingly, this subaltern counterpublic is being recognised by an international public.

The mega-events that sparked this activism in Rio are now over, but the struggle over the access to and management of urban spaces and territories is not. As the current Brazilian government threatens to reverse many of the gains towards equality achieved during the Pink Tide, this struggle continues on the platforms established by journalists-as-activists in recent years. Indeed, the methodology and infrastructure for protest and activism based on social media and mobile technology is one of the most significant legacies of the 2014 World Cup and the 2016 Olympics.

Concluding Thoughts

As the Brazilian Pink Tide now recedes, the country is in economic crisis and the Worker Party's president Dilma Rousseff was removed by a questionable impeachment process in August 2016.[5] The current right-wing government of Michel Temer has since introduced austerity politics that threaten to reverse many of the gains towards a more equal Brazil achieved during the last couple of decades. Nevertheless, prior to these developments Brazil made significant gains in the inclusion of the formerly excluded by raising the minimum wages, introducing the conditional cash transfer programme Bolsa Familia (see de Lavra Pinta (Chap. 6), this volume), as well as quotas for Afro-Brazilians in prestigious public universities. All of this was helped along by impressive economic growth. Nevertheless, these policies have not been sufficient to eradicate poverty and erase the conceptual and social distinction between favela and "the asphalt", the formal neighbourhoods.

As the reconfiguration of public spaces ushered in by the hosting of mega-events made clear, nor did the Pink Tide reduce historical inequalities with regards to access to these spaces. If anything, the eviction and security policies of recent years did much to reverse any gains by clearing out poor people from attractive areas (Ystanes 2016a, b; de Magalhães 2013; Rolnik 2015; Barbassa 2015). Militarising the spaces where poor people live either officially through "pacification" (Salem 2016; Larkins 2015; Sørbøe 2013) or unofficially through paramilitary militias (Vieira 2016; Martín 2016), was equally destructive for residents. It is interesting in this regard that when the army occupies a favela as part of the "pacification" process they claim the territory by planting the Brazilian flag there. This symbolic gesture illustrates the extent to which favelas are considered external to the rest of Brazil. The high incidence of police violence and deaths at police hands in "pacified" favelas, as well as the apparent acceptance of this reality by the rest of the population, further emphasises the unequal value placed on human lives.

When the Olympics kicked off in August 2016, the city had been in mega-event preparation mode ever since it was awarded the Pan American Games in 2002. This was the same year the Labour Party candidate Luiz Inácio Lula da Silva was elected president and the processes referred to as the Pink Tide were most actively set in motion in Brazil. These parallel and in many ways incompatible developments are informative. The deepening inequalities arising from the reconfigurations of urban spaces as preparations for the mega-events reveal the shallowness of the reforms of the Pink Tide. While significant gains were made with regard to identity politics as well as economic inequality, the clearing out of poor and Afro-descendant residents from attractive areas as the city prepared for the mega-events spoke volumes about the challenges still ahead for those who desire a more equal Brazil. Mass media's lack of interest in the fate of those who are adversely affected by these developments, further emphasise that inequality is not just inscribed in the urban landscape, but also in the lifeworlds of those who inhabit this landscape.

The rise of journalism-as-activism constitutes a challenge to these structures. By weaving together digital and "real life" events, this is not merely the production of a discourse where the most educationally privileged and politically conscious favela residents participate. It facilitates and informs about activities and events that are firmly located within local communities, and reaches and includes people who are not present on social media. Indeed, these practices, digital and "in real life", contribute to widening the sphere of public contestation, and provide virtual and local spaces where stories about violence, inequality and exclusion can be told. As such, digital community journalism can potentially help erode the exclusionary modes of public debate that currently dominate Brazilian mass media and challenge persistent inequality.

Acknowledgements Earlier versions of this text have been presented at the original workshop organised in Bergen, at the 2015 LASA (Latin American Studies Association) congress in San José and at the ESPM (Escola Superior de Propaganda e Marketing) in Rio de Janeiro. I am grateful to all of those who participated in these events for their comments, and to Michele de Lavra Pinto for the invitation to speak at ESPM. Alejandro Huidobro Goya and Iselin Åsedotter Strønen also read and commented upon different draft versions. I extend my most heartfelt gratitude to all these keen readers and listeners, who contributed significantly to improving the text. The Research Council of Norway's SAMKUL programme (Cultural conditions underlying social change) generously funded the research project this chapter grew out of.

Notes

1. In Portuguese: "...falaram que era bandido mas morreu mais um inocente, aqui tem trabalhador e também tem estudante mas pra eles se tá no morro tu já é traficante".
2. The drawing can be seen here: https://tinyurl.com/lwhpcqa.
3. Alemão and Maré are names of large favela complexes, whereas Rocinha is the name of Rio's largest favela. Voz da Comunidade means "voice of the community". *Comunidade* (community) is an often-used term for favela that was originally intended to escape the stigma associated with being a favela resident. In Rio, however, most social media activists use the term "favela", and focus on challenging the injustices suffered by the residents of these places and cultivating a positive self-image through the use of music, art and other cultural expressions. The title Voz da Comunidade thus plays on the idea that the purpose of this news outlet is to give voice to favela residents.

4. Although it must be added that later Habermas modified this view.
5. See the Introduction, as well as Costa's (Chap. 3) and Sørbøe's (Chap. 5) in this book, for more on the impeachment of Dilma Rousseff.

References

Barbassa, Juliana. 2015. *Dancing with the Devil in the City of God: Rio de Janeiro on the Brink*. New York: Touchstone.

Benites, Afonso. 2014. Polícia Brasileira Mata Cinco Pessoas a Cada Dia. *El País*. https://tinyurl.com/lv6ew43

Boykoff, Jules. 2016. *Power Games: A Political History of the Olympics*. London/New York: Verso.

Brasil, Luisa. 2015. Empregadores Domésticos Rejeitam Morador de Favela. *O Dia*. http://odia.ig.com.br/noticia/economia/2015-02-12/empregadores-domesticos-rejeitam-morador-de-favela.html

Brito, Guilherme. 2014. Sininho E Outros Ativistas Suspeitos de Atos Violentos, No Rio, São Detidos. *O Globo*. http://g1.globo.com/rio-de-janeiro/noticia/2014/07/ativistas-suspeitos-de-atos-violentos-em-protestos-sao-detidos-no-rio.html

Caldeira, Teresa Pires do Rio. 1988. The Art of Being Indirect: Talking About Politics in Brazil. *Cultural Anthropology* 3 (4): 444–454.

Caldeiro, João Pedro. 2013. 65% Dos Moradores de Favelas No Brasil São de Classe Média. *Exame*. http://exame.abril.com.br/economia/noticias/65-dos-moradores-de-favela-sao-de-classe-media

Castells, Manuel. 2015. *Networks of Outrage and Hope: Social Movements in the Internet Age*. Cambridge/Malden: Polity Press.

Coelho, Janet Tappin. 2016. Rio de Janeiro Citizens to Receive New App to Record Police Violence in City's Favelas. *The Independent*. https://tinyurl.com/kdhc4uf

Comité de Candidatura Rio 2016. 2009. *Rio de Janeiro 2016. Dossiê de Candidatura Do Rio de Janeiro a Sede Dos Jogos Olímpicos E Paraolímpicos de 2016*. http://www.rio2016.com/sites/default/files/parceiros/dossie_de_candidatura_v1.pdf

Cornelissen, Scarlett. 2012. 'Our Struggles Are Bigger than the World Cup': Civic Activism, State-Society Relations and the Socio-Political Legacies of the 2010 World Cup. *British Journal of Sociology* 63 (2): 328–248.

Deak, Andre. 2014. Apagão Na Democracia. *Brasil Post*. http://www.brasilpost.com.br/andre-deak/apagao-na-democracia_b_5581013.html

de Magalhães, Alexandre Almeida. 2013. *Transformações No 'problema Favela' E a Reatualização Da 'remoção' No Rio de Janeiro*. Universidade do Estado do Rio de Janeiro.

Duarte, Rachel. 2013. Juventude Brasileira Grita Contra Genocídio de Jovens Negros. *Sul21*. http://www.sul21.com.br/jornal/juventude-brasileira-grita-contra-genocidio-de-jovens-negros-no-brasil/

Duarte, Alssandra, and Carolina Benevides. 2013. Polícia Mata Cinco Pessoas Por Dia No Brasil. *O Globo*, November 3. https://tinyurl.com/kvmmgk7

Fraser, Nancy. 1990. Rethinking the Public Sphere: A Contribution to the Critique of Actually Existing Democracy. *Social Text* (25/26): 56–80.

Gaffney, Christopher. 2010. Mega-Events and Socio-Spatial Dynamics in Rio de Janeiro, 1919–2016. *Journal of Latin American Geography* 9 (1): 7–29.

———. 2014. Global Parties, Galactic Hangovers: Brazil's Mega Event Dystopia. *Los Angeles Review of Books*. https://lareviewofbooks.org/essay/global-parties-galactic-hangovers-brazils-mega-event-dystopia

Gibson, Owen, and Jonathan Watts. 2013. World Cup: Rio Favelas Being 'Socially Cleansed' in Runup to Sporting Events. *The Guardian*. http://www.theguardian.com/world/2013/dec/05/world-cup-favelas-socially-cleansed-olympics

Glenny, Misha. 2016. *Nemesis: One Man and the Battle for Rio*. New York: Alfred A. Knopf.

Green, Maia. 2003. Globalizing Development in Tanzania. Policy Franchising Through Participatory Project Management. *Critique of Anthropology* 23 (2): 123–143.

Habermas, Jürgen. 1991. *The Structural Transformation of the Public Sphere: An Inquiry into a Category of Bourgeois Society*. Cambridge, MA: MIT Press.

Inman, Phillip. 2012. Brazil's Economy Overtakes UK to Become World's Sixth Largest. *The Guardian*. http://www.guardian.co.uk/business/2012/mar/06/brazil-economy-worlds-sixth-largest

Insurgencia. 2014. Drogas, UPP E Criminalização Da Pobreza Em Debate. *Insurgencia. Tendência Interna Do PSOL*. http://www.insurgencia.org/drogas-upp-e-criminalizacao-da-pobreza-em-debate/

Klein, Naomi. 2007. *The Shock Doctrine: The Rise of Disaster Capitalism*. London/New York: Penguin.

Larkins, Erika Mary Robb. 2015. *The Spectacular Favela: Violence in Modern Brazil*. Oakland: University of California Press.

Martín, Maria. 2016. Como a Milícia Se Infiltrou Na Vida Do Rio. *El Pais*. http://brasil.elpais.com/brasil/2016/07/21/politica/1469054817_355385.html?rel=mas

Ng'weno, Bettina. 2007. *Turf Wars. Territory and Citizenship in the Contemporary State*. Stanford: Stanford University Press.

Nunes, Rodrigo. 2014. The Worst Kind of World Cup Legacy: Brazil's New Political Prisoners. *Huffington Post*. http://www.huffingtonpost.com/rodrigo-nunes/the-worst-kind-of-world-c_b_5620976.html

Olsen, Maren Næss. 2012. Verden i Krise, Brasil På Ferie. *Morgenbladet*. http://morgenbladet.no/samfunn/2012/verden_i_krise_brasil_pa_ferie

Pearlman, Janice. 2010. *Favela. Four Decades of Living on the Edge in Rio de Janeiro*. Oxford: Oxford University Press.
Prado, Raphael. 2014. PM Do Rio E de SP Mata Mais Que Todos Os Países Com Pena de Morte Somados. *Folhapolitica.org*, January 8. https://tinyurl.com/m6n2d2b
Puff, Jefferson. 2014. 'Genocídio' de Jovens Negros É Alvo de Nova Campanha Da Anistia No Brasil. *BBC*. http://www.bbc.co.uk/portuguese/noticias/2014/11/141108_genocidio_jovens_negros_anistia_jp_rb
Ramos, Paulo. 2012. A Violência Contra Jovens Negros No Brasil. *Carta Capital*. http://www.cartacapital.com.br/sociedade/a-violencia-contra-jovens-negros-no-brasil/
Rolnik, Raquel. 2015. *Guerra Dos Lugares: A Colonização Da Terra E Da Moradia Na Era Das Finanças*. São Paulo: Boitempo Editorial.
Salem, Tomas. 2016. *Taming the War Machine: Police, Pacification and Power in Rio de Janeiro*. Thesis Submitted for the MA Degree at Department of Social Anthropology, University of Bergen.
Savell, Stephanie. 2014. The Brazilian Military, Public Security, and Rio de Janeiro's 'Pacification.' *Anthropoliteia.net*.
Sawyer, Suzana. 2003. Subterranean Techniques. Corporate Environmentalism, Oil Operations, and Social Injustice in the Ecuadorian Rain Forest. In *In Search of the Rain Forest*, ed. Candace Slater, 69–100. Durham/London: Duke University Press.
Shaer, Matthew. 2015. 'The Media Doesn't Care What Happens Here'. *The New York Times Magazine*. http://tinyurl.com/ora26mr
Sørbøe, Celina Myrann. 2013. *Security and Inclusive Citizenship in the Mega-City. The Pacification of Rocinha, Rio de Janeiro*. Thesis Submitted for the MA Degree at Department of Literature, Area Studies and European Languages, University of Oslo.
Stepan, Nancy Leys. 1991. *'The Hour of Eugenics'. Race, Gender, and Nation in Latin America*. Ithaca/London: Cornell University Press.
Thanyá, Yasmin. 2014. Eu Não Mereço Morrer Assassinado. *Brasilpost.com.br*, April 24. http://tinyurl.com/llubhhy
Timerman, Jordana. 2014. In Brazil, Where Police Killings Are Commonplace, Cell Phone Cameras Play a Powerful Role. *The Atlantic/Citylab*. https://tinyurl.com/mmxpg2o
Tsavkko Garcia, Raphael. 2014. Dozens of Activists in Brazil Were Arrested Not for Protesting the World Cup, but for Possibly Planning to Do So. *Global Voices*. http://globalvoicesonline.org/2014/07/22/brazil-preemptively-arrests-activists-before-world-cup-final/
Vaz, Thiago. 2014. Criminalização Da Pobreza E Violência Do Estado. *Observatório Da Imprensa*. http://www.observatoriodaimprensa.com.br/news/view/_ed794_criminalizacao_da_pobreza_e_violencia_do_estado
Vieira, André. 2016. 'Milícia É Sempre Governo, Nunca Oposição', Diz Freixo. *Brasil de Fato*.

Ystanes, Margit. 2011. *Precarious Trust. Problems of Managing Self and Sociality in Guatemala*. Dissertation Submitted for the Degree of Philosophiae Doctor (PhD) at the University of Bergen.
———. 2014. Saving Guatemala's 'Mayan Forest': The Environmental Crisis and Contested Development. In *Crisis in the Nordic Nations and Beyond: At the Intersection of Environment, Finance and Multiculturalism*, ed. Kristín Loftsdóttir and Lars Jensen, 121–142. Farnham: Ashgate.
———. 2015. 'Problemet Er at vi Ikke Aner Hvor Dette Bærer': Dystopiske Fremtidsforestillinger i Sportsarrangementenes Tid. *Norsk Antropologisk Tidsskrift* (3/4): 221–239.
———. 2016a. Brasils Problematiske OL-Arv. *Manifest Tidsskrift*.
———. 2016b. Mega-Events and Urban Poverty: Legacy Projects in Rio de Janeiro. *CROP Poverty Brief* (31), April.

Open Access This chapter is licensed under the terms of the Creative Commons Attribution 4.0 International License (http://creativecommons.org/licenses/by/4.0/), which permits use, sharing, adaptation, distribution and reproduction in any medium or format, as long as you give appropriate credit to the original author(s) and the source, provide a link to the Creative Commons license and indicate if changes were made.

The images or other third party material in this chapter are included in the chapter's Creative Commons license, unless indicated otherwise in a credit line to the material. If material is not included in the chapter's Creative Commons license and your intended use is not permitted by statutory regulation or exceeds the permitted use, you will need to obtain permission directly from the copyright holder.

CHAPTER 5

Urban Development in Rio de Janeiro During the 'Pink Tide': Bridging Socio-Spatial Divides Between the Formal and Informal City?

Celina Myrann Sørbøe

INTRODUCTION

A few weeks after the 2016 Olympic Games in Rio de Janeiro, Brazil, residents from the upper middle-class neighbourhood São Conrado organised a protest. The combination of 'Rio residents', 'sports events' and 'protests' has appeared in countless headlines since June 2013, when millions of Brazilians took to the streets in mass demonstrations. A cacophony of demands, from broad citizenship issues to state inefficiency and corruption to protesting the disproportionate spending on the hosting of mega sports events, were fronted. Demonstrations have continued to bring Brazilians to the streets, but the agendas of protesters have radically changed character:

C.M. Sørbøe (✉)
Norwegian Institute for Urban and Regional Research, Oslo and Akershus University College of Applied Sciences, Oslo, Norway

© The Author(s) 2018
M. Ystanes, I.Å. Strønen (eds.), *The Social Life of Economic Inequalities in Contemporary Latin America*, Approaches to Social Inequality and Difference, DOI 10.1007/978-3-319-61536-3_5

> Away with the bus stop! São Conrado does not accept a final stop/bus stop. Disorder for the residents of the neighbourhood. Noise, filthiness, occupied lanes, traffic. The municipality does not listen to us!!! We demand action.

The above message appeared on several banners that were draped on buildings in São Conrado in September 2016, demanding that the local bus stop would be removed. The City obliged to the demand, and according to one of its users, the bus stop was moved to:

> A dark, one-way street behind an old hotel that has been abandoned for decades. It is a deserted street, with no sidewalk, next to a forest (…) unlit, and without a shelter for people to sit and wait for the bus.

Anyone who has travelled on the over-crowded, under-air-conditioned buses in Rio's blistering summer heat knows that they are not the prioritised means of transportation for those with alternatives. The majority of the users of the bus stop are not the residents of São Conrado, but those of neighbouring Rocinha, Rio and Brazil's largest *favela* (urban informal settlement). While only metres away from each other, the two neighbourhoods seem worlds apart. In a 2016 Social Progress Index measuring human development, Rocinha scored 44.9 on a scale from 0 to 100. That ranked Rocinha in 29th place of 32 administrative regions in the city. São Conrado's region ranked second with a score of 85.18 (IPS 2016). This contrast between São Conrado and Rocinha illustrates the prevalence of uneven urban development and socio-economic differences in the city. The recent protest in São Conrado also testifies to a deep-rooted class struggle that has resurfaced in later years.

With the 2002 election of the Worker's Party's (PT) Inácio 'Lula' da Silva as President, many hoped Brazil's entrenched inequalities could be confronted. Lula placed Brazil at the forefront of the centre-left 'Pink Tide' in Latin America. The socially oriented policies introduced in Lula's first term increased minimum wages and strengthened worker's rights. Cash transfer programmes helped keep children from underprivileged families in school, while affirmative action granted their elder siblings access to universities. Lula's second term operationalised an ambitious developmentalist agenda, implementing national development programmes in industries and infrastructure. In Rio, these programmes were connected with the city's preparations for the 2014 FIFA World Cup and the 2016 Olympics. The City pledged to use the unique opportunity of the mega sports events to respond to the legacy of socio-spatial inequalities, and targeted favelas with investments in infrastructure, security and social housing. Rocinha was one of the favelas at the receiving end of investments.

The PT years did bring a profound change to the composition of the Brazilian society through the programmes of redistribution, social inclusion and poverty reduction. As argued throughout this book, the 'Pink Tide' in Brazil was however marked by continuities as much as ruptures. The inequality-reducing measures introduced may have eased the lives of the poorest while there was economic and political will to uphold these policies. But they were less successful building a lasting foundation for inequality reductions beyond economic concerns. From 2013 onwards, PT became the scapegoat for the deepening political and economic crises enveloping the country, and the party's reign ultimately came to a brutal end with Dilma's impeachment in September 2016 (Jinkings et al. 2016). Advancements that did take place in terms of efforts at addressing social justice and constructing citizenship are currently being rolled back in what can be termed a revanchist (Smith 1996) counter-reaction to the gains made by the poorer segments of society. This chapter will reflect on these issues through the case of Rocinha.

Part 1: Decades of Change

The Divided City

The name Rocinha means 'little farm' and stems from the initial occupation of the territory in the 1930s by small-scale farmers. Rocinha's growth accelerated from the 1950s, a period when rapid urbanisation brought millions of rural workers from the agricultural states in the northeast to the large industrial centres in the centre-south, such as Rio de Janeiro and São Paulo (Leitão 2009). Unable to find affordable housing, the migrants innovated and built their homes on the steep hillsides wedged between the middle- and upper-class neighbourhoods lining Rio's shoreline. According to the latest census (IBGE 2010), one quarter of Rio's population resides in favelas. Rocinha's privileged location, between São Conrado and Gávea, two of the most affluent neighbourhoods of the city, has for good and for bad continually placed the spotlight on the community.

Urban informality is often associated with marginality, precariousness, socio-economic vulnerability and conflict in what Ananya Roy (2011, 224) has termed an 'apocalyptic and dystopian narrative of the slum' (see, e.g. Neuwirth 2005; Davis 2006). Urban informal settlements have often been presented as 'diseases on the social body', providing urban reformers justifications for razing them (Stepan 1991; Holston 2009). In the 1960s and 1970s, the government initiated forced removals in many of the centrally located favelas in Rio, and Rocinha was no exception. The community suffered three partial removals in this period, but residents returned to Rocinha because of its location. The removals therefore did not stall the favela's growth. Rather, it accelerated as the construction boom in Rio's infrastructure and real estate sectors provided work opportunities, including in the construction of São Conrado. The latter expanded in the 1960s, and is today a high-end neighbourhood of gated communities and luxurious shopping centres.

In the decades that have passed, starch differences have consolidated between the two neighbourhoods. The favela's narrow, winding pathways contrast with the formal city's straight streets and avenues. The favela's makeshift economy, where everything from basic services such as sewage, water and electricity to transportation, commerce and security has largely been arranged informally, differs from the urban economy of the formal city. There, business is mainly on the books and workers' wages and working conditions conform to labour laws and standards. A 33-year-old man born and raised in Rocinha takes it so far as to claim that "there is a frontier here, where all that is missing in order to prevent people from crossing is border customs". Perhaps more important than material differences, he refers to symbolic, behavioural and cultural barriers that have excluded favela residents from mainstream society (see also Larkins 2015). A perception of favela residents as a dangerous 'other' (Said 1979) representing a threat to 'civilised society' has prevailed since the favelas first appeared over a century ago (Valladares 2005; Leite 2012). This perception was reinforced when the international drug trade found a stronghold on the unmapped, unpatrolled hillsides of Rio's favelas from the 1980s onwards. Drug traffickers often had the resources to maintain order and provide social assistance in areas where public services were limited at best. As armed drug gangs started filling the vacuum of the weak state presence, regular residents within these territories were seen as accomplices of the drug traffickers because of neighbourhood relations, kinship or economic and political ties. The police took a militarised approach to combating the drug trafficking in Rio's favelas, and the social conflict in the city became formulated as a 'war' (Machado da Silva and Leite 2008). This war has legitimised illegalities in the state's handling of the favelas.

In his writings on what he terms a 'state of exception', Agamben (1998) describes a condition under which normal principles of law and order are superseded by exceptional acts or displays of force in the name of protecting citizens. Judith Butler (2004, 98) points out that this can produce a state of 'desubjectivation' where "certain subjects undergo a suspension of their ontological status as subjects". Drug traffickers were envisioned not merely as common criminals but as enemy combatants at war with the state. Due to their perceived connection with drug trafficking, regular favela residents also became a kind of nonperson stripped of citizenship, a condition Agamben calls 'bare life' (1998, 11). An illustrative occurrence is a large police operation in Rocinha on May 20, 2016. Around 3:30 pm on that Friday afternoon, the BOPE special police force entered Rocinha with military helicopters and trucks in an intense shoot-out with local drug traffickers. Rio's largest newspaper *O Globo* reported on the event under the headline *"shoot-out in Rocinha scares students at PUC "*, the catholic university in the nearby upper-class neighbourhood Gávea (see Papo Reto 2016). The angle of the article, focusing on the fear of upper middle-class students in an adjacent neighbourhood rather than the fate of Rocinha residents caught in the crossfire, is telling of how favela residents have been rendered as 'bare life'.

Politics of Citizenship

There are still stark socio-spatial differences in Rio and Brazil, entrenched inequalities do not erase easily. But since the 1980s, Brazil has come a long way in establishing a legal framework and institutions that work to promote a more inclusive society. Citizenship has been a key concept.

With the end of the military dictatorship in the mid-1980s, social movements of all sorts, including favela, workers', landless', urban, health, feminist, black and student movements, emerged as protagonists of a new kind of politics. The reference to citizenship was not only a tool in their specific struggles but also a powerful link among them. The notion of citizenship in terms of 'cultural' inclusion, political representation and especially social rights (see Stokke forthcoming), became the mean through which the traditionally excluded masses gained a voice in the public sphere. The fruits of their struggle were manifest in the 1988 Constitution, often referred to as the 'Citizen Constitution' (Dagnino 2010). It recognised social and economic rights such as housing, employment, education and health. In terms of specifically urban challenges, it also incorporated new ideas about the 'social function' of cities and urban property. The 2001 City Statute further recognised the 'right to the city' (Lefebvre 1968; Harvey 2008; Júnior 2005), the right of all urban dwellers to appropriate urban space and to participate centrally in its production (Purcell 2003). As a result, the 1990s and 2000s saw important advancements in policies and politics towards the favelas. Favela residents called for public investments with the Constitution in hand, and removal policies were put to an end. The public debate shifted to concentrating on the necessity of integrating the favelas in the city (Burgos 1998). When Inácio Lula da Silva from the Worker's Party (PT) won the presidency on a pro-poor platform in 2002, many were optimistic that the old divides between the favela and the formal city could slowly be erased.

PT Under Lula: Combining Social Concerns for the Poor with Economic Concerns for Growth

The election of Lula represented an historic opportunity for significant change in Brazil. The worker's union leader, who was illiterate until the age of ten and did not receive much in terms of formal education, represented something radically new in Brazil and in Latin America. At the same time, there were powerful forces of continuity. As Strønen and Ystanes point out in the introduction to this volume, the scope of possibility the Pink Tide governments operated within was largely defined by traditional elites. The re-democratisation of Brazil was a gradual opening (*abertura* in Portuguese) rather than a rupture, and the country preserved the historic structures of an oligarchic-bourgeois political society (see Teles and Safatle 2010). Lula had previously run for president three times without success. In order to win in 2002, he modified his once radical socialist orientation and reached out to the conservative political and financial elites. In an open letter addressed to the Brazilian people, but whose intended audience was rather these elites, Lula promised to adhere to fiscal responsibility, make low inflation a priority, and generally play by the rules of the market (Singer 2012). A pragmatic dealmaker, Lula accepted the neoliberal reality but sought to address the downsides of those policies through redistributing to the poorer segments of society. The elimination of the previous radicalism of PT and the search for a broad government coalition mark a transition from *petismo* to *lulismo*— 'the Lula way of governing' (Sampaio jr., 2012; Singer 2012).

Mega Sports Events and Entrepreneurial Governance

In Rio de Janeiro, both the governor from 2007 and the mayor from 2009 were from PMDB, the business-oriented party within Lula's broad governing alliance. The three levels of government were thereby aligned for the first time in decades and would converge around a common project: the hosting of mega sports events. Brazil and Rio de Janeiro bid successfully on both the 2014 FIFA World Cup and the 2016 Olympics, the largest sports spectacles in the world. This would present a unique window of opportunity for investments in Rio's favelas.

Lula's great ambition was to take Brazil out of the shadow of being the eternal 'land of the future' (Zweig 2017) to becoming an economic and political power to be reckoned with. His hope was that the 2016 Olympics would become a stamp of approval on the South American giant's coming of age, just as the Beijing Olympics of 2008 marked China's revival as a world power (Broudehoux 2007). Rio's local level government, on the other hand, had its own interests in hosting these events. Compelled to compete on the global arena over increasingly mobile capital, cities have adapted entrepreneurial styles of action and communication (Harvey 1989). The summer Olympics is the 'holy grail' of the entrepreneurial city competition, and Rio has bid on the event since the 1990s as part of its entrepreneurial governance (Vainer 2011).

The marketing of Rio as a potential host city depended on constructing an image of an exotic but tame city. This required that Rio confronted the statistics where it exhibited poor rankings, such as indicators on crime, violence and inequality. These were all issues that to a large degree were associated with the favelas, which had become an 'anti-postcard' (Ventura 1994) for Rio de Janeiro and for Brazil. Public policies in the favelas had to be revised. Interventions in the favelas became a central part of the Olympic development plans. Rio's Olympic bid pledged to use the Olympics both to improve living conditions for the poor and improve security in the city, leaving the city with a 'social legacy' after the Games (Braathen et al. 2013). Programmes were developed at all three levels of government targeting the favelas in particular, the main references being the federal Program of Accelerated Growth (PAC), the state Police Pacification Program (UPP) and the municipal Morar Carioca (Rolnik 2011). An additional 'legacy' from these interventions would hopefully come in the form of 'branding' Rio within the entrepreneurial city competition. In the next section, we will look at how the PAC and UPP programmes have materialised in Rocinha.

Part 2: Towards Urban Integration?

Rocinha: From Favela to Formality?

With his long white beard and never-faulting khaki shorts and sandals, 70-year-old José Martíns de Oliveira is an easily recognisable resident of Rocinha. A member of the community for nearly half a century, Martíns has accompanied Rocinha's growth from a once-small community to a densely populated neighbourhood of nearly 200,000 residents. Rocinha today is a far shot from the ramshackle wooden houses Martíns encountered when he migrated to Rio from north-eastern Ceará in 1968, when he tells me "there was no water, no transportation, no banks, commerce or supermarkets". Today Rocinha offers all the services found in the formal city. While today's unfinished brick houses still may not look like much from the outside, appearances can deceive. Nearly all residents have access to electricity and running water. Inside, flat screen TVs, sound systems, and latest-model refrigerators and other domestic goods are common. The latter items are a visual confirmation of the improved material living standards brought on by PT's socially oriented policies. The family allowance *Bolsa Família*, higher minimum wages and facilitated access to credit has allowed low-income families to purchase once unattainable goods. According to Meirelles and Athayde (2016), the average income of favela residents rose by 54.7 per cent between 2003 and 2013.

Different urbanisation programmes have provided improvements in Rocinha since the 1980s, but the largest one by far to reach the community is the federal Program of Accelerated Growth (PAC), initiated by Lula in the very beginning of his second term in 2007. PAC's main investments were large-scale projects within the areas of construction, energy, transport and logistics, but it also had a subprogramme called PAC-Favela that provided urban upgrading in some of Rio's favelas. Rocinha was promised investments for US$ 400 million through two phases of PAC. PAC's stated aim in Rocinha was to "transform physical interventions of urban upgrading (…) into processes of sustainable development" (EMOP 2007). PAC was to build on grassroots-driven struggles for urban developments in Rocinha that date back to the mid-2000s, when a 'Socio-Spatial Master Plan for the Sustainable Development of Rocinha' was produced. The architect behind the Master Plan, Carlos Luis Toledo, is well-known for his strong belief in participatory planning, and the Master Plan was the result of nearly 2 years of discussing Rocinha's needs with residents in a bottom-up manner. According to a community leader, "[Toledo] did something that rarely happens, which was to hold assemblies, here in the community, discussing with the residents. It was democratic, there was participation". The process thus marked a step away from clientelist practices that have tended to steer interventions in Rio's favelas, where politicians have exchanged upgrading projects or other services for votes (Maricato 2000). The Master Plan's main proposals included completing infrastructure and facilities of basic sanitation, ensuring better accessibility, establishing limits on Rocinha's horizontal and vertical growth, and constructing a series of urban facilities, all while 'valuing Rocinha's culture and identity' (see Toledo 2011).

In the same period the PAC programme was being implemented in Rocinha, another initiative to intervene in Rio's favelas was developed at the state level: the Police 'Pacification' Program (UPP). UPP was designed as a combination of proximity policing with a social component, the municipal programme UPP Social (later re-named Rio+Social) that would provide social services like job training and cultural activities. The stated goal was to take back state control over territories controlled by drug traffickers to provide the local population "peace and public safety", seen as "necessary for the full exercise and development of citizenship" (Henriques and Ramos 2011, 243). It thus aspired to break with the logic of 'war' that had steered police interventions in favelas. The BOPE special police force occupied Rocinha in November 2011 to prepare for the implementation of the UPP, which was inaugurated in September 2012.

The combination of the improved security through UPP, the PAC investments in infrastructure, and policies that aimed at reducing income inequalities, presented a promise of significant changes in Rocinha. Together they constituted a politics of citizenship; that is, a pursuit of redistribution, representation and recognition as three interrelated dimensions of injustice and citizenship politics (Stokke forthcoming). How and to what degree did these programmes and policies live up to their expectations?

PAC and Participatory Development

PAC started as a prolongation of the Master Plan, and Toledo was hired to oversee the process. However, as the process went from the planning stage to the implementation of PAC works, it changed considerably. Toledo claimed "the government chose what was not our priority", and Martíns lamented that "the PAC works were implemented from the top-down". While the Master Plan explicitly listed basic sanitation as the community's most urgent need, the State Company of Public Works (EMOP) cherry-picked for execution prestigious infrastructure projects such as a large sports complex and a footpath designed by the internationally renowned architect Oscar Niemeyer, which connects Rocinha and São Conrado. It is an 'architectonical masterpiece symbolically and physically bridging the formal and the informal city' according Ruth Jurberg, responsible for PAC-Rocinha at EMOP, while Martíns regards it an expensive 'white elephant' replacing an already existing, fully functioning bridge that had strong historic and cultural value for the community. Many residents have denounced the PAC projects of being 'for tourists to see': architectonical masterpieces that are doing a specific symbolical work with impacts that reach beyond the immediate locality. As one resident puts it,

> They are works that you can see, basic sanitation on the other hand you cannot. If you show off a cable car in a favela, the foreigners taking photos, it is something that calls attention. It is just that it is not what the resident needs.

The cable car he refers to was a proposal from the federal government when a second round of PAC investments were promised Rocinha in 2012. Local civil society groups rejected the idea of the cable car in several preliminary hearings, asking for the completion of works that had been contracted through PAC but stalled in 2011 when 70 per cent of the work had been completed yet the initial budget was overrun by about 35 per cent (Daflon and Berta 2011). They also asked for PAC 2 to prioritise basic sanitation. Nevertheless, when Dilma officially launched PAC 2 in Rocinha in June 2013, half of the budget was earmarked for the construction of a cable car.

UPP: 'Opening Up' the Favela

As for the UPP 'pacifying' police, it pledged to pacify police and drug traffickers. Of equal importance for the Olympic city, it also pacified the anxieties of the middle classes and tourists in adjacent formal neighbourhoods, who reported feeling safer as the drug-related violence was displaced out of centrally located pacified favelas into the peripheries of the city (Cavalcanti 2013, 205). Real estate prices in São Conrado increased by nearly 200 per cent after the pacification of Rocinha (Ibid., 2014).

The UPP police was however less successful in making residents of Rocinha experience increased safety. According to data from the Institute of Public Safety, the rates of crime increased significantly in Rocinha from 2011 to 2012 (Rousso 2012). The pacification also increased insecurity for residents in a different sense, through 'opening up' the favela for a range of outside actors.

While the hills and mountainsides of the favelas were seen as wasteland a century ago when the favelas first emerged, they are today considered prime pieces of real estate in central areas of the city (see Rolnik 2016). As areas to a large degree outside of the formal economy, they also represent areas of capitalist interest. As Governor Cabral bluntly put it in 2011, when commenting on the public interventions in Rocinha, "we have to keep doing construction projects, but capitalism has to enter more and more" (Schmitt 2011). On the heels of the BOPE special police force that occupied Rocinha in 2011 came another invading force, the so-called formalisation task forces that were to formalise businesses and real estate (Urani et al. 2011), along with corporate actors eager to tap into the lucrative favela market. Services like the *gato* networks providing affordable electricity, internet, cable TV and motorcycle taxi services were formalised with a resulting multiplication of costs. This is what Harvey (2003) has termed an 'enclosing the commons', a privatisation of services that used to be informally taken care of. Local business owners struggle to compete with national and international franchises that have established a local presence, offering 24-month down payments on credit-bought electronics. A resident interviewed in 2012 remarked the following:

> The big companies that enter ruin the local economy. A product in Casa Bahia [electronics store] might be 900 Reais [250 USD], while it is 500 Reais [130 USD] in a local store. But because you can pay in instalments there, a lot of people prefer it. Local business is not surviving…it is not better for the community, but people are short sighted.

Urban Entrepreneurialism and the Favela's Place in the City

The public interventions in Rocinha formed a three-part strategy focusing on urban infrastructure, security and formalisation of the informal economy. This package of interventions has provided security and the necessary infrastructure to attract market forces and investments into the favela. Rocinha today is among the top tourist attractions in Rio, and a range of (mostly non-resident run) agencies provide 'favela tours' to give foreigners an exotic taste of the 'authentic' Rio (Larkins 2015). The UPPs have also made the city of Rio as a whole, and in particular areas of the city close to pacified favelas, safer (at least for a while). As a consequence, these interventions have helped with the rebranding of Rio as an Olympic city in order to attract international capital, tourists and investments. Along the way, the promise of enhanced citizenship for local residents seems to have lost focus in favour of other interests guiding the interventions.

In spite of the legal framework guaranteeing the 'right to the city' and popular participation in governance, the grassroots-driven struggles for urban development in Rocinha that led to the Master Plan in 2004–2006 were all but co-opted by elite interests. The visual prestige projects that have been completed, along with the proposed cable car, provide a branding factor far more favourable to the entrepreneurial city governance than invisible sewage improvements. Another likely reason for the large-scale projects is that they have good conditions for graft and super profits. The massive *Lava Jato* corruption investigation that exploded in 2014 has exposed the corrupt connections between politicians and domestic firms who gained lucrative contracts through state development programmes, and the PAC works in Rocinha have been connected to this scandal (Agência Brasil 2017).

As for the UPP, it constitutes a police practice that is exercised according to the spatial configuration of the city. While promoted as a programme to spur an approximation process between different parts and populations of the city, one can ask to what degree a differentiated policing of space can counter the differentiated citizenship in the city. Rather, it can be argued that such location-specific policing reinforces divides (Samara 2011). The logic steering the pacification programme can also be connected with Rio's entrepreneurial mode of governance. Rather than abandoning the logic of 'war', it installed a militarised state of exception in pacified favelas (Freeman 2014). It can thus be argued that the programme serves to protect the rest of the city, tourists and capital rather than ensuring increased security for favela residents. A 33-year-old journalist born and raised in Rocinha describes residents' disillusionment with the recent government interventions as follows:

> PAC entered with an absurd force, and the hope was that there would be a great change (…). Afterwards the pacification came, and we started believing in it (…) but we saw that everything that was being done was for the sake of the World Cup and the Olympics. We saw that if there were structural

changes in Rocinha, it was for the sake of tourism. If security was to be improved, it wouldn't be for the favela but for the 'asphalt',[1] it is about securing the criminals within the favelas so they don't go to the asphalt. Everything was because of the World Cup and the Olympics. We always thought so (…) [and] we saw that it was exactly what happened, everything was very superficial. PAC didn't do half of what should have been done, UPP came in saying it would guarantee security and we did not get security, and the other services that were promised never came.

To summarise, the recent public interventions for enhanced citizenship in Rocinha have addressed economic inequalities through policies of redistribution. This has led to a degree of social inclusion through lifting people out of poverty and providing them entry into middle-class consumer markets. The interventions have however been less successful in building a foundation for addressing inequalities beyond economic concerns. While some residents have experienced material enfranchisement and heightened access to goods and services, one can ask, following Larkins (2015, 157), to what degree their new consumptive habits has bestowed them acceptance into the middle or upper classes or whether their skin colour and place of residence trump their increased purchasing power as a marker of class status (see Bourdieu 1984).

Part 3: Challenging Entrenched Inequalities

'Not Far Enough': The June Uprisings

On June 25, 2013, thousands of Rocinha residents marched roughly 5 kilometres to the upscale neighbourhood Leblon where they occupied Governor Cabral's home. The theme of the demonstration was 'Basic Sanitation, Yes! White Elephants, No!', a clear rejection of PAC's prioritisation of large-scale, visual projects over basic sanitation improvements. The demonstration happened in the midst of the massive 'June uprisings', an unprecedented wave of mass protest that rocked Brazil. When a small protest against the increase to the bus fare in São Paulo in early June was met with massive police repression, it became the 'last drop' of Brazilians' increasing frustrations with a deepening 'urban crisis' (Rolnik 2011), government inefficiency, corruption and overspending on mega sports events. By the end of the month, millions of Brazilians from across the socio-economic scale took to the streets in hundreds of cities all over the country.

Both the shape and demands of the 'June uprisings', as well as the responses to and consequences of them, varied across the cities in Brazil. In Rio, the demonstrations synthesised the increasing discontentment with the mega event-driven urban governance and a deep disjunction between the politicians and their vision for the city and the interests of the population they were supposed to represent. The prospect of the benefits of the interventions that would come with turning Rio into an 'Olympic city' allowed for stepping outside the institutional framework (Vainer 2011), and as seen through the case of Rocinha there was little or no dialogue with the population when it came to the selection of investments and projects. While the *Bolsa Família* increased minimum wages and other federal programmes improved the living conditions of the poorest of the poor, this increased income, which enabled the growth of consumption, did not solve the precarious nature of public education, health care, security or public transport, nor did it address the fragmentation that characterises the duality of the urban landscape in Rio.

In addition to the demonstration on June 25, Rocinha had another large demonstration in July 2013, this time against the UPP police. On July 14 the UPP had taken local resident Amarildo da Souza Silva in for questioning, and he never returned home. It was later revealed that he was tortured, murdered and his body disappeared by the UPP police. His disappearance would mark a watershed for the UPP programme's legitimacy. Young favela men of Afro-Brazilian heritage, mainly those living in favelas and other marginalised communities, continue to be associated with violent crimes and are disproportionally targeted by extra-judicial executions and other human rights violations committed by the police in Rio's favelas (Amnesty International 2015). While it was far from the first case of its kind, the timing—in the midst of a city in revolt—spurred massive mobilisations that would gain international repercussion. People from around the world posted pictures on social media holding up signs demanding to know: 'Where is Amarildo?'

The two demonstrations in Rocinha, as part of the wider 'June uprisings', expressed frustrations with the limitations of the inequality-reducing measures introduced under *lulismo* and its alliance with urban entrepreneurialism in Rio. At the same time, they show some of the strides forward that had been made. As outlined in the introduction of this volume, the protests reflect how popular movements—building on decades of struggles for the citizenship rights people are granted in the legal framework but do not see reflected in their everyday lives (see Dagnino 2010)—managed to take advantage of the political space opened up by socially progressive governments. The PT governments did have an important impact in terms of placing citizenship on the agenda and challenging entrenched inequalities. They did introduce policies and politics to contest the privileges of occupational status, of masculinity, of whiteness and of heterosexuality. The symbolism of having an uneducated ironworker and a woman as presidents can also not be ignored in a country where the majority of the people have not seen themselves reflected in the traditional class of white, middle-aged, male politicians. As a result, the traditional upper and middle classes have found themselves sharing universities, airports, shopping centres and other venues with the 'new' middle class (the so-called class C, see Ricci 2013) that grew from *lulismo* politics. As long as the PT governments answered also to the upper classes' interests through maintaining a strong economy and low rates of unemployment, they remained silent. With the deepening economic and political crises from 2014 onwards, elaborated on in the chapter of Costa (this volume), this would change.

'Too Far': Revanchism

According to Chaui (2016, 21), the traditional middle class in Brazil has always had a weak position, and has therefore substituted their lack of economic and political power for the search of symbols of prestige within the consumerist society. With the economic crisis, it became increasingly problematic to maintain this lifestyle. People who had accumulated debts with high interest rates in the consumption-led, credit-fuelled economy found themselves in a difficult position. This can result in frustrations pointing in different directions. In June 2013 it was expressed as an anger directed 'upwards', against the economic and political elites. Gradually, however, this has been replaced by an anger directed 'downwards'. Their position threatened, the middle class 'waged a war' (Ibid.) on people they perceived to have encroached on their privileges. The conflict has a clear class distinction and can be read in light of what Neil Smith (1996) terms revanchism; a discourse of revenge on behalf of the bourgeois political elite and their supporters against those who benefited the most from the redistributive policies, affirmative action and antipoverty legislation introduced under PT.

From 2014, an unremitting rejection of the PT governments took centre stage in street demonstrations. There is a clear class distinction between those who participated in the June 2013 protests and the anti-PT protests from 2014 onwards. The grand majority were white with levels of income and education high above the average (Mello and da Costa 2017). In September 2016, after months of anti-PT demonstrations, Dilma was impeached (on highly questionable grounds, see Jinkings et al. 2016). Dilma's successor, former Vice President Michel Temer (PMDB), wasted little time before scaling back many of the social policies put in place by PT and unveiling an agenda of liberal economic reforms. These austerity measures were presented as necessary to tackle the budget deficit and restore market confidence in Brazil, arguing that PT and its extensive social welfare policies had drained the Brazilian economy. I will however argue they are best understood within a framework of revanchism, where the object is to reverse the victories and safeguards of the working class and the poor that were achieved during the 13 years of PT governments and to preempt further redistributive reforms.

As a result, those who rose to the 'new' middle class during the PT years now find their new class position to be quite uncertain. For the case of Rocinha, this chapter started with outlining a recent request to (re)move a bus stop in São Conrado. The protest is an illustration of how the strides forward of the poorer segments of society have been met with a revanchist counter-reaction on behalf of the middle and upper classes. The protest against the bus stop is just one among many situations where residents of Rocinha feel their rights violated or less respected than those of their neighbours. It is neither the most serious nor offensive one in a context of deep structural inequalities, rampant police violence and profound social and racial discrimination. Residents of Rocinha however explicitly place the protest against the bus stop within a context of class relations. "They want to take our buses. They treat us like crap, in fact, if they could put up a high wall so that they could not see us, it would be perfect [to them]," a 30-year-old man tells me. A 29-year-old female resident sees it as a "classic case of class struggles, not accepting the poor dividing the same territory". She also argues this protest would not have happened five years ago. The climate of protest that has characterised Brazil since June 2013 has given revanchist segments of society a newfound confidence in the streets as a place to raise their demands.

As to the other public interventions in Rocinha, PAC 2 is unlikely to materialise as the Temer government has abandoned state investment programmes in favour of privatisations. While this puts an end to the contested cable car, urgent needs for basic sanitation investments are also not being responded to. The UPP police, on the other hand, have largely lost legitimacy and their presence has been scaled back due to the severe economic crisis of the State of Rio. The weakened police presence has opened up for drug traffickers from different factions reclaiming control over pacified favelas, and violence is resurging. Residents of Rocinha thus experience a sense of increased insecurity both in the literal sense and in terms of uncertainty as to what their future beholds.

Final Remarks

This chapter has taken the community of Rocinha and its relation to neighbouring São Conrado as the starting point for reflecting on the inequality-reducing measures introduced since Lula became president in 2003. Public interventions in Rocinha during the PT years came with the promise of reducing social and spatial divides between the favela and the surrounding city and enhancing citizenship rights. The generation of 20-something in Rocinha that became adults during the PT years has seen important changes in their lifetime, and many are better off than their parents and grandparents. At the same time, many are disillusioned with the PAC and UPP programmes' failure in living up to their expectations and frustrated with the limits of their own social mobility. The advancements that did take place in terms of a (limited) upward mobility of poorer segments of society is currently being rolled back, while 'cultural' discrimination is coming to the forefront through a revanchist counter-reaction.

To conclude, it must however be remarked that the last years have seen important advancements in terms of creating a climate of debate on the historical, structural foundations of inequality. When Dilma was impeached and her successor appointed a cabinet consisting of only elder, white men from the traditional political class, it spurred harsh criticism and clearly showed an elite that is out of touch with the strides forward Brazil has indeed seen these last decades. What we are left with is an increasingly polarised and politicised social landscape, with hard lines of debate, societal unrest and protests. This is unlikely to decrease in the years to come.

Note

1. The formal city is often referred to as the 'asphalt' because of the paved streets, as opposed to the narrow pathways in the favelas.

REFERENCES

Agamben, Giorgio. 1998. *Homo Sacer: Sovereign Power and Bare Life*. Stanford: Stanford University Press.

Agência Brasil. 2017. *TCERJ aponta superfaturamento em obras do PAC na Rocinha, Manguinhos e Alemão*. http://agenciabrasil.ebc.com.br/geral/noticia/2017-01/tce-rj-aponta-superfaturamento-em-obras-do-pac-na-rocinha-manguinhos-e-alemao. Last accessed 10 Apr 2017.

Amnesty International. 2015. *Brazil: You Killed My Son. Homcides by Military Police in the City of Rio de Janeiro*. Anistia Internacional Brasil.

Bourdieu, Pierre. 1984. *Distinction: A Social Critique of the Judgment of Taste*. Cambridge, MA: Harvard University Press.

Braathen, Einar, Celina Sørbøe, Tim Bartholl, Ana Carolina Christovão, and Valeria Pinheiro. 2013. *Favela Policies and Social Mobilizations in Rio de Janeiro*. NIBR Working Paper Series 2013:111. Oslo: Norwegian Institute for Urban and Regional Research.

Broudehoux, Anne Marie. 2007. Spectacular Beijing: The Conspicuous Construction of an Olympic Metropolis. *Journal of Urban Affairs* 29 (4): 383–399.

Burgos, Marcelo Baumann. 1998. Dos parques proletários ao Favela-Bairro: as políticas públicas nas favelas do Rio de Janeiro. *Um século de favela*, 25–60.

Butler, Judith. 2004. *Undoing Gender*. Brighton: Psychology Press.

Cavalcanti, M. 2013. À espera, em ruínas: Urbanismo, estética e política no Rio de Janeiro da 'PACificação'. *Dilemas: revista de estudos de conflito e controle social* 6 (2-ABR): 191–228.

Chaui, M. 2016. A nova classe trabalhadora brasileira e a ascensão do conservadorismo. In *Por Que Gritamos Golpe? Para entender o impeachment e a crise política no Brasil*, ed. I. Jinkings, K. Doria, and M. Cleto. Boitempo: São Paulo.

Daflon, Rogério, and Ruben Berta. 2011. Na Rocinha, construção de planos inclinados, creches e mercado está parada. *O Globo*, July 19. Available online at: http://oglobo.globo.com/rio/na-rocinha-construcao-de-planos-inclinados-creches-mercadoesta-parada-2714033. Last accessed 10 Apr 2017.

Dagnino, Evelyn. 2010. Citizenship: A Perverse Confluence. In *Deconstructing Development Discourse. Buzzwords and Fuzzwords*, ed. A. Cornwall and D. Eade. Oxford: Practical Action Publishing Ltd.

Davis, M. 2006. *City of Quartz: Excavating the Future in Los Angeles*. New York: Verso Books.

EMOP. 2007. *Trabalho Technico Social*. http://www.emop.rj.gov.br/trabalho-tecnico-social/plano-de-desenvolvimento-sustentavel-pds/. Accessed 10 Apr 2017.

Freeman, James. 2014. Raising the Flag over Rio de Janeiro's Favelas: Citizenship and Social Control in the Olympic City. *Journal of Latin American Geography* 13 (1): 7–38.

Harvey, David. 1989. From Managerialism to Entrepreneurialism: The Transformation in Urban Governance in Late Capitalism. *Geografiska Annaler B* 71 (1): 3–17.
———. 2003. Accumulation by Dispossession. In *The New Imperialism*, 137–182. Oxford: Oxford University Press.
———. 2008. The Right to the City. *New Left Review* 53: 23–40.
Henriques, Ricardo, and Silvia Ramos. 2011. UPP social: ações sociais para a consolidação da pacificaçãoe. In *Rio: a hora da virada*, ed. A. Urani and F. Giambiagi, 242–254. Rio de Janeiro: Campus/Elsevier.
Holston, James. 2009. Insurgent Citizenship in an Era of Global Urban Peripheries. *City & Society* 21 (2): 245–267.
IBGE. 2010. *Censo 2010*. http://www.ibge.com.br/home/estatistica/populacao/censo2010/default.shtm. Accessed 5 Apr 2017.
IPS. 2016. *Índice De Progresso Social No Rio De Janeiro. Resumo Executivo*. Available at: https://www2.deloitte.com/content/dam/Deloitte/br/Documents/about-deloitte/IPS_RJ_ResumoExecutivo.pdf. Accessed 5 Apr 2017.
Jinkings, I., K. Doria, and M. Cleto, eds. 2016. *Por Que Gritamos Golpe? Para entender o impeachment e a crise política no Brasil*. São Paulo: Boitempo.
Júnior, Nelson Saule. 2005. *O Direito à Cidade como paradigma da governança urbana democrática*. http://www.polis.org.br/uploads/750/750.pdf
Larkins, Erica M.R. 2015. *The Spectacular Favela: Violence in Modern Brazil*. Berkeley: University of California Press.
Lefebvre, Henri. 1968. *Le Droit à la ville*. Paris: Anthropos.
Leitão, Gerônimo EA. 2009. *Dos Barracos de Madeira aos Prédios de Quitinetes: Uma análise do processo de produção da moradia na favela da Rocinha, ao longo de cinquenta anos*. Editora da UFF.
Leite, Márcia Pereira. 2012. Da 'metáfora da guerra' ao projeto de 'pacificação': favelas e políticas de segurança pública no Rio de Janeiro. *Revista Brasileira de Segurança Publica* 6 (2): 374–389.
Machado da Silva, Luiz Antonio, and Márcia Pereira Leite. 2008. Violência, crime e política: o que os favelados dizem quando falam desses temas? In *Vida sob cerco. Violência e routina nas favelas do Rio de Janeiro*, ed. Luiz Antonio Machado da Silva. Rio de Janeiro: Editora Nova Fronteira S.A.
Maricato, Ermínia. 2000. Urbanismo na periferia do mundo globalizado: metrópoles brasileiras. *São Paulo em perspectiva* 14 (4): 21–33.
Meirelles, Renato, and Celso Athayde. 2016. *Um país chamado favela*. São Paulo: Editora Gente Liv e Edit Ltd.
Mello, William J., and da Costa, Altemar M. 2017. *Class Struggle in Brazil: Who Will Defend the Working Class?* http://nonsite.org/editorial/class-struggle-in-brazil. Accessed 10 Apr 2017.
Neuwirth, R. 2005. *Shadow Cities: A Billion Squatters, a New Urban World*. London/New York: Routledge.

Papo Reto. 2016. *Versão corrigida*. https://100ko.wordpress.com/2016/05/22/versao-corrigida-troca-de-tiros-na-rocinha-assusta-alunos-da-puc/. Accessed 5 Apr 2017.
Purcell, M. 2003. Citizenship and the Right to the Global City: Reimagining the Capitalist World Order. *International Journal of Urban and Regional Research* 27 (3): 564–590.
Ricci, Rudá. 2013. O *Maior Fenômeno Sociológico do Brasil: A Nova Classe Média*. Available online http://www.escoladegoverno.org.br/artigos/209-nova-classe-media. Accessed 10 Apr 2017.
Rolnik, Raquel. 2011. Democracy on the Edge: Limits and Possibilities in the Implementation of an Urban Reform Agenda. *International Journal of Urban and Regional Research* 35 (2): 239–255.
———. 2016. *Guerra dos lugares. A colonização da terra e da moradia na era das finanças*. São Paulo: Boitempo Editorial.
Rousso, Bruno. 2012. *Rocinha: 1 ano após ocupação, homicídios, estupros e roubo a casas sobem até 100% R7 Notícias*. Available online: http://noticias.r7.com/rio-de-janeiro/noticias/rocinha-1-ano-apos-ocupacaohomicidios-estupros-e-roubo-a-casas-sobem-ate-100-20121113.html
Roy, Ananya. 2011. Slumdog Cities: Rethinking Subaltern Urbanism. *International Journal of Urban and Regional Research* 35 (2): 223–238.
Said, Edward. 1979. *Orientalism*. 1978. New York: Vintage, 1994.
Samara, Tony Roshan. 2011. *Cape Town After Apartheid: Crime and Governance in the Divided City*. Minnesota: University of Minnesota Press.
Sampaio Jr., P. A. 2012. Desenvolvimentismo e neodesenvolvimentismo: tragédia e farsa (Developmentalism and New Developmentalism: Tragedy and Farce). *Serviço Social & Sociedade*, São Paulo (112): 672–688.
Schmitt, S. 2011. Estado e presidente Dilma finalizam o PAC 2 da Rocinha. *O Globo*, November 8.
Singer, Andre. 2012. *Os Sentidos do Lulismo. Reforma Gradual e Pacto Conservador*. São Paulo: Companhia das Letras.
Smith, Neil. 1996. *The New Urban Frontier: Gentrification and the Revanchist City*. Florence: Psychology Press.
Stepan, N.L. 1991. *"The Hour of Eugenics": Race, Gender, and Nation in Latin America*. Ithaca/London: Cornell University Press.
Stokke, Kristian. Forthcoming. Politics of Citizenship: Towards an Analytical Framework. *Norwegian Journal of Geography*.
Teles, Edson and Vladimir Safatle (orgs). 2010. *O que resta da ditadura: a excecão brasileira*. São Paulo: Boitempo.
Toledo, Luis Carlos. 2011. http://bentorubiao.org.br/habitacao/wp-content/uploads/2011/11/17.-Projetos-participativos-de-urbaniza%C3%A7%C3%A3o-de-favelas.pdf. Accessed 5 Apr 2017.

Urani, A., F. Giambiagi, and A. Souza, eds. 2011. *Rio: A hora da virada*. Rio de Janeiro: Elsevier Editora.

Vainer, Carlos. 2011. Cidade de exceção: reflexões a partir do Rio de Janeiro. In *XIV Encontro Nacional da ANPUR*. Rio de Janeiro.

Valladares, Licia do Prado. 2005. *A invenção da favela: do mito de origem a favela.com*. Rio de Janeiro: FGV.

Ventura, Zuenir. 1994. *Cidade Partida*. São Paolo: Companhia das Letra.

Zweig, Stefan. 2017 [1941]. *Brasilien. Ein Land der Zukunft*. Königstein: Ausgabe im SoTo Verlag.

Open Access This chapter is licensed under the terms of the Creative Commons Attribution 4.0 International License (http://creativecommons.org/licenses/by/4.0/), which permits use, sharing, adaptation, distribution and reproduction in any medium or format, as long as you give appropriate credit to the original author(s) and the source, provide a link to the Creative Commons license and indicate if changes were made.

The images or other third party material in this chapter are included in the chapter's Creative Commons license, unless indicated otherwise in a credit line to the material. If material is not included in the chapter's Creative Commons license and your intended use is not permitted by statutory regulation or exceeds the permitted use, you will need to obtain permission directly from the copyright holder.

CHAPTER 6

Meanings of Poverty: An Ethnography of Bolsa Familia Beneficiaries in Rio de Janeiro/Brazil

Michele de Lavra Pinto

INTRODUCTION

The so-called Pink Tide that swept across the Latin American continent at the turn of the millennium took on different facets in different countries, although certain basic ideals remained as a common thread. The imperative of poverty reduction was one of them. In Brazil, the *Bolsa Familia* programme (hereafter, BFP) completed 14 years of existence in 2017. Its expansion to reaching over 13 million households in 2016 is an indication of the program's success in numerical terms. Yet so, the relative success of the program also testifies to the numerous obstacles and difficulties that remain with regards to overcoming the impacts of poverty in a country of such vast proportions and with such deep-rooted inequalities as Brazil. Indeed, the BFP also highlights that poverty is a complex and historical social phenomenon with multiple dimensions that cannot be measured by material benchmarks alone.

M. de Lavra Pinto (✉)
ESPM (Escola Superior de Propaganda e Marketing),
Rio de Janeiro, Brazil

© The Author(s) 2018
M. Ystanes, I.Å. Strønen (eds.), *The Social Life of Economic Inequalities in Contemporary Latin America*, Approaches to Social Inequality and Difference, DOI 10.1007/978-3-319-61536-3_6

This chapter presents the results of ethnographic research carried out between 2012 and 2015 with several families living in a *favela* (low-income, informal neighbourhood)[1] in the southern zone (Zona Sul) of the city of Rio de Janeiro. The aim is to first describe key aspects related to the BFP (types of benefits paid and inclusion criteria in the programme) in order to subsequently unveil the meanings of "being poor" and "poverty" through the eyes of the beneficiaries, residents of the favela and the social workers managing the programme. Therefore, the study will show the kind of vision "the poor" have of themselves, their economic conditions and the social differences in their daily life in the favela. As is also illustrated by Costa's chapter (this volume), the BFP has not contributed to a radical redistribution of resources during Brazil's engagement with the Pink Tide. Now, as the Pink Tide unravels, Brazil remains one of the most unequal countries in the world. However, the ethnographic material presented here shows that BFP has made a significant difference in improving life conditions for the poorest segments of society. Even so, this study of how recipients conceptualise their situation and their identity is illustrative of the manners in which economic and social stratification, as well as multifaceted precariousness, remain fundamental features of life in Rio de Janeiro's favelas.

The History of Welfare Programmes in Brazil

There is an increasing number of studies in Brazil that discuss and analyse the effects of public policies, including conditional cash transfer programmes in education, health, work, and their impacts in eradicating poverty and/or reducing inequality in Brazil (see, e.g. Jaccoud 2006; Reis 2005; Sprandel 2004; Hoffman 2006). The studies are frequently based on quantitative data generated by the *Pesquisa Nacional por Amostra de Domicílios Contínua* (Brazilian National Household Survey Continuos).

This interest is justified, since the issue of poverty is pointed out as a problem to be overcome by governments, especially in developing countries. Regarding the cash transfer programmes in Brazil, these policies have historically been presented as forms of social protection. The first discussion of a cash transfer programme in Brazil began in 1975, when the economist Antônio Maria da Silveira published the paper "Redistribution of income" with the objective of gradually eradicating poverty through government intervention (Silva et al. 2008, 93). The idea was based on a study of "negative income tax" by the North-American author Milton Friedman; a proposal that he endorsed in his book Capitalism and Freedom (1962).

The Brazilian Constitution of 1988 states that "Social assistance shall be provided to those who need it, regardless of contributions to social security" (Brazilian Constitution of 1988, art. 203). Hence, the right to such policies and their benefits was formally assured to whomever may require them, regardless of any prior contribution. Under the new constitutional provisions, the social assistance policy began to organise its implementation under two pillars: the provision of services and the granting of monetary benefits" (IPEA 2010, 78). According to Silva et al. (2008), the context of widening social rights for social policies was instituted at an unfavourable moment from the point of view of the fiscal crisis of the State, which began in the 1980s and grew in the 1990s; when the implementation of neoliberal policies gained pace in Brazil.[2] The neoliberal era in Brazil began in earnest with the election of Fernando Collor de Mello in 1989 (who was impeached on corruption charges and briefly replaced by Vice President Itamar Franco), and continued through Fernando Henrique Cardoso's two successive governments, from 1995 to 2002.

In 1995, the first year of Fernando Henrique Cardoso's presidency, the priority was to maintain economic stability and the Plan to Combat Hunger and Misery (*Plano de Combate à Fome e a Miséria*) from the previous government. This programme was then substituted by the Solidarity Community Programme (*Comunidade Solidária*) (Lahóz 2002). The Solidarity Community Programme aimed at articulating and linking the State with civil society, as well as implementing social programmes in the poorest municipalities of the country by integrating municipal-, state-, and federal governments. In 2001, during the second term of Fernando Henrique Cardoso, federal programmes with decentralised implementation in the municipalities were created (Silva et al. 2008, 98). According to Peres, "the Solidarity Community Programme survived to the end of the Fernando Henrique Cardoso government (2002). In January 2003 it became linked to the Ministry of Food Safety" (Peres 2005, 1). During 2003, the programme was gradually disarticulated and substituted by the Lula administration's Zero Hunger Programme (*Programa Fome Zero*).

Amongst the programmes developed under the umbrella of the Zero Hunger Programme, was a school allowance programme called School Stipend (*Bolsa Escola*). In order for each child or adolescent to be granted this fund, the parents or legal guardians of the child were required to present proof of the child's school attendance (at least 85 per cent), and to earn the minimum salary (established by the government) or less. The Gas Help (*Auxílio Gás* or *Vale Gás*) programme provided financial aids for purchasing cooking gas every two months to families that had a maximum income of half the minimum salary. This policy helped families that were already assisted by the *Bolsa Escola* and other programmes that integrated the Social Protection Network (*Sistema de Proteção Social*, integrating all the social programs). Additionally, it is also worth noting the *Programa Bolsa Alimentação* (Food Grant Programme), which was coordinated by the Ministry of Health (*Ministério da Saúde*) and carried out through the municipalities. The Bolsa Alimentação programme had a duration of six months, which could be prolonged for subsequent periods, provided that the beneficiary fulfilled health conditionalities (weighing and measuring small children in the household every month, following the vaccination calendar, pregnant women undergoing prenatal screening, etc.). The money from these programmes had a predetermined end (i.e. purchasing gas, food, and school material) and directing such funds to different products was prohibited. Therefore, in addition to the conditionalities, there was also a "control" of the expenditures of the benefit.

In 2003, in the early days of the government of then-President Luiz Inácio "Lula" da Silva, the unification process of national cash transfer programmes began to spread across several ministries. The unification process took place until 2007, when the transfer of the main programmes to the BFP was completed (Silva and Lima 2010). However, until the complete merger of the programmes, other social assistance processes were important for the unification and implantation of the BFP, among them the creation of the Ministry of Social Development and Fight against Hunger (*Ministério do Desenvolvimento Social e Combate à Fome*) in 2004. According to Silva et al. (2008), starting in 2003 the federal government established qualitative and quantitative changes in the construction of a national policy of cash transfer. During four successive Workers' Party governments (President Luiz Inácio "Lula" da Silva [2003–2010]; President Dilma Rousseff [2011–2016 until the impeachment]), the BFP was not the most important in terms of the volume of resources invested, but it is said to have had the greatest impact on the lives of the poorest families (Weissheimer 2006). In political discourse, the programme became cast as an antithesis to the social policies and neoliberal matrix developed during the Fernando Henrique Cardoso government. When Luiz Inácio "Lula" da Silva was re-elected for a second term in 2006,[3] his re-election was widely attributed to the success of these programs, as the majority of his voters came from the poorest part of the population. Nevertheless, and reflecting class based social cleavages in Brazil, the BFP was criticised by certain sectors of

Brazilian society as something negative that encouraged the poor to not work and/or have more children.

Indeed, since its introduction, BFP has been the subject of extensive debate and controversy in the Brazilian media. Pires and Dias (2015) analysed how the BFP was represented in a large national newspaper (*O Estado de São Paulo*) in the period between 2003 and 2013. According to the authors, in 2003, the newspaper focused on the "escape mechanism" of the BFP and called it the "handout programme", since one of its characteristics was not setting a maximum time limit for receiving benefits. Such criticisms, over the years, cooled to the point where, in 2013, the main candidate of the opposition to the presidency proposed the constitutionalisation of the benefit, which was seen as a positive factor for the re-election campaign of then-president Dilma Rousseff (Pires and Dias 2015).

At the current political and economic moment in Brazil, characterised by budget cuts and political instability arising from the impeachment process against President Dilma Rousseff, the BFP is back on centre stage of public debate. Some advocate for its maintenance, while others regard it as a "handout programme" and "unemployment programme", and/or they support cuts in the programme budget, which in 2016 was around R$ 28 billion. However, it should be noted that my research was conducted at a time when this attention, although existent, was not as much in evidence.

Bolsa Família Programme: Benefits and Eligibility Criteria

The BFP has been modified since its creation, although without losing the principle of cash transfer with conditionalities and autonomy of beneficiaries regarding the expenditure of money. Who then can request the benefit and which are the inclusion criteria? And what is the central measure of poverty deployed by the programme?

The main criterion established by the programme is *per capita* income. That is, a poverty line was established in which families with a monthly income per person between BRL 85.01 (EUR 25.24) and BRL 170.00 (EUR 50.48)[4] may apply for the BFP. By establishing *per capita* income as the main criterion of inclusion and exclusion, the BFP seeks to reach the population that it considers to be poor and, therefore, in the most dire need of the benefit. This way, the programme anchors itself on a one-dimensional poverty criterion, determining that the poor and extremely poor are included in the income range established by the programme. The programme registers other information about families such as the location of their residence, housing conditions, levels of education, and employment, but these features are not taken into account for assessing eligibility for the programme.

According to the Ministry of Social Development (*Ministério de Desenvolvimento Social*),[5] the city of Rio de Janeiro, with a population of 6,476,631 inhabitants (IBGE 2015), had a total of 479,693 families registered in the BFP in 2016. In February 2017, 233,766 families received the benefit, which represents a coverage of 79.7 per cent of the estimate of poor families in the municipality, with an average benefit in the amount of BRL 162.40 (EUR 48.22) (MDS 2017).[6] In Copacabana and Ipanema, where the Pavão-Pavãozinho favelas are located, 3589 families were enrolled in 2015 and 1814 received the benefit.[7] Here, data from the Reference Center for Social Assistance (*Centro de Referência de Assistência Social*, or CRAS) obtained by the researcher, lists approximately 265 families to be beneficiaries in 2016, of which 122 are in a situation of extreme poverty. According to CRAS's estimates, the most common profile for a beneficiary is a female between 30 and 39 years of age with an incomplete basic education, who has between two and four children, and who make a living through informal work.

The amount that each family recieves through the BFP varies, and is based on the profile registered in the Single Registration System (*Cadastro Único*) used by the programme. Among the information used for the calculus is the monthly income per person, the number of family members, household composition—the total number of children and adolescents up to the age of 17—, and the number of pregnant women. Although the financial aid received is not extensive, the families interviewed for this study consider it a "fixed" income that help them in numerous situations, for example to pay for electricity, public transport, food and rent, among other expenses.

The regulation of the programme establishes the following types of benefits: the Basic Benefit is granted only to extremely poor families (monthly income per person below or up to EUR 25.24). The Variable Benefit from 0 to 15 years amounts to EUR 11.58 and is granted to families with children or adolescents from 0 to 15 years of age. The Variable Benefit for Pregnant Women amounts to EUR 11.58 and is granted to families with pregnant women. Payment is made in nine consecutive instalments, provided that the pregnancy has been identified before the ninth month.[8] Furthermore, the Nutritional Variable Benefit consists of EUR 11.58, and is granted to families with children between 0 and 6 months in their household.[9]

These benefits are limited to five per household. There is a variable grant for families with adolescents aged 16–17 consisting of EUR 11.36 (limited to two per household), and a special benefit for overcoming extreme poverty. The calculations differs from case to case, and is granted to households that are enrolled in the programme but remain in extreme poverty despite other benefits. This benefit is intended to boost families' income in order to overcome the extreme poverty threshold. As this outline of the programme's main features indicates, the amount of cash benefits recieved by individual households vary, but we should also add that in addition to the Bolsa Familia programme, the Unified Registry provides access to other governmental programmes and social policies at federal, state, and local levels. Such benefits are paid on monthly basis.

In order to receive the Bolsa Familia allowance, each recipient is given a debit magnetic-stripe card issued by the Federal Bank, *Caixa Econômica Federal*. It has the name of the recipient and the Social Identification Number (NIS) printed on it. For registration, it is necessary to present identity documents, proof or declaration of address, and proof of income. The NIS is a number assigned to every citizen seeking some kind of state assistance. Once the NIS is generated, the citizen, according to their income, is able to register for social programmes or make requests such as exemption from fees in civil service examinations, social tariffs for electricity bills, and so on. For the head of the household, it is necessary to present a social security number (CPF) or voter's registration card. For the other members of the family, any identification document, such as identity card, voter's registration card, birth or marriage certificate, CPF,[10] or employment record card can be presented. The documentation must be submitted in one of the CRAS in the municipality where the applicant resides, which are responsible for identifying and registering families (MDS 2015).

In Rio de Janeiro, the CRAS are under the direction of the Municipal Social Welfare and Development Office (*Secretaria Municipal de Desenvolvimento e Assistência Social*, MSWDO). They are responsible for, among other things, directing families to town hall social services, which include several social programmes, such as *Bolsa Familia*. The CRAS are also under the direction of the Social Development Coordination (*Coordenadoria de Desenvolvimento Social*), whose competence includes participating in the planning of programmes and projects in their local area, implementing local social policy actions, conducting research, and coordinating, supervising, and evaluating the implementation of all the social development programmes and projects. The methods used to identify eligible households involve obtaining information from local people, schools, residents' association, trade unions, or from the families who apply for registration at the MSWDO themselves.

Conceptualisations of Poverty: Criteria and Definitions

"Poverty" and "extreme poverty" are not new terms; however, they have been mentioned many times since the creation of the BFP. Both in research and in conditional cash transfer programmes in other context, "poverty" and "extreme poverty" are defined as conditions that need to be overcome. Thus, there is a significant generation of statistical data that attempt to identify and measure poverty rates (Neder 2006; Neri 2011). This reality based on figures is important and necessary; however, it also represents power because they may legitimise access and assistance in the area of public policies (Desrosieres 2010). Therefore, it is important to have in mind that no perspective on "the problem of poverty" is neutral. Rather, it remains an issue open to conflicts, struggles and disputes over how to define it, which terms to use, and how solutions are defined and implemented.

This is evident when we examine what the literature has to say about the indices used to measure poverty. Neri (2010) emphasises that there are some poverty measures taking several dimensions into regard, for example "sanitation" and "electricity", while other more simple measures focus on a single dimension—usually the income. In Latin American literature, for example, the concepts of Basic Needs Index and Human Poverty Index have frequently been used (Neri 2010). The Ministry of Social Development uses a synthetic indicator called the Family Development Index as a means of approaching the families that have—based on their income level—become enrolled in Bolsa Familia. The index is compiled from six aspects: vulnerability, access to knowledge and work, availability of resources, child development, and housing conditions.

For some authors, such as Rocha (2007), there is no "unambiguous" definition of poverty. The starting point for discussion on the issue should be a conceptual explanation, which depends on the standard of living and how basic human needs are met. According to Rocha, "to determine who is poor in a defined social group is to establish a common list of a minimum set of public services and goods necessary for survival" (Rocha 2007, 23). In the social science literatures, different forms of qualitative analysis have been employed to analyse poverty. DaMatta (1995) emphasises the importance of culture and history in the definition of poverty in Brazil. Studies of poverty elsewhere support this point; poverty is always conceptualised in particular ways depending on the social, cultural, and historical context (see, e.g. Anderson and Broch-Due 1999; Broch-Due and Schroeder 2000; Milton 2007; O'Connor 2002; Lautier 2002).

On a global basis, the United Nations and the World Bank define a "poor" country based on income levels. On individual levels, the World Bank's international poverty line is currently USD 1.90 per day. Despite the advantage of simplicity, it is argued that, by focusing solely on income, we are also implicity framing the discussion about poverty to a question of purchasing power. Certainly, the level of income is relevant as it determines the purchasing power of consumers and whether they have enough to feed themselves. However, increases in income does not automatically translate into better access to basic services such as health and education, among others. Rego and Pinzani (2013, 149) emphasise that the problem of analysing poverty only based on income is that this criterion does not account for the level of well-being of individuals, making their definition and criteria inaccurate. There is ample scope for determining poverty criteria, thus creating the need for a multidimensional view of poverty and deprivation, as stated by Sen (2000).

Based on this perspective, a team of researchers of The Oxford Poverty and Human Development Initiative, with the support of the United Nations, created an indicator called "Multidimensional Poverty Index". This indicator, according to Rattner (2010), seeks to build a picture of poverty based on the fraction of households that lack basic goods and services (whether the house has a cement floor, a bathroom and electricity). Other questions seek to assess issues regarding education and health. Rattner (2010) also highlights that there is no unanimity as to results and how to determine poverty. A simple definition would be, "people who do not have enough to lead a dignified life" (Rattner 2010, 76). But what is "enough", which goods and services characterise it, and who should decide these questions—researchers, governments, or international agencies? My contention is that these are far more complex issues than what can be measured by numbers, and that the poor themselves should have the final word on their conditions and expectations on poverty.

"Being Poor": Meanings and Perceptions in the *Favela*

The implementation of public policies in the favelas is not something new in the history of Rio de Janeiro (see, e.g. Magalhães 2013). Valladares (2000, 2005) explains how favelas were introduced and treated in the political and social debate in the city. The author also discusses how knowledge about the favelas has been perceived and constructed throughout the twentieth century, and how a negative image of these communities, associating the place and its people with poverty, dirt and trickery, has been forged. Silva stresses that favelas are often studied under two different approaches: "one that intends to formulate 'solutions' to the 'social problems' in the communities and another that seeks to generate political and ideological lines of action" (Silva 2011, 699). However, favela dwellers are not a homogeneous population (see, e.g. Larkins 2015; Pearlman 2010). Nevertheless, the association between the favela and poverty in Brazil is constructed automatically by most of the Brazilian population, including those who are agents in social assistance programmes.

Residents of the Pavão-Pavãozinho favelas interviewed for this study did not always hold the perception that being a resident of the favela was synonymous with being poor, nor that it denoted eligibility for the BFP. This shows a plurality of perceptions and criteria related to the term poverty across and within social groups. Some of these differences can be discerned in the meanings that favela residents attribute to poverty and to being poor.

In the favela, accounts of being poor and of poverty are related to income, but they go beyond it as well. According to one resident, not having a decent bathroom in your house is a sign of extreme poverty. When being invited into private homes in the favela, you often find that the bathrooms only have a toilet and no shower, or that the toilet is broken. Often there is a lack of water. Other homes have bathrooms constructed as outhouses, and many have water containers on the outside of the house. In one of the houses I visited, the woman gave her children baths using a large water container outside the front door. Utilisation of water containers was also reported by Cunha: "these containers are used to store water, as a way for residents to work around the many days that they did not have water in their houses" (Cunha 2011, 16). In some areas, a turn-taking system of water collection known as a "maneuver" is used, consisting of a "local system in which residents redirect the course of water each day to a certain area of the favela, since the public system does not reach all houses" (Cunha 2011, 16, see also Cunha 2014).

By assessing levels of poverty in a concrete fashion by people's relative access to basic services and needs, people in the favelas deploy categorisations of poverty that resembles that of Gutíerrez, who considers poverty as a descriptive category based on comparative indicators vis-à-vis other individuals (Gutíerrez 2007). In that regard, housing issues need to be emphasised as an emic indicator of poverty for residents. For residents of Pavão-Pavãozinho (beneficiaries of BFP or not), the characteristics of houses and their location in the favela indicate who the poor people are.

Based on observations and the accounts of local residents, it was evident that the poorest families possessed wood houses in the areas with most difficult access and at the highest elevations, known as "Caranguejo" and "Vietnã". In addition to precarious constructions, the access by narrow and steep stairs impeded delivery of purchases and mail. According to Maria, a resident who lived adjacent to "Caranguejo" and who was a beneficiary of the BFP, the closer one lived to "the asphalt", as the formal neighbourhoods are referred to as,[11] the more expensive the house was:

> *Poor people like me can't get down; I'm waiting to be called to get a PAC apartment [Programa de Aceleramento do Crescimento, PAC—Program for Growth Acceleration]. Here is an area of risk, so I should go live in the apartments. For now, I'm staying here.*

The PAC was created in 2007 during the second term of President Luis Inácio Lula da Silva (see also Sørbøe, this volume, for more on this programme). It aims to resume the planning and execution of social, urban, logistical, and energy infrastructure projects. The housing program My House, My Life (*Minha Casa, Minha Vida*) is part of the PAC (www.pac.gov.br) and the programme was also present in Pavão-Pavãozinho. However, since there were not enough new housing units available for all residents living in risk areas, people continued to live in residents that had been marked as dangerous by the Civil Defense.

Another possibility for people living in areas of risk was to be contemplated for a PAC unit in neighbourhoods further away from the south zone (Zona Sul). However, most of the residents preferred to stay in their residences in the south zone. This part of the city was associated with easier access to services (water, electricity, and trash collection), social programmes, proximity to the beach and recreation and sometimes to work and income, in addition to emotional ties. And a resident recounts: "[…] my life is here. I work nearby and I get to the beach easily. I grew up here, how will I get a job if I live far away? I prefer to pay rent and stay here as long as possible". However, residents reported that there has been an increase in the value of housing in recent years—some have already left due to this. A resident, whose family receives the benefit of the BFP, reports that she remains in Pavãozinho because her husband performs odd jobs in the favela, she receives food donations, and the money from BFP helps them to pay the rent (BRL 350.00; EUR 105.46). Their house consists of a single room with bathroom, providing shelter for two adults and five children. The family is extremely poor and also receives help from neighbours who donate clothes and milk powder for the children, among other items.

Some people living in the PAC apartements already built by the government in the Cantagalo favela complained about the condominium fee that they need to pay, as this comes at the top of their already heavily strained budgets. Other residents agree with the fee, but they complain that in addition to the buildings there should be parking garage and playground space. According to José, who lives in a government-subsidised apartment, the building lacks automobile parking space for those who own a car as he does.

> *I lived on the X Street in Pavão; my house was torn down to widen the street. My car is on the other side because I cannot park here. The authorities do not know our reality. There is everything here [in the favela]: poor people and the new middle class (C class) like me. Aren't they talking about the Class C on television? Well, I purchased my used car with a lot of sacrifice, but I have no parking space for it. In the government's opinion, everybody is poor and has no money to buy a car in the favela. Those who live in the favela must ride a bus or walk.*

The difference between the poor and those who are a little better off also involves the ownership of certain assets, such as a car. However, household size—and more specifically the number of people in the household—is a strong indicator of poverty. Added to this, there is the difficulty of continuing living in the favela since there has been a steep increase in the value of housing and rents in Rio de Janeiro, mostly due to the hosting of the 2014 FIFA World Cup and 2016 Olympics (see Sørbøe (Chap. 5) and Ystanes (Chap. 4), this volume, for more on the effects of mega-event hosting in Rio). It is evident from the reports (of beneficiaries and non-beneficiaries) that the poorest have more difficulty in continuing to live in the south zone because of these processes. Thus, two parallel processes have been taking place: on the one hand, the poorest residents have seen their situation improved by the Bolsa Familia cash transfers, and on the other hand, life in south-zone favelas has become increasingly expensive as gentrification takes hold, forcing many of the poorest to leave for less attractive locations. The hosting of mega-events therefore highlights the fragility of the gains in social welfare achieved by the Workers' Party governments, putting the structural and political dimensions of the favela residents housing situations into sharp relief. Harvey (2004), in his analyses of Baltimore, the United States, reports on similar processes in relation to large-scale urban development processes, generating a "fever of construction" "no matter what", a shift from the centre to the suburbs, and unordered growth, inequality, and poverty (Harvey 2004, 9–10). This in turn led to an urban crisis. Harvey (2004) illustrates how space comes to be perceived of as capital's material resource, and he highlights the dispersal of manufacturing from centres to suburbs, multinationals' interests, and fiscal austerity as some of the causes of the urban crisis in Baltimore.

In contrast to this perception of space as an asset to be exploited by capital, Lefebvre (2001) points out that space is something that people creates. He emphasises man as the subject of history, who not only reproduces but also produces his and her surroundings. As previously mentioned, local protection network makes it difficult for people to move to a new home distant from the present one (whether or not beneficiaries of Bolsa Familia), even when they live in dangerous circumstances. According to Lefebvre (2001), social relationships are not uniform in time and space; they depend on the reality to which they are subjected. In this sense, the author suggests that space contains the social relations and is a product of them; therefore, reality is historically constructed, which involves having a mental representation of the city and the urban as their material expression. He also points out that a locality is a set of differences, that is, the point of coexistence of plurality and simultaneity of patterns and the different ways of living the urban life. However, space is also a place of conflict, in which exploitation is not particular to the "working class but is found among all social categories" (Lefebvre 2001, 138).

In the Pavão-Pavãozinho favelas, families are distinguished by income level, assets, and the level of education (participation in higher education is considered a milestone). These differences are evidently also found in other communities and populations, favelas or not. However, it is important to highlight these dimensions of favela realities in order to counteract reifying and simplistic perceptions of the favela as a homogenous space of uniform (poor) material and human conditions. Silva (2011) describes the existence of a "favela bourgeoisie", when referring to access to local resources, both economic, political and material. This heterogeneity amongst residents creates different viewpoints, assessment and needs; an issue that became evident in my research as I attended meetings of the residents' association. For example, the demand for a parking space in the favela was a recurrent topic at those meeting. Residents who owned a car complained that spaces used to park cars became prohibited since the Pacifying Police Unit (*Unidade de Polícia Pacificadora*—UPP) was set up in Pavão-Pavãozinho.

The residents justify this claim by saying that the favela has changed and that its residents now have cars. Jussara, a nurse who works at two different hospitals, said that after purchasing her car, for which she is still paying, it is possible to meet her tight schedule at both hospitals. However, the favela does not have a parking space where she could leave her car. Jussara added that they

> *"could leave their cars on the 'X' street before, but it is not allowed now and we have no other option. The available space at the entrance must be used to build a parking space. Many people have a car here. They [referring to the Municipality of Rio de Janeiro] think that everyone is poor and that no one has a car here; we have to have the same rights as those who own a house on the 'asphalt'".*

At another meeting of the residents' association, waste disposal was discussed as the highest ranking priority. Waste and rubbish is found spread on the slopes across the favela and many people tend to blame "the others" for this situation, especially the poorest who are living in the high part of the favela. However, evidently, the most fundamental cause for the waste situation is the deficiencies in basic public services for garbage disposal in the favela.

Another demand was the expansion and improvement of the local family care clinic (a health centre serving the communities of Pavão-Pavãozinho, Cantagalo and adjacent places). According to residents who attended the meeting, the attendance at the family clinic should include sex education, as the number of pregnant adolescents in the community was noticeable. One of the residents agreed with the initiative; however, she emphasised that there is a lot of information about contraceptive methods nowadays, and that pregnancy is in fact a way to get more money from Bolsa Familia. "These girls do not want to study and work, the government pays the stipend. So they get pregnant in order to receive more money. This is poor people's behaviour; they are used to get everything for free", she claimed. Her statement, in spite of being from a favela herself, echoes that of the middle- and upper classes' view on the poor as being lazy, cunning and feeding off the state, illustrating how deeply rooted these imageries are in the Brazilian public.

The per capita income in favelas in the south zone of Rio is higher than the maximum income elegibility criteria established by the BFP. As a consequence, the number of families receiving the benefit is lower that in other favelas in the north and west zone. This led many favela residents to believe that only the poorest people of the favela recieve the benefit of the BFP. Consequently, this perception fuelled a certain stigma of poverty associated with being a BFP beneficiary, as local residents attributed it to being very poor to the extent of struggling to afford food and being dependent upon food donations. "Only very poor people have difficulties satisfying their basic needs", said Jonas, a resident of Pavão-Pavãozinho. This view was shared by many of the social workers who work for Bolsa Familia; that is, that access to conditional cash transfer programmes should primarily be destined to those facing difficulties in obtaining food.[12] However, this perception did not imply that the social workers did not recognise that other households benefiting from the programme also needed the money. Indeed, the also displayed "solidarity" with the beneficiaries that exceeded the stipulated maximum income of BRL 170.00. During the research, cases arose when the family had an increase in income exceeding the maximum level, prompting the social worker to suggest that the beneficiaries should provide that information at a later point in order to be able to continue receiving the stipend until the deadline for the re-registration process. This reflects that in the social workers' opinion, who became well aware of the everyday life realities of living in poverty, the meanings of poverty are not based solely on per capita income established by the programme. These meanings are also based on the story of each family in a detailed case report. Thus, sometimes learning about people's family histories made it possible for social workers to take a multidimensional approach to the concept of poverty beyond the strictly monetary criteria established by the programme.

Another variable described by residents and beneficiaries as poverty indicator relates to not having at least one stable source of income in the family, because "guaranteed money helps a lot, it is financial security" in difficult times (see, e.g. Lavra Pinto 2013). According to Maria Claudia, life was different when her husband had a permanent job. "The Bolsa Familia benefit is our only income, but it is not enough. I pray he will soon find a formal job because depending on the BFP is much humiliation." Aparecida, another beneficiary also reports on the precariousness in which the family lives and the lack of formal work:

> *I do not like to receive BF: It's humiliating. Our lives are being watched, no one likes that. If I had studied I would be a public servant [...]. Money in the bank, monthly salary to buy what my kids ask for [...]. Wow, it would be awesome!*

Even with these differences in income and access to goods and services, the fact of being a favela resident qualifies the "applicant" to access the BFP registration. For example, the information that a person resides in a favela allows him/her to see the social workers working for the programme, and if the income is within the criteria established by law, this person will eventually be registered in the programme. The relationship between poverty and favela is generated almost automatically by those who work for the BFP. In many ways, their conceptualisation of the favelas they work in has not caught up with the profound changes in standard of living that many favela residents have seen during the Pink Tide. Interestingly, favela residents sometimes question the notion of poverty based on income, as applied by the programme.[13] For example, there are stories circulating about people who request the benefit although they are not in need of it. According to a beneficiary of Pavão-Pavãozinho, her neighbour draw monthly benefits from the BFP, but she does not need it because "she owns her home, her husband works and she is retired". About her own situation, however, she notes:

> *I do deserve it, because I have no formal job and I pay rent, I am poor, but not miserable; food is not missing, but without the benefit it would be difficult to pay the electricity bill [now that the 'cat'- illegal electricity connection—is over], and other bills.*

Thus, she does not question low income as a criterion, but invokes dimensions she also thinks should be included in the evaluation of a person's poverty; homeownership, the income of others in the household, access to informal solutions and age. Another beneficiary reports the same as her neighbour: a woman she knows does not need the money because she "has money in the bank and pays health insurance [...]". About her own situation, she notes: "I am so poor, I have only the BF benefit and if I get sick, I use the public health system". These statements are recurrent. In some cases, social workers visit the homes of beneficiaries to check the "actual" family conditions.

In many ways, the concept of assistance that beneficiaries are suggesting, and that social workers are sometimes providing, is similar to the socialist-era Hungarian system described by Haney (2000). Here, beneficiaries could appeal to a whole range of issues that social workers could help them address, and a lack of money was just one of them. Domestic violence, strained kinship or marital relations, neglect and work-related problems were all issues for which people could receive the assistance of social workers. Later, as neoliberal reforms were introduced and welfare became based on a strict assessment of economic need, the concept of poverty, and of need, narrowed. Similarly, the ethnographic material presented here shows that while access to the BFP is granted based on an assessment of economic need, beneficiaries as well as social workers often have a more multidimensional understanding of poverty. They might agree with Simmel (1998), who argues that in sociological terms, poverty refers less to people with low income and more to individuals who are dependent on assistance. For him, poor people are not those who have specific needs or privations, but those who receive assistance or should receive it.

For residents in Pavão-Pavãozinho, the lack of a formal source of income, difficulty to buy food, the receipt of BF (or other federal, state, or municipal benefit), and the type and location of the house in the favela are indicators of whether families and individuals are considered as "poor". These representations and definitions are multidimensional, and it is important to point out that the comparisons are made between the residents themselves (whether they are beneficiaries or not). Surely, if the comparison were made with the inhabitants of the "asphalt" (middle-class residents of nearby neighbourhoods), all the favela residents would be considered "poor".

Final Considerations: *Bolsa Familia* and the Pink Tide

The insights about the dynamics guiding the BFP offered in this chapter, provides a glimpse of its role in reducing poverty and inequality in Brazil during the Pink Tide period. It is estimated that the programme has contributed to bringing 36 million people out of the extreme poverty. According to the Human Development Index (HDI), it points to the growth of the Brazilian HDI, from 0.683 in 2000 to 0.755 in 2014, a rise of more than 10.5 per cent (Human Development Report 2014). The contributions of BFP in achieving these improvements is evident in guaranteeing a minimum income to families in poverty, and in strengthening the capacity of people to invest in schooling and in the healthcare of children through conditionalities.

Although the research period (2012–2015) has not covered the current political moment, it is worth mentioning that the future of the BFP is uncertain. The neoliberal orientation of the government of President Michel Temer, indicates that the programme will be revised. However it is not yet known what exactly will be changed. However, beneficiaries are currently reporting increasing difficulties in accessing the benefits and that families have also stopped receiving it. At the current moment in Brazil, the Bolsa Familia programme is on the threshold between the achievements of the Pink Tide period and the return to power of a party that tries to implement neoliberal measures.

Notes

1. The Favelas of Pavão-Pavãozinho are located in the neighbourhood of Copacabana. They have a population of 5567 inhabitants distributed in 1840 households.
2. According to Naomi Klein (2007), neoliberal ideas started to be implemented in Brazil as early as after the coup in 1964, and much of the economic policy of the military regime was designed by economists educated under Milton Friedman in Chicago.
3. In the 2006 presidential election between Geraldo Alckmin (PSDB) and Luiz Inácio Lula da Silva (PT), Lula was elected in the runoff with 60.83 per cent of the votes (TSE 2006). For an analysis of the electoral result, see for example Holzhacker and Balbachevsky (2007).
4. The Bolsa Familia allowances are updated for 2016, following the increase in July 2016.
5. Under the Michel Temer government, after June 2016 the *Ministério de Desenvolvimento Social e Combate à Fome* (Ministry of Social Development and Fight Against Hunger) became the *Ministério de Desenvolvimento Social e Agrário* (Ministry of Social and Agrarian Development), and then renamed to *Ministério de Desenvolvimento Social* (Ministry of Social Development).
6. The numbers referring to the BFP change every month, since families enter and leave the programme for various reasons. However, the total amount of beneficiary families has remained around 13 million (MDS 2016).
7. Data from CRAS São Sebastião, 2015.
8. It should be noted that pregnant women are identified by the local health service they belong to and sent to the BFP.
9. Payment is made in six consecutive monthly instalments, provided that the child has been identified in the *Cadastro Único* (Single Registration) up to the sixth month of life.
10. The CPF has 11 numbers and serves as a credit identifier, through which it is possible to check debts (if any) of the user with any company, in addition to being requested in numerous places where it is necessary to prove identity.
11. The term "asphalt" is used as favela residents use it, to denote Zona Sul residents who do not live in the favela, even if they live in close proximity.
12. According to a report from the Brazilian Institute for Social and Economic Analysis (IBASE 2008), beneficiary households of the BFP have consumed more animal and dairy products, cookies, oil, sugar, and processed foods (see, e.g. Lavra Pinto and Pacheco 2009).
13. The applicant who does not have a proof of earned income must fill in and sign a declaration that informs about the number of people in the household and per capita income.

REFERENCES

Anderson, David M., and Vigdis Broch-Due. 1999. *The Poor Are Not Us. Poverty & Pastoralism in Eastern Africa*. Oxford/Nairobi/Athens: James Currey/ E.A.E.P./Ohio University Press.

Broch-Due, Vigdis, and Richard A. Schroeder. 2000. *Producing Nature and Poverty in Africa*. Stockholm: Nordiska Afrikainstituttet.

Cunha, Juliana B. 2011. O PAC e a UPP no complexo Pavão-Pavãozinho-Cantagalo: processo de implementação de políticas públicas em uma favela da zona sul da cidade do Rio de Janeiro. In *XI Congresso Luso Afro Brasileiro de Ciências Sociais*. Salvador. https://www.file:///E:/1308347052_ARQUIVO_paperConlab.pdf. Accessed Mar 2016.

———. 2014. *"Nossa casaca é dupla-face": dinâmica sócio espacial e política local no processo de implementação do PAC e da UPP em uma favela da cidade do Rio de Janeiro*. São Paulo: Tese Doutorado em Antropologia Social – Universidade de São Paulo.

DaMatta, Roberto. 1995. *On the Brasilian Urban Poor: An Anthropological Report*. Kellog Institute, Democracy and Social Policy Series, Working Paper.

Desrosieres, Alain. 2010. *Est-il bom, est–il méchant?* Le role Du nombre dans Le gouvernement de La cite néolibérale. Comuunication au Seminaire L'informazione prima dell'informazione. Conoscenza e Scelte Pubbliche, Univerwsite de Milan Bicocca.

Gutiérrez, Alicia. 2007. *Pobre como sempre: estratégias de reprodução social da pobreza*. Córdoba: Ferreira Editor.

Haney, Lynne. 2000. Global Discourses of Need: Mythologizing and Pathologizing Welfare in Hungary. In *Global Ethnography: Forces, Connections, and Imaginations in a Postmodern World*, ed. Michael Burawoy et al. Berkeley/Los Angeles/London: University of California Press.

Harvey, David. 2004. Os espaços de utopia. In *Espaços de Esperança*. São Paulo: Edições Loyola.

Hoffman, Rodolfo. 2006. Transferência de renda e a redução da desigualdade e da pobreza. In *Revista Parcerias estratégicas*/CGEE. Brasília, 22 (6).

Holzhacker, Denilde Oliveira, and Elisabeth e Balbachevsky. 2007. *Classe ideologia e política*: uma interpretação dos resultados das eleições de 2002 e 2006. *Opinião Pública* 13 (2).

IBASE. 2008. *Relatório Repercussões do Programa Bolsa Família na Segurança Alimentar e Nutricional das Famílias Beneficiadas. Documento síntese*, Junho 2008. Rio de Janeiro: Instituto Brasileiro de Análises Sociais e Econômicas. http://www.ibase.br/userimages/ibase_bf_sintese_site.pdf. Accessed October 3, 2017.

Instituto Brasileiro de Geografia e Estatística (IBGE). 2015. *Estimativa da população* 2015. Accessed 15 Dec 2016.

Instituto de Pesquisa Econômica Aplicada (IPEA). 2010. *O Brasil em 4 Décadas*. Brasília: Ipea.
Jaccoud, Luciana. 2006. Indigência e Pobreza: efeitos dos benefícios previdenciários, assistenciais e de transferência de renda. In *Desafios e Perspectivas da Política Social*, ed. Anna Maria T. Medeiros Peliano. IPEA: textos para discussão, (1248). https://www.cebes.org.br/anexos/desafios%20E%20perspectivas%20 da%politicasocial.pdf. Accessed Aug 2009.
Klein, Naomi. 2007. *The Shock Doctrine: The Rise of Disaster Capitalism*, 80–81. London/New York: Penguin.
Lahóz, André. 2002. Renda e Consumo. In *A era FHC, um balanço*, ed. Bolíver Lamounier and Rubens Figueiredo. Cultura Ed: São Paulo.
Larkins, Erika Mary Robb. 2015. *The Spectacular Favela: Violence in Modern Brazil*. Oakland: University of California Press.
Lautier, Bruno 2002. *Pourquoi faut-il aider les pauvres?* Une étude critique Du discours de La Banque mondiale sur La pauvreté. Revue Tiers Monde, T. XLIII, (169), janvier-mars.
Lavra Pinto, Michele de. 2013. O público e o privado: o 'baralhamento' no cotidiano das famílias beneficiárias do Programa Bolsa Família. *Política & Trabalho. Revista de Ciências Sociais* 38 (4).
Lavra Pinto, Michele de, and Janie K. Pacheco. 2009. Consumo, moralidade e o Programa Bolsa Família: padrões e percepções de um grupo de baixa renda. In *Juventude, Consumo & Educação 2*, ed. Michele de Lavra Pinto and Janie K. Pacheco. ESPM: Porto Alegre.
Lefebvre, Henri. 2001. *O direito à cidade*. São Paulo: Centauro.
Magalhães, Alexandre de. 2013. *Transformações no "problema favela" e a reatualização da "remoção" no Rio de Janeiro*. Centro de Ciências Sociais. Instituto de Estudos Sociais e Políticos. UERJ.
Milton, Cynthia E. 2007. *The Many Meanings of Poverty. Colonialism, Social Compacts, and Assistance in Eighteenth-Century Ecuador*. Stanford: Stanford University Press.
Ministério de Desenvolvimento Social e Combate à Fome. 2015. *Relatório do Bolsa Família Rio de Janeiro*. http://www.mds.gov.br/. Accessed Nov 2015.
———. 2016. *Relatório do Bolsa Família*. http://www.mds.gov.br/. Accessed Dec 2016.
———. 2017. *Relatório do Bolsa Família Rio de Janeiro*. http://www.mds.gov. br/. Accessed Feb 2017.
Neder, Henrique Dantas. 2006. *Indicadores sociais no Brasil*: uma análise de sua evolução em período recente. *Revista Parcerias estratégicas, Brasília* 22 (6).
Neri, Marcelo. 2010. *CPS&EPGE*. https://www.fgv.br/cps. Accessed 20 Dec 2012.
———. (ed.) 2011. *Miséria, Desigualdade e Estabilidade*: o segundo real. Rio de Janeiro: CPS/FGV. https://www.fgv.br/cps/pesquisas. Accessed 28 Sept 2011.

O'Connor, Alice. 2002. *Poverty Knowledge: Social Science, Social Polity, and the Poor in Twentieth-Century U.S. History*. Princeton: Princeton University Press.
Pearlman, Janice. 2010. *Favela. Four Decades of Living on the Edge in Rio de Janeiro*. Oxford: Oxford University Press.
Peres, Thais Helena de Alcântara. 2005. A proposta de um outro modelo para as políticas sociais. *Civitas Revista de Ciências Sociais*, Porto Alegre 5, n. 1 (2).
Pires, André, and Tainah Biela Dias. 2015. *De Bolsa Esmola à Constituição Federal*: o Programa Bolsa Família no jornal O Estado de São Paulo (2003–2013). *Fronteiras – estudos midiáticos* 17 (2).
Rattner, Heinrich. 2010. Como medir e combater a pobreza? *Revista Espaço Acadêmico* 112 (9).
Rego, Walquiria L., and Alessandro Pinzani. 2013. *Vozes do Bolsa família: autonomia, dinheiro e cidadania*. São Paulo: Unesp.
Reis, Elisa P. 2005. Pobreza e Exclusão. In *Exclusão Social e Mobilidade no Brasil*, ed. Estanislao Gacitúa-Marió and Michael Woolcock. Brasília: IPEA/Banco Mundial.
Relatório Repercussões do Programa Bolsa Família na Segurança Alimentar e Nutricional das Famílias Beneficiadas. 2008. *Documento síntese* (6). https://www.ibase.br. Accessed 14 Aug 2010.
Rocha, Sonia Maria Rodrigues da. 2007. *Pobreza no Brasil: afinal, de que se trata?* Rio de Janeiro: Ed. FGV.
Sen, Amartya. 2000. *Desenvolvimento como liberdade*. São Paulo: Cia das Letras.
Silva, Luiz Antônio Machado da. 2011. A política das favelas. In *Revista de Estudos de Conflitos e Controle Social* 4 (4), out/nov/dez.
Silva, Maria Ozanira da Silva e, and Valeria Ferreira Santos de Almada Lima. 2010. *Avaliando o Bolsa Família: unificação, focalização e impactos*. São Paulo: Cortez.
Silva, Maria Ozanira da Silva e, et al. 2008. *A política social brasileira no século XXI: a prevalência dos programas de transferência de renda*. 4ª ed. São Paulo: Cortez.
Simmel, Georg. 1998. *Les pauvres*. Paris: Press Universitaires France.
Sprandel, Marcia A. 2004. *A pobreza no paraíso tropical: interpretações e discursos sobre o Brasil*. Rio de Janeiro: Relume Dumará.
Tribunal Superior Eleitoral. 2006. www.tse.jus.br/eleicoes/. Accessed 15 Mar 2016.
Valladares, Licia do P. 2000. *A gênese da Favela Carioca. A produção anterior às Ciências Sociais. RBCS* 15 (10).
———. 2005. *A invenção da favela*. Rio de Janeiro: FGV.
Weissheimer, Marco Aurélio. 2006. *Bolsa Família: avanços, limites e possibilidades do programa que está transformando a vida de milhões de famílias no Brasil*. São Paulo: Editora Perseu Abramo.

Open Access This chapter is licensed under the terms of the Creative Commons Attribution 4.0 International License (http://creativecommons.org/licenses/by/4.0/), which permits use, sharing, adaptation, distribution and reproduction in any medium or format, as long as you give appropriate credit to the original author(s) and the source, provide a link to the Creative Commons license and indicate if changes were made.

The images or other third party material in this chapter are included in the chapter's Creative Commons license, unless indicated otherwise in a credit line to the material. If material is not included in the chapter's Creative Commons license and your intended use is not permitted by statutory regulation or exceeds the permitted use, you will need to obtain permission directly from the copyright holder.

PART III

Subjectivities and Structures

CHAPTER 7

Political Polarisation, Colonial Inequalities and the Crisis of Modernity in Venezuela

Iselin Åsedotter Strønen

Introduction

The Bolivarian process in Venezuela opened up a political space for the contestation of historically informed socio-cultural hierarchies articulated through notions of class, ethnicity, gender and "race." At the same time, socio-economic hierarchies were challenged through reduced levels of poverty[1] and increased access to social welfare. Concurrently, political polarisation in the course of the Bolivarian process accentuated the colonial legacy of class-based and racial hierarchies. This gained particular visibility through opposition supporters' portrayal of Chávez' predominantly poor and coloured followers in highly contentious and contemptuous terms. Reversely, Chávez' followers frequently deployed an "upwards"

I want to thank the participants at the workshop "Rethinking Inequalities in Latin America" (Bergen, March 5–6, 2015) for an inspiring start-up to the realisation of this book. I am also grateful to Margit Ystanes for valuable comments on the draft version of this chapter. Moreover, my deepest gratitude goes to all the people in Venezuela who have generously shared their time, experiences and knowledge and made me feel at home in the Caracas barrios through successive fieldworks in the period 2005–2015. The ethnographic research informing this chapter has been funded by the Norwegian Research

I.Å. Strønen (✉)
University of Bergen and the Chr. Michelsen Institute (CMI), Bergen, Norway

© The Author(s) 2018
M. Ystanes, I.Å. Strønen (eds.), *The Social Life of Economic Inequalities in Contemporary Latin America*, Approaches to Social Inequality and Difference, DOI 10.1007/978-3-319-61536-3_7

class-contemptuous discourse, revering the country's whiter and wealthier for being stupid, superficial, unpatriotic and lacking of character and morals (Strønen 2017). However, whilst the tit-for-tat pejorative descriptions between different political camps were out there in the open for everyone to see, it is paramount to go beyond these surface expressions of conflict in order to understand their origins and deeper implications and meanings. In order to do so, we need to take into account the historical formation of Venezuelan society since its colonial inception as well as its subsequent development trajectories up to and into the Pink Tide.

This is precisely what this chapter aims to do, through a discussion that is structured around two main axes of analysis. The first axis of analysis is, in alignment with the overall focus in this edited volume, a contextual analysis of the historical formations of racial- and class-based inequalities in Venezuela, followed by a discussion of how these formations were remoulded and re-accentuated during the socio-economic crisis and neo-liberalisation of Venezuelan society in the 1980s and 1990s. The second axis of analysis is concerned with exploring how the historical formations of different life worlds in Venezuela—undercut by economic, spatial and socio-cultural inequalities—translated into the formation of radically opposite interpretations of the meaning of the Bolivarian process and an accentuated polarisation of Venezuelan society.

Seen from within—that is, the emic view, as it was conceptualised by its believers and followers—the Bolivarian process gained its strength from simultaneously addressing the politics of recognition as well as the politics of redistribution (de Sousa Santos 2001; Fraser and Honneth 2003). Through a political ideology affirming that socio-cultural discrimination and socio-economic exclusion constitute and re-enforce one another,

Council through the research project "Flammable Societies: The Role of the Oil and Gas Industry in the Promotion of Poverty Reduction and Social Volatility" and by the Norwegian Ministry of Foreign Affairs as part of the research project "Everyday Maneuvers: Military-Civilian Relations in Latin-America and the Middle East." I am deeply grateful to the project leaders, John Andrew McNeish and Nefissa Naguib, respectively, for their generosity and support. I also want to extend my gratitude to CMI and its director Ottar Mæstad for generous fieldwork funding in 2012–2013. Additional funding for field research has been awarded by the Lauritz Meltzer Research Fund and the Inger Haldorsen Memorial Fund.

supporters of the Bolivarian process positioned themselves as historical subjects that had been systematically marginalised within a local-global matrix shaped by colonial- and neocolonial structures of domination. The historical and global framing of the contemporary struggle that the Bolivarian process represented provided for an emerging structure of feeling (Williams 1989) that weaved individual suffering and hardships into a collective political story about the past, present and future.

However, whilst this paradigmatic change was experienced as emancipatory for the popular classes, the Bolivarian process was experienced as threatening by those sectors of the population whose socio-cultural and political dominance was challenged and undermined. Evidently, there is clearly a crude political-economy component to this, in the sense that the Chávez government challenged entrenched capitalist and class interests in the country. An understanding of political opposition to the Chávez government is inseparable from the struggle for control over the country's oil sector (see Tinker Salas 2009), and inseparable from the nexus between Venezuelan capitalist interests, their transnational networks and allies, and their ideological and interest-based adherence to free-market politics. It is also inseparable from middle-class resentments against weakened control over access to the state apparatus and public institutions (which, reflecting the accentuated levels of corruption in Venezuelan society since the 1970s, are widely seen as a honey jar[2]), and their resentment against state money being channeled in the direction of the "underserving poor" (Katz 1989).

However, interest-based opposition alone cannot count for explaining the aggravated hostility and fear-mongering that characterised opposition to the Chávez government and its supporters. Moreover, opposition to the government was evidently also informed by heterogeneous sets of reasons by different actors and groups, many of them expressing legitimate concerns about the problematic aspects of the Chávez era. However, in the context of the focus of this edited volume, the main argument that I want to develop is that racialised and class-contemptuous expressions of political opposition were constitutive of the hierarchical formation of the Venezuelan post-colonial state, whilst simultaneously shaped by the preceding political trajectories and the particular political ideology and aesthetics framing the Bolivarian process itself. Simultaneously, I contend that there is another dimension that needs to be addressed in order to understand the deeper meaning behind political divisions in Venezuela; namely the crisis of modernity as it is unfolding in Latin America at large.

Indeed, as I will argue towards the end of the chapter, the formation of radically different political realities in Venezuela reflects a growing global schism between those who "live inside" the imagery of a globalised, cosmopolitan capitalist modernity, and those who feel excluded by it. In Venezuela, and elsewhere at the continent before and during the Pink Tide, accumulated local/global differentiation translated into attempts to carve out new political and social models and imaginaries that also managed to incorporate subaltern life worlds, histories and aspirations. As the Pink Tide now by most accounts is ebbing, and Venezuela is finding itself in the largest crisis amongst all the former Pink Tide countries, it is necessary to take a broader and historically informed look on the underlying structures and processes that undergirded the divisive nature of the Bolivarian process. However, before I reach that point in the discussion, I will lay out the broader contextual framework for understanding Venezuela's particular socio-political formations during the Pink Tide, starting with a broad overview over key political trajectories in the latter part of the twentieth century.

The Neoliberal Era and Its Context

In some significant respects, Venezuela followed a different political and economic development trajectory during the latter part of the twentieth century than other South-American nations. For one, the country did not have any authoritarian regimes coming to power by violent means as most of its neighbours. For long, the country appeared, at least on the surface, as a relatively socially stable and harmonious society, leading scholars to coin the expression the "Venezuelan exceptionalism" (Ellner 2010:2). Following the authoritarian Marcos Pérez Jimenez's fall in 1958, political stability was maintained by a political pact between the two dominant parties, Acción Democrática (AD) and COPEI. This pact, entered in 1958, was created to exclude political competition from the right and the left. Notably, this involved excluding the communist party and leftist currents who had participated in bringing down Pérez Jiménez. For the next 40 years, AD and COPEI alternated in government offices until Chávez' arrival to power in 1998. During the 1960s and 1970s, the country was characterised by a strong state-interventionist approach and a populist-nationalist ideological vein, in particular articulated and channeled by Acción Democrática. The country's growing abundance of oil wealth provided post-1958 governments with significant economic leeway, at the same time as a growing petroleum economy led to the abandonment of the countryside and booming urban informal growth. To a certain extent, social conflict was smoothed out through extensive clientelism and patronage systems and the co-optation or oppression of oppositional or radical currents. A brief period of guerilla warfare was crushed by the state by the end of the 1960s (Ciccariello-Maher 2013), and social struggle did not really gain public momentum again until the 1980s.

Venezuela implemented structural adjustment reforms dictated by the International Monetary Fund (IMF) later than its neighbouring countries. The first round came in 1989 during the second Carlos Andrés Pérez administration (AD) (1989–1992) in the form of a "shock treatment", whilst additional reforms came during the Caldera government (COPEI) (1994–1998) in the 1990s (Ellner 2010:90). Carlos Andrés Pérez had presided over the golden years in Venezuelan history as president in the period 1974–1979. The price hikes on oil due to the Arab oil embargo filled the state's coffins, at the same time as Pérez mortgaged the country's future oil rents in exchange for foreign loans in order to develop his ambitious development plans.

Thus, ironically, the debt burden that would later propel Carlos Andrés Pérez into an uneasy (and to him personally, disastrous[3]) marriage with the IMF was originally principally accumulated by himself. When global oil prices slumped in the early 1980s, the country found itself in an economic quagmire. A run on the country's currency, the *bolívar*, and massive capital flight eventually forced the subsequent Herrera government (1979–1984) to devaluate on February 18, 1983, known as the Black Friday. In the immediate following years, the Herrera and later the Lusinchi government (1984–1989) resisted the adaption of IMF prescriptions. However, the economy continued to deteriorate. Both governments prioritised paying off foreign debt (some of it considered illegal) bleeding dry public coffers, and the exchange system set up to protect the bolívar was subject to rampant corruption and mismanagement. Public firms were run into the ground to the extent that some argued that it was done deliberately in order to pave the way for subsequent privatisation (Ellner 2010:79–81). At the same time, corruption and mismanagement escalated (Ellner 2010:82). During these years, poverty and inequality rates escalated quickly, and even parts of the middle classes found themselves slumping into poverty.

In the 1989 presidential elections, Carlos Andrés Pérez was elected to a second term, echoing popular sentiments opposing further austerity policies and promising that he would restore the prosperity of his first presidential époque. However, in the backroom, he had brokered a secret structural adjustment deal with the IMF. Key aspects of the plan included the lifting of price controls on basic goods, "flexibilisation" of the labour system, the elimination of subsidies on gasoline, the privatisation of state enterprises and the social security system and the removal of restrictions on foreign investments (Ellner 2010: 91–94).

On the morning of February 28, the price of bus tickets rose steeply due to the sudden increase in the price of gasoline. This was a few days before the end-of-month paycheck, and most people were both broke and exhausted by years of escalating struggles and hardships. A riot started on the bus station of the satellite town of Guarenas outside of Caracas and quickly spread to Caracas and other urban centres across Venezuela. People were used to government clamp-down on popular protests, but this time, they were met with unprecedented state violence. *El Caracazo*, as the riot came to be known, claimed between 1000 and 3000 lives by unofficial accounts (the official accounts were highly unreliable). Subjecting parts of shantytowns (*barrios*) to a military siege for several days, el Caracazo has been called "the largest and most violently repressed revolt against austerity measures in Latin American history" (Coronil 1997: 376). In following years, social protest and disenchantment with the political system at large translated into increasing repudiation of the Puntofijo model, at the same time as the effects of the neoliberal policies set in, resulting in accentuated levels of inequality and social insecurity (Lander 2005).

After the Caracazo, many soldiers, who themselves came from lower socio-economic strata, became disgruntled with the government for having been sent out "to kill their own." In 1992, Hugo Chávez, then a military officer who had led a secret dissident group within the military for ten years, led an aborted civil-military revolt against the government of Carlos Andrés Pérez (see Strønen 2016). The rebels were citing the massive onslaught on the civilian population during the Caracazo as part of the reason for why, in their view, the government had lost its constitutional legitimacy. Chávez was imprisoned, and immediately converted into a popular hero. Upon being released from prison in 1994, he formed a political party, Movimiento Quinta República (MVR), and won the presidential elections in 1998 with 56 per cent of the vote.

The Chávez Government

Chávez did not run for president on an explicitly anti-neoliberal programme. Rather, he initially signalised interest in Tony Blair's "Third Way" and was in the beginning also supported by parts of the country's middle classes and business community (Tinker Salas 2015:172). However, this quickly changed as he made it clear that he was not interested in making a pact with the "old establishment." The decisive split eventually came with the passing of 49 laws by decrees in the fall of 2001. Significantly, the decrees extended the state's regulatory control over the agricultural and fishery sector, as well as Venezuela's principal economic asset: the hydrocarbon sector. In effect, this meant the reversal of a gradual privatisation process that had been taking place throughout the 1990s, putting the government at a definitive collisions course with some of the most powerful sectors in the country, as well as foreign interests and capital tied to the oil sector.

The aborted coup in 2002 and the oil strike/sabotage in 2002–2003 (Tinker Salas 2015:158–162) prompted a radicalisation both in the government and amongst Chávez' supporters. In 2005, Chávez declared himself a socialist at a mass meeting at Mar de Plata, Argentina. During Chávez' tenure, several reforms from the neoliberal era were reversed, including the renationalisation of the pension system, the ports and key companies in telecommunications, electricity and heavy industry. Several banks were taken over by the state, and land reforms distributing land and credits to peasants were enacted on the countryside. Renegotiated deals and agreements with foreign oil companies provided the Venezuelan state with majority stakes in all joint ventures, and taxes and royalties were raised. New policies within health and education, the so-called social missions (D'Elia and Cabezas 2008; Muntaner et al. 2011), were pursued through building up new programmes and policies outside established institutional frameworks. The argument for doing so—and not without merit—was that existing state institutions were too rigid, inefficient and governed by staff from the Puntofijo era who in effect were in opposition to the government. However, the lack of institutionalisation of social programmes and policies would also later emerge as one of the Achilles heels of the Bolivarian process. Nevertheless, at the time, the extensive state-community cooperation in the course of the development of the social programmes was vital for forging a new sense of socio-political inclusion in the popular sectors. Concurrently, the social missions also represented unprecedented access to social welfare and services in the popular sectors, having real and substantive impact on many people's lives (Strønen 2017).

Crafting a Bolivarian Space

Chávez' arrival to power generated a new era of popular mobilisation and organisation in Venezuela. Social movements had relatively limited manoeuvring space during the Puntofijo era and were frequently subjected to political repression and censorship (Lopez-Maya et al. 2002; Ciccariello-Maher 2013). After 1999, a broad and diverse grassroots movement, comprising urban dwellers, peasants, indigenous groups, and diverse cultural and political movement with roots in the popular sectors became vested with a new form of legitimacy and public visibility in the country. Indeed, "Bolivarianism" offered previously marginalised sectors a new historical narrative and new moral grounding for asserting themselves as a historical subject, *el pueblo*, whose time had come to claim rectification for accumulated injustice.

In the same period, successive left-leaning governments were brought to power on the backbone of popular mobilisation in neighbouring countries, creating the sensation that a continental shift was taking place. The Bolivarian process was at its height in the years following the defeat of the 2002 coup, the 2002/2003 oil strike/sabotage and the 2004 recall referendum against Chávez. In the fall and winter of 2005/2006, I did fieldwork amongst popular movements in western Caracas on a day-to-day basis (Strønen 2006). Caracas' barrios and the city's political centre west of Sabana Grande were teeming with revolutionary fervour, and marches, popular assemblies, mobilisations and events were taking place at a grand scale. The social missions were in the process of being developed, both in health, education, sports, culture and alimentation, and many people were deeply involved in housing and infrastructure projects through the so-called Urban Housing Committees (Comités de Tierra Urbana, CTU) and Participative Committees for the Transformation of Habitat (Comité de Participación de Transformación de Habitat, CPTH). As one woman worded it:

> The most special thing with this process is that people, like my mother aged 70, who never before in her life and gone out [to do work in the community]…with this process she got motivated, and in some form or another, in her own manner, is doing social work…people participate from their homes, people participate in the assemblies, and people participate both in their homes and in their assemblies (Strønen 2006:67).

Innumerable times I was told by enthusiastic activists that Venezuela was the epicentre for a global historical shift, proving wrong Francis Fukuyama's famous postulate about "the end of history." The political aesthetics of the revolution was crafted through revolutionary music and jingles, political wall paintings, public concerts draped in revolutionary symbolism, the revival of popular revolutionary singers (Alí Primera, Silvio Rodríguez), political programming on state TV, political discourse from above and political discourse from below. In barrio streets and barrio houses, and at street corners, bars and restaurants in the western city centre, political discussions were the order of the day. Intense political manoeuvring and strategising was taking place amongst popular sector activists as they were discussing how to further their causes within the political space that had been opened up by the Chávez government. In no way was this a harmonious and straightforward process; rather, conflicts and intense negotiations were the order of the day both horizontally and vertically. However, what characterised these processes was the sensation of living in a critical moment in history, whereby historical power structures had been seriously destabilised. What was at stake was to steer the process in such a way that it would lead to long-lasting socio-political change, and to seize the moment to rectify historical injustices.

I have previously coined the concept "a Bolivarian space" in order to capture the symbolic, political, cultural and social space of interaction that was carved out in the interface between the Chávez government and its principally popular constituency. More precisely, I have described the Bolivarian space as:

> the complex conundrum of political discourses, practices, policies, historical narratives and ideological templates shaping the interaction between the state and the popular grassroot in Venezuela under the Chávez government. This is not a top–down process whereby Chávez imposed a political idea from above. Rather, it is a flow of multi-directional processes that are shaped by popular efforts to appropriate the political space opened up by the Chávez government's pro-poor political alignment (Strønen 2017:5).

Within that space, the templates of neoliberalism and global capitalism were framed in explicitly negative terms, both as political systems of domination and subordination in an orthodox left-wing, anti-imperialism sense, but also through articulating the lived experiences of its localised outcomes. The popular sectors in Venezuela were deeply traumatised by the social havoc they experienced during the 1980s and 1990s (Lander 2005). Personal stories of hardships, hunger, violence, death, vulnerability and desperation were interwoven with a collective historical narrative about having been under siege by hostile and callous politicians and a brutal economic system. To them, "neoliberalism" and "capitalism" were not descriptive terms for particular economic and political regimes of governance. Rather, these concepts epitomised a lived experience within a particular social order that was experienced as detrimental to their life projects and dignity. Significantly, the years leading up to el Caracazo in 1989, and the experience of living through el Caracazo, were conceptualised not only as a brutal state clampdown on a spontaneous reaction to extended suffering. It was also conceptualised as a demonstration of the brutal callousness of the system itself, which by default designated poor people to suffer whilst protecting the interests of the rich. As Rosa, a Chávez supporter from one of Caracas' western barrios worded it:

> So the second government of Carlos Andrés Pérez was the final thrust…the poor got even poorer, because they didn't raise the wages, the businesses did whatever they wanted with their workers, they came and told you a story that "look, there isn't any money to pay you with, we cannot pay you the Christmas bonus"…The poor have always waited for Christmas bonus so that you can buy the things that you are going to need for the rest of the year…the poor went without buying a new pair of shoes the whole year, not a shirt, do you understand? Because you couldn't, we were like the Indians, we worked in order to be able to eat, and that was it. But in December the workplace paid out our four bucks [of Christmas bonus] and you went out and bought two shirts, two jeans, stacked the cupboards with food so that it would last longer, things like that. Do you understand?

> And then, well…the final thrust came when Carlos Andrés Pérez appeared on national television and delivered that bomb about the measures that had to be taken, what we had to do with the loan that the International Monetary Fund had given us…. The loans that they had asked the International Monetary Fund for…so we had to obey the normative [structural adjustment plans] that they implemented, and it was so outrageous, because it was the poor who had to do the sacrifice, right? We would have to pay for their riches, we will have to pay their taxes, we will have to pay all their expenses… and the next week the prices on the bus tickets went up, and then [el

Caracazo] exploded…it was like ten years where more and more things came up combined, do you understand? People were already like a pressure cooker that was about to explode any minute.

Rosa's narrative brings out how many people conceptualised the structural and political underpinnings of poor people's suffering. Concurrently, the association between the politicians of the past, and their continuous presence in opposition ranks, was epitomised in the slogan that was coined after the 2002 coup: *no volverán*—"they will not come back." To many people in the barrios, the Bolivarian process *was* (and is) a class war, because if the opposition ever returned to power, they were bound to reinstall a self-serving neoliberal regime and oppress popular protest with violence if necessary as they had done in the past.

Altering the "Natural Order"

The account above is quite unidimensional in the sense that it says nothing about the multiple conflicts, struggles and contradictions that characterised both "the Bolivarian space" as well as the unfolding of the Bolivarian process and the actions of the Chávez government as such. However, this is a subject that I have treated extensively elsewhere (Strønen 2016, 2017). In the context of this chapter, the purpose of the section above is to tease out a broad panorama of the qualitative shifts in the texture of relations (Gupta 1995:215 in Sharma and Gupta 2001) between formal power and the formerly marginalised segments of the populations.

By way of contrast, the former political and economic elites, and many from the middle and upper classes, felt threatened and alienated not only by Chávez per se but also by the alteration of what they had historically perceived as the "natural social order." This had always been a hierarchical social order defined and controlled by the whiter and wealthier, circumscribed by a long colonial and post-colonial legacy that naturalised sociocultural and socio-economic inequalities. The white and economically privileged did not only dis-recognise the legitimacy of Chávez—being of afro-indigenous heritage and a poor socio-economic background—but they also felt deeply uncomfortable with the new role that Venezuela's poor and coloured held in Venezuelan society. This, in turn, translated into accentuated political polarisation in the country with profoundly classist and racialised overtones (Fernandes 2010, Duno-Gottberg 2009, 2011). Expression such as negros, monkeys and savages were commonplace, accentuating Cannon's observation that "race, or rather racism, is an essential but extremely subtle, ingredient in opposition discourse rejecting Chávez and those who follow him" (Cannon 2008:732). However, in order to understand the historical context for these racialised expressions of conflict, it is necessary to explore how they reverberate with historical templates informed by the country's historical legacy.

Class and Race in Venezuela

Historically, the Venezuelan myth of national racial heritage was that of *café con leche* (coffee with milk) (Tinker Salas 2009:133), allegedly a product of centuries of slow racial mixing (Wright 1990:1). Racial origins in Venezuela overlap to a large degree with people's class. The majority of poor inhabitants are black or *mestizo* (of a mixed race), whilst the higher classes are for the most part whiter and more European-looking.

In the post-emancipation period, Venezuelan elites regarded blacks as inferiors because they were associated with their status as slaves, perceived of as a separate cast designed to work for the whites (Wright 1990:5). Hence, the elites did not consider themselves racist, but rather attributed their contempt for blacks to the fact that they were poor—a just socio-economic classification in the elites' eyes, rather than a racial categorisation (Wright 1990:5). This perception of race and status coincides with what has come to be the dominant racial interpretative scheme in Latin America. As Mullings writes, "the Latin American model [has] generally 'privileged culture over race,' in which extensive racial discrimination coexists with the absence of formal laws enforcing racism and an official ideology denying racism" (Mullings 2005:678) (Photo 7.1).

By the mid-twentieth century, Venezuelan elites had accepted a fluid concept of racial distinctions that allowed a socio-racial flexibility on the scale of the status hierarchy (Wright 1990:5). Processes of miscegenation served as a racial transitional buffer between white elites and black masses, preventing people from "getting stuck" in endogenous racial categorisations (Wright 1990:5). This also impeded the enforcement of racial segregation (Wright 1990:5).

According to Wright, blacks and non-whites have played a larger role in political and social institutions in Venezuela than elsewhere in the Latin American continent (Wright 1990:9). Black and coloured people held important positions amongst regional and national elites after Venezuela's independence in 1830. The lack of a strong central state allowed black and coloured individuals to establish themselves as regional caudillos deriving

Photo 7.1 Statue of Simón Bolívar in Paseo de los Próceres in Caracas. Note the wall carvings behind him. Bolívar liberated Venezuela and several of the surrounding countries from the Spanish Crown. He was from a wealthy creole family, and, driven by his political ambitions and his (for the time) progressive, egalitarian views, he split off from his class background. This is also what has given him such mythical qualities in the context of the Bolivarian process (Photo by the author)

their power from military might (Wright 1990:10). Moreover, *pardos* (the racial amalgam of Europeans, blacks and Indians) were also found in the federal agencies and military organizations (Wright 1990:10).

However, starting in the 1890s, leading intellectuals talked about the need to "whiten the race" by encouraging the immigration of white Europeans whilst blocking the immigration of non-whites (Wright 1990:2; Tinker Salas 2009:133; Derham 2010:69). They were influenced by a Spencerian positivism and by related European racial theories, and openly stated that they perceived Venezuela's political instability and economic stagnations as a consequence of the predominance of a mixed population (Wright 1990:10). Attributing racial dispositions to genetic deficiencies (Derham 2010:69), they didn't perceive blacks and *pardos* as compatible with democratic self-rule, and advocated for a strong centralist government that they eventually found in Juan Vicente Gómez's regime (Wright 1990:10). Following Gómez's death in 1935, the subsequent heads of state took a more "open-minded" stance on the correlations between race and democratic inclinations, allowing Acción Democrática to form its party with a leadership drawing from mixed-race and middle-class groups. Moreover, Acción Democrática soon found alliances with *pardos* and black masses (Wright 1990:10), turning the notion of racial democracy into their official party ideology (Wright 1990:11). Within Acción Democrática there were central figures that favoured the "whitening" strategy, such as Arturo Uslar Pietri, Alberto Adriani and Andrés Eloy Blanco (Wright 1990:12; Derham 2010:69). However, the focus nevertheless shifted from differences based on race to those based on class, forming the basis for a "colour-blind" cultural nationalism (Wright 1990:11).

These changes were seen as threatening by the white elites, not necessarily because of the threat of colour but rather because of the threat of the mobilisation and rise of the lower classes (Wright 1990:11). During Acción Democrática's short governmental interlude between 1945 and 1948, the party tried to carry out reforms that impacted immigration laws and those public facilities that were designed to cater to North American oil workers, thus improving conditions for the non-whites (Wright 1990:11). The state bureaucracy was opened to non-whites, and the economic expansion created job opportunities for these groups (Wright 1990:11–12). As Acción Democrática and COPEI consolidated their governance following 1959, racial democracy became the dominant official ideology.

The Venezuelan lower classes occupied a legitimate position in the social landscape until the social breakdown in the 1980s. They were portrayed as *el pueblo*, "as virtuous, albeit ignorant, and therefore in need of guidance" (Coronil and Skurski 2006:199). The masses were contained and controlled with a carrot or stick approach, that is, either through populist discourse and clientelistic paternalism, or with violence. However, as social unrest increased from the early 1980s, the poor and coloured were increasingly blamed for the country's ills (Cannon 2008:736). Concurrently, the founding myths of the modern Venezuelan nation state—cross-class harmony and racial democracy—started to crack.

Savagery and Civilisation

Coronil and Skurski (2006:123) quote Sofia, a Harvard-trained lawyer, on uttering after el Caracazo: "I would have killed all those savages, as I am sure that they would have killed us if they had a chance. They hate us." The "savagery" and "civilisation" tropes hold deep roots in the construction of a Venezuelan national cosmology, as in the rest of Latin America. In political discourse, and particular at critical political conjunctures where class conflicts are surfacing, these tropes have been used to evoke notions of the poor masses as representing savagery in contrast to the civilised nature of the middle and upper classes.

The dual imageries of savagery and civilization are a legacy of the colonial reality established in the New World after the Spanish conquest, whereby "the Indian and African *irracionales* became compliant to the reason of small number of white Christians" (Taussig 1987:5, cursive in original). As Quijano (2000) has noted, Latin America was never fully really decolonised after independence. Rather, preceding over the construction of emerging nation states, white Creoles selectively imported the Enlightenment ideas that fit best their needs and local realities. Equality was not part of this imaginative or interest-based horizon, since the ruling elites thrived on subordination and economic exploitation of those considered ethno-racially and socially inferior (Grosfoguel 2000:368). This translated into the crafting of political, economic and cultural, as well legal structures that favoured white (male) elites (Grosfoguel 2000:368; Wiarda 1971), and the continuation of classificatory schemes that placed colonial subjects outside the imagined political community of the nascent nation states (Grosfoguel 2000:368).

Serving as an interpretative scheme for classifying and attributing supposedly inherent qualities, capacities and ideas to different social groups, the savagery/civilisation juxtaposition has run as an (sometimes explicit) undercurrent in Venezuelan political discourse. More precisely, this dichotomy has been articulated by the powerful to question the civilisational potential and hence the social legitimacy of the supposedly more savage and less civilised masses. As Coronil and Skurski (2006) have demonstrated, the most sublime expression of the civilisation/barbary tropes in Venezuelan national cosmology is found in the novel Doña Bárbara (1929) by Rómulo Gallegos, considered the greatest expression of Venezuelan identity (Coronil and Skurski 2006:91). The novel depicts the struggle for the "domestication of unconquered nature and uncivilized humans" (Coronil and Skurski 2006:92), transcended into a struggle for the nation's soul. Indeed, as Coronil has argued in "The Magical State" (1997), the very idea of the modern Venezuelan nation state after 1959 was based on the rejection of the barbarous past represented by the caudillos of the nineteenth and early twentieth century. The new era, as represented by Acción Democrática and COPEI, was cast as a civilisatory mission designed to bring the country out of its backwardness and on the road to prosperity, modernity and development. However, as the myth of social harmony lost grip in the 1980s, the increasing tensions between the elites and the poor transformed *el pueblo* from a noble mass, as they had become depicted within the nationalist-populist discourse, to an unruly mass that threatened the civilisational harmony of the nation. As Coronil and Skurski demonstrate through a minute analysis of the public reactions to the so-called Amparo massacre in 1988 and *el Caracazo* in 1989, both instances "made salient suppressed conceptions of the poor as disposable savages" (Coronil and Skurski 2006:123). The trope of "uncivilised savages" continued to be expressed in the Chávez era, but then in the context of a political turning of tables whereby the dominant classes no longer found themselves in a position of social hegemony. Yet so, even if the poor were in a position to vocally express their contempt against the underlying schemes and assumptions articulated through these tropes, that does not imply that the dominant classes adapted a self-reflective stance on the founding premises of their social models. Rather, the opposite happened. Popular political agency in the context of the Bolivarian process was labeled as politically illegitimate and irrational, advanced by socio-culturally inferior groups—a tautological relation that reinforced its/theirs illegitimacy.

The Denial of Political Legitimacy

Oppositional labeling of Chávez' supporters commonly included the usual usage of expressions such as "negros" and monkeys (*monos*). Other common expressions were *hordas* (hordes), *chusma* (lowlife, scum), *turba* (mob), *marginales* (marginals), *ordinarios* (simple) and *lumpen* (poor, vulgar, brute). Yet another expression, *tierruos* (from *tierra/*soil), refers to when *barrio* inhabitants could be identified by their soiled feet (because *barrio* streets were not asphalted) upon entering the city centres. Yet another idiosyncratic expression is *pata en el suelo* (hoof on the ground), referring to a person who cannot afford to buy shoes and thus walks barefoot.

The racial dimension of political opposition was also evident in the frequent portrayal of Hugo Chávez, and other coloured political leaders, as monkeys in cartoons (Fernandes 2010:118–119). A few years after Chávez took office, the US embassy in Caracas hosted a party where the guests were entertained with a puppet show portraying Chávez as a gorilla. Colin Powell, the United States foreign minister at the time, was not amused—perhaps for obvious reasons—and publicly reprimanded the embassy (Ali 2013). Furthermore, Hugo Chávez was frequently referred to as "*mico mandante*" by government opponents. The expression was derived from *mi comandante* (my commander)—an expression Chávez' followers often used when referring to him, whilst *mico* is a small monkey. The pun therefore translates to "monkey-in-charge."

Behind the obvious racist as well as class-contemptuous slant of these characteristics is a deeper meaning that harks back to the incomplete decolonisation process inscribed in the Latin American polity. Scholars have drawn attention to how both oppositional groups and affiliated private media consistently have portrayed themselves as "civil society groups," whereas government supporters have been described as hordes, mobs and scum. As Fernandes notes, the exclusionary notion of civil society deployed by elite groups "has various race, class, and gender associations that mark out certain social groups and classes as unfit for participation in the public sphere" (2010:121). The exclusionary usage of the civil society concept is also symptomatic of its broader application in the neoliberal era; it is associated with certain social groups exercising "civil freedom," but within the confines of class-defined symbolic markers and liberal values. This appropriation of the right to exercise "civic agency" was also remarked upon by Chávez' supporters. To them, it illustrates the global dimension of Venezuelan class conflicts; they interpreted "civil society" as an ideological concept embracing a particular group of global citizens (see also Chatterjee 2004 for an analysis of its historical origins and its colonial adaption). From the point of view of many popular sector activists I spoke to, the opposition's active and exclusionary branding of themselves as civil society was used as a worldwide marketing strategy in order to gain international support for their cause; thereby legitimising and bolstering oppositional and middle-class political agency whilst simultaneously negating popular and pro-government agency.

The depiction of members of the popular classes as "hordes" was a recurrent feature in media representations of Chávez' supporters, harking back to the old civilisation/barbary dichotomy. As Duno-Gottberg writes about how the private Venezuelan media portrayed the popular mobilisation during the 2002 coup: "As a mob, they were undifferentiated, faceless" (Duno-Gottberg 2009:160). They were cast as barbaric, irrational and violent, and deprived of political rationale (Duno-Gottberg 2009:160). Whilst these recurring media representations reflected deep-seated historical templates, they also reinforced political polarisation in the country through playing up to deep-seated fears about "the others." Before the coup in 2002, inhabitants in rich neighbourhoods organised themselves in armed self-defense groups, fearing the "hordes'" invasion and pillage of their residences (see Bartley and Ó Briain 2003). People were warned to keep an eye on their domestic servants in case they were collaborating in preparing an attack. Of a more recent date, a middle-class friend of mine told me of how residents in a gated condominium close to the city centre gathered during the riots referred to as "las guarimbas" in 2014. These protests started up as peaceful protests by oppositional student groups, but soon turned into violent riots. The riots caused massive destruction of public property and 43 casualties, most of them security personnel, government supporters and innocent passers-by. However, fearing that government supporters would descend on the city centre where most of the protests were taking place, the residents were discussing how they could strike back on an attack on their building. The suggestion gathering the most momentum was that they would stand on the roof and throw boiling cooking oil down on the "invaders." As it turned out, the hordes never arrived.

Deserving and Undeserving Poor

The denial of not only the political legitimacy of the popular classes but also of their social legitimacy also undergirded widespread resentments against government spending on the poor. Commonly, government supporters were referred to as *resentidos* (resentful), implicating that they were "envious" towards the rich, and by extension, trying to get their hands on wealth that they did not deserve nor had worked for. Oscar, a community activist in the popular parish of 23 de Enero, once spoke about a friend of his and her experience as a poor student attending what is traditionally a university for the privileged:

> Look, a friend of mine who studies in la [Universidad] Católica, en la Andrés Bello, she is from a humble origin but she is there on a scholarship, she told me how they talk…she hears different expressions from *mono* (monkey) to *esos pobres de mierda* (those shitty poor) who want to take everything away from us, those lazy people, what they want is what we produce…

Similar sentiments, yet in a stronger language, can be discerned in a commentary written by "Lara Lopez" under a YouTube video showing a discussion about the 2013 elections of Nicolás Maduro:

> Chavistas take off to Cuba so you can continue to eat shit…CONFORMISTS you are thugs and whores who don't want a better country because you live in misery and feel envy for those who have worked hard for everything they have achieved, and you have expropriated it!! Marginal thieves, just like your ex-president and mister potato face (Maduro). YOU ARE A FRAAAAAUD.[4]

Underlying these portrayals of the poor one can identify deep-seated notions echoing the idea of a culture of poverty (Lewis 1966), namely, that the Venezuelan poor were poor due to laziness, low morals and sloth. Within this interpretative scheme, government "hand-outs" only served to bolster these character traits. This view was expressed through referring to government supporters as having a *bozal de arepa*. Arepa, Venezuela's prime staple food, is a flat, round bread baked on corn flour, and the significance of this saying is that they were led haplessly like a horse or a donkey by an arepa-filled muzzle offered by the government.[5] These ideas are not unique to Venezuela; as noted in the introduction to this volume, the Brazilian middle and upper classes also revolted against the idea the poor would get access to state benefits and consumer items that they did not "deserve." Likewise, the Venezuelan poor were framed as undeserving recipients of state-supported material well-being, and by the same sleight of hand, the fundamental issue of the historical constitution of Venezuela as a fundamentally unequal society, and the question of how to challenge this legacy, was removed from view.

Differentiated Life Worlds

One of the first days upon my arrival to Venezuela in 2005, I was told by Maria, a Chávez supporter in her mid-40s:

> They [the opposition/middle and upper class] never knew anything about the living conditions in the rest of the society. They didn't have to use public transport because they had their own cars. They didn't need to use public hospitals because they were insured at private clinics. They didn't have to care about pensions or social security because they had money. They didn't have to worry about crime because they had their private security firms. They knew nothing about all this and they don't understand what is happening here because they don't understand the background for it. It is like Chávez once said: even if we placed the opposition on a pedestal covered with diamonds, they would still hate us.

Her words underlined the fundamental characteristics of Venezuelan society; it is built upon a fundament of entrenched social, spatial and social-cultural inequalities. In turn, this translates into completely different life experiences and perspectives through which different social groups ground their identities and political subjectivities. To many in the middle and upper classes, popular sector neighbourhoods are perceived as dangerous and uncivilised spaces, occupied by uneducated, unsophisticated people. Most middle-class people that I met during my time in Venezuela were shocked to hear that I actually lived in a popular sector neighbourhood, and occasionally "lectured" me on the violent nature of these areas as well as its residents' less-refined intellectual capacities (Photos 7.2 and 7.3).

However, most middle-class people had never set their foot in a barrio, and would never do so. A friend of mine once said that rich people, rushing by in their SUVs on their way home to eastern Caracas, probably just close their eyes when they pass the Western barrio communities, pretending they are not there. In Venezuela, as in other Latin American countries, the spatial and social divisions between different social groups frequently preclude middle and upper class contact with people on the other side of the social fence, except from encounters marked by defined status ascriptions such as labourers, waiters, shop clerks and domestic servants. As Maria alluded to above, the poor and the rich live their lives on widely divergent social and spatial arenas. Indeed, the secluded view from the predominantly prosperous eastern valley of Caracas[6] meant that many people would still, after two decades of social misery and unrest during the 1980s and 1990s, repeatedly state that "Chávez destroyed the harmonious society that we once had."

Photo 7.2 Typical *barrio* homes (Photo by the author)

THE CRISIS OF MODERNITY

Tinker Salas eloquently summarises a widely held explanatory model amongst opponents to the Chávez government:

> Many opposed to Chávez expressed a view of society that created a false distinction between an educated and enlightened opposition fighting to save the country and defend democracy and an uneducated multitude led by a charismatic yet unscrupulous popular leader who retained support by squandering government funds on his followers (Tinker Salas 2015:172).

Indeed, these views reflected that opposition supporters perceived of themselves as the gatekeepers and embodiment of the mythical model version of the modern Venezuelan nation state; a state that was moulded upon a class-defined social hegemony and Venezuela's compliance with the founding tenants of contemporary global modernity; liberal democracy and free-market politics. The Bolivarian process was incomprehensible for many from the upper and middle classes, as well as for many of the

Photo 7.3 Gated mansions in an affluent neighbourhood in the east of Caracas (Photo by the author)

country's intellectuals, who were oriented towards "consumption patterns, value orientations, and enjoyment of the 'modern' global good life" (Lander 2005:33). The new political orientation, away from Westernised imageries of modernity, Western political alliances as well as the allusions to nationalism, was interpreted as "an anachronism in a globalizing world, a return to unfeasible and historically Third World postures" (Lander 2005:33). To them, Chávez represented an uncivilised, caudillistic political order, and the socialist façade of the Bolivarian process represented a position on the wrong side of the global ideological fence.

However, in the final part of this chapter, I want to reflect upon the deeper implications of the dichotomised perception of local and global realities that were crystalising in the Chávez era. I suggest that, in essence, these also reflect the crisis of modernity in the Latin American continent. For the better part of the twentieth century, Venezuela was living the expectation of developmentalism and modernity; an expectation that harks back to the very foundation of Latin American nation states. As Hellinger has written:

> The model of political modernization bequeathed to political science by the French revolution and Enlightenment, suggests that Latin America will only progress once its traditional, personalist culture is replaced by civic culture populated with rational, educated citizens capable of completion in both the economic and political marketplace...secular modernist like Betancourt, Rómulo Gallegos, Luis Beltran Figueroa, and others sought to tame la barbarie and, aided by oil rents, build a modern, Western democratic society. (Hellinger 2001:9)

What is important to capture is the increasing divergence between the official, middle- and upper-class narrative about the emerging modern Venezuelan society at the time and the actual experiences of living in that society from a subaltern perspective. The foundational myth of Chavismo rests on the schism that developed as Puntofijismo, and the social sectors it represented, increasingly alienated the popular sectors from an illusory cross-class society. Acción Democrática initial paternalistic attempt to save the popular sectors from themselves turned into an alienation of those very same sectors, as the chosen political and economic model turned into a system of exclusion rather than inclusion. For the popular sectors, liberal democracy became a facade for elite accumulation by dispossession (Harvey 2005) that was blatantly intensified during the neoliberalisation of Venezuelan society. Moreover, the state's predisposition to crush dissent through violence and repression made it clear that it was not only unwilling to respond to popular sector needs, but it was also effectively outlawing them from the Venezuelan polity.

It was on this background that Chávez' portrayal of the world as historically and structurally unjust struck a deep chord amongst the popular sectors, because they never came to enjoy the fruits of global capitalism and liberal democracy as promised to them. From the popular sector's perspective, this ideology rather served to disguise the oppressive economic mechanisms that had relegated them to poverty, and to cover the violent oppression of subaltern dissent that was taking place across the world—a violence that had been deeply inscribed on their own social body. Thus, the espousal of a worldview aligned with the "Third World," or what Hellinger has called *tercermundismo* (2001), rather than with western notions of modernity, allowed the popular sectors to create a

Photo 7.4 Labour Day in Western Caracas, May 1, 2011 (Photo by the author)

twenty-first century identity that incorporated them into a global narrative about subaltern struggle (Photo 7.4).

In the Introduction (this volume) Strønen and Ystanes refer to the proliferation of alternative political horizons and projects emerging as part of the Pink Tide. As Motta has argued, these heterogeneous proposals represent different ways of imagining and practising the relationship between the market, the state and society (Motta 2009:43). It constitutes an opposition to "the cultural logics, social relations, and institutions that underpin and sustain the 'system'" (ibid.) altogether, because "the system" (the state-capital nexus, as it has worked so far in Latin American history) is by default an oppressor to subaltern lives, needs and claims. On the other hand, the Latin American middle and upper classes have become progressively enmeshed in what may be epitomised through what de Sousa Santos calls "Americanization, as a hegemonic form of globalization" (de Sousa Santos 2001:185). In essence, this worldview hinges upon Euro-American notions of liberal democracy, market capitalism, consumer society and the global media sphere. Through the lenses and normative frameworks of "Americanization," subaltern struggles appear politically incomprehensible and illegitimate, advanced by socio-culturally unsophisticated and inferior groups.

Note that it is not my intent here to suggest that it is possible to draw up clear-cut binaries between "inside and outside" modernity. The complexities surrounding identity politics and symbolic representations of modernity in Venezuela are also extensively discussed in Strønen (2017). My aim is, however, to highlight how differentiated life worlds also shape different political, social, cultural and epistemological groundings for orienting, assessing and positioning oneself in the world. This schism became utterly visible in Venezuela, where the two different political camps came to ground their political struggle—for or against the Bolivarian process—on the basis of different conceptualisations of their nation, society and the world. This schism provides for a continuously unstable grounding for any future project of national building, implying that the contemporary crisis of governance and stand-off (as this chapter is written in April 2017) between the Maduro government and the opposition only serves to mask much deeper challenges for Venezuela's political future.

Conclusion

This chapter has taken as a point of departure the socio-economic and socio-cultural hierarchies that characterised the formation of Venezuelan society since its inception. Through the ways in which race, racism and class became antagonistically articulated as part of the political polarisation following Chávez' electoral victory, these hierarchical social matrixes gained renewed salience. Through the crafting of what I have termed a Bolivarian space, new collective consciousness and political subjectivities grounded in the counter-hegemonic identity politics and claims for redistribution gained political force and visibility. At the same time, this generated a counter-reaction amongst the dominant classes who had previously enjoyed political and cultural hegemony. However, I have also suggested that the cleavages that crystalised in the course of the Bolivarian process are reflecting the crisis of modernity in Latin America at large. As the promised gains of developmentalism, and subsequently free-market politics and liberal democracy, failed to materialise, Latin American nation-building projects are founded upon highly unstable grounding. Indeed, there is a growing schism between those who are progressively enmeshed in hegemonic forms of globalisation, and those who are searching for alternative social, political and epistemological social models. In conclusion, the Pink Tide époque in Venezuela during Chávez' presidency represented a paradigmatic rupture in the nation's history, at the same time as it made visible and accentuated the inherently unequal, hierarchical and differentiated life worlds that characterise the Latin American polity.

Notes

1. Poverty levels have now risen again after the onset of the economic crisis in the country. However, this is not the topic of this chapter as I am focusing on the particular dynamics characterising the Chávez era.
2. See Strønen (2017) for a discussion of the historical origins of and social meaning of corruption in Venezuela.
3. Pérez eventually stepped down facing a trial on corruption charges in 1993, but it has been suggested that he to a certain extent was designated as the scapegoat for the political and economic crisis at large.
4. YouTube. 2013. Ana Mercedes Díaz. Ex jueza electoral venezolana en Bayly. Video uploaded April 10. http://www.youtube.com/watch?feature=player_embedded&v=rFfZ0HwSupk, accessed December 20, 2013.
5. I have discussed elsewhere both how to understand Chávez in relation to the concept of populism, as well as the historical legacy of clientelism in the Chávez government's relationship to its constituency and vice versa (Strønen 2017).
6. The city valley of Caracas is marked by an east-west divide, whereby the majority of the poor live in the west, and the east is predominantly affluent. The invisible, yet palpable line is drawn east of the pedestrian street of Sabana Grande.

References

Ali, Tariq. 2013. Tariq Ali: Hugo Chávez and Me. *The Guardian*, March 16. http://www.theguardian.com/world/2013/mar/06/hugo-chavez-and-me-tariq-ali. Accessed 20 Feb 2017.

Cannon, Barry. 2008. Class/Race Polarisation in Venezuela and the Electoral Success of Hugo Chavez: A Break with the Past or the Song Remains the Same? *Third World Quarterly* 29 (4): 731–748.

Chatterjee, Partha. 2004. *The Politics of the Governed. Reflections on Popular Politics in Most of the World.* New York: Colombia University Press.

Ciccariello-Maher, George. 2013. *We Created Chávez: A People's History of the Venezuelan Revolution.* Durham/London: Duke University Press.

Coronil, Fernando. 1997. *The Magical State: Nature, Money, and Modernity in Venezuela*. Chicago: University of Chicago Press.
Coronil, Fernando, and J. Skurski. 2006. *States of Violence*. Ann Arbour: University of Michigan Press.
D'Elia, Yolanda, and Luis Fransisco Cabezas. 2008. *Las Misiones Sociales en Venezuela*. Caracas: Instituto Latinoamericano de Investigaciones Sociales (ILDIS).
Derham, Michael. 2010. *Politics in Venezuela. Explaining Hugo Chávez*. Oxford/Bern/Berlin/Bruxelles/Frankfurt am Main/New York/Wien: Peter Lang.
Duno-Gottberg, Luis. 2009. Social Images of Anti-Apocalypse: Bikers and the Representation of Popular Politics in Venezuela. *Contracorriente* 6 (2): 144–172.
———. 2011. The Colour of Mobs. Racial Politics, Ethnopopulism, and Representation of the Chávez Era. In *Venezuela's Bolivarian Democracy. Participation, Politics and Culture under Chávez*, ed. D. Smilde and D. Hellinger. Durham/London: Duke University Press.
Ellner, Steve. 2010. *Rethinking Venezuelan Politics. Class, Conflict, and the Chávez Phenomenon*. Boulder/London: Lynne Rienner Publishers.
Fernandes, Sujatha. 2010. *Who can Stop the Drums? Urban Social Movements in Chávez' Venezuela*. Durham/London: Duke University Press.
Fraser, Nancy, and A. Honneth. 2003. *Redistribution or Recognition? A Political-Philosophical Exchange*. London: Verso.
Gallegos, Rómulo. 1929. *Doña Bárbara*. Barcelona: Editorial Araluce.
Gupta, Akhil. 1995. Blurred Boundaries: The Discourse of Corruption, the Culture of Politics, and the Imagined State. In *The Anthropology of the State. A Reader*, ed. A. Sharma and A. Gupta. Oxford: Blackwell Publishing.
Grosfoguel, Ramon. 2000. Developmentalism, Modernity, and Dependency Theory in Latin America. *Nepantla: Views from the South* 1 (2): 347–374.
Harvey, David. 2005. *A Brief History of Neoliberalism*. Oxford: Oxford University Press.
Hellinger, Daniel. 2001. *Chávez, Globalization and Tercermundialismo*. Paper Presented at the Congress for Latin American Studies Association, Washington, DC, 2–8 Sept 2001.
Katz, Michael. 1989. *The Undeserving Poor. America's Enduring Confrontation with Poverty*. New York: Oxford University Press.
Lander, Edgardo. 2005. Venezuelan Social Conflict in a Global Context. *Latin American Perspectives* 32 (2): 20–38.
Lewis, Oscar. 1966. *La Vida: A Puerto Rican Family in the Culture of Poverty*. San Juan/New York: Random House.
Lopez-Maya, Margarita, David Smilde, and Keta Stephany. [1999] 2002. *Protesta y cultura En Venezuela. Los Marcos de Acción Colectiva en 1999*. Caracas: FACES-UCV, CENDES, FONACIT.

Motta, Sara. 2009. Old Tools and New Movements in Latin America: Political Science as Gatekeeper or Intellectual Illuminator? *Latin American Politics and Society* 51 (1): 31–56.

Mullings, Leith. 2005. Interrogating Racism: Toward an Antiracist Anthropology. *Annual Review of Anthropology* 34: 667–693.

Muntaner, Carles, et al. 2011. History is Not Over. The Bolivarian Revolution, "Barrio Adentro," and Health Care in Venezuela. In *The Revolution in Venezuela. Social and Political Change under Chávez*, ed. Thomas Ponniah and J. Eastwood. Cambridge/London: Harvard University Press.

Quijano, Anibal. 2000. Coloniality of Power, Eurocentrism, and Latin America. *Nepantla: Views From the South* 1 (3): 533–580.

Santos, Boaventura de Sousa. 2001. Nuestra America: Reinventing a Subaltern Paradigm of Recognition and Redistribution. *Theory, Culture and Society* 18: 2–3.

Strønen, Iselin Å. 2006. *For Us This is Utopia Coming True. Venezuela's Bolivarian Revolution and Popular Movements in a Caracas Barrio*. Master Thesis Submitted at the University of Bergen.

———. 2016. "A Civil-Military Alliance": The Venezuelan Armed Forces Before and During the Chavez-era. *CMI Working Paper* 2016:4. Chr. Michelsen Institute, Bergen.

———. 2017. *Grassroots Politics and Oil Culture in Venezuela: The Revolutionary Petro-State*. New York/London: Palgrave Macmillan.

Taussig, Michael. 1987. The Genesis of Capitalism amongst a South American Peasantry: Devil's Labor and the Baptism of Money. *Comparative Studies in Society and History* 19 (2): 130–155.

Tinker Salas, Miguel. 2009. *The Enduring Legacy: Oil, Culture, and Society in Venezuela*. Durham: Duke University Press.

———. 2015. *Venezuela. What Everyone Needs to Know*. Oxford: Oxford University Press.

Wiarda, Howard. 1971. Law and Political Development in Latin America: Toward a Framework for Analysis. *The American Journal of Comparative Law* 19 (3): 434–463.

Williams, Raymond. 1989. *Resources of Hope. Culture, Democracy, Socialism*. London: Verso.

Wright, Winthrop. 1990. Café con Leche. In *Race, Class and National Image in Venezuela*. Austin: University of Texas Press.

Audiovisual

2003. *The Revolution will not be Televised*. Dir. Kim Bartley and Donnacha O'Briain. Galway: Power Pictures

Open Access This chapter is licensed under the terms of the Creative Commons Attribution 4.0 International License (http://creativecommons.org/licenses/by/4.0/), which permits use, sharing, adaptation, distribution and reproduction in any medium or format, as long as you give appropriate credit to the original author(s) and the source, provide a link to the Creative Commons license and indicate if changes were made.

The images or other third party material in this chapter are included in the chapter's Creative Commons license, unless indicated otherwise in a credit line to the material. If material is not included in the chapter's Creative Commons license and your intended use is not permitted by statutory regulation or exceeds the permitted use, you will need to obtain permission directly from the copyright holder.

CHAPTER 8

Market Liberalisation and the (Un-)making of the 'Perfect Neoliberal Citizen': Enactments of Gendered and Racialised Inequalities Among Peruvian Vendors

Cecilie Vindal Ødegaard

Peru was not part of the so-called Pink Tide in Latin America, but opted for deepening its neoliberal orientation initiated with Alberto Fujimori's policy reforms in the 1990s. Since then, governments have envisioned modernisation and progress through an emphasis on market liberalisation and implemented tax, royalty and policy regimes accommodating for privatisation and foreign investments. Social reforms initiated in the 1990s took the form of 'liberal-informal' regimes based on (partial or total) privatisation of the financing and provision of services, as well as state-financed social programmes targeting particular segments of the population (Rousseau 2007:97). Alongside these developments, small-scale businesses among the poor were increasingly encouraged by the state, NGOs and commercial enterprises through the provision of micro-credit arrangements and training in marketing skills. Through this expansion of neoliberal rationality, governments aimed to instigate 'development'

C.V. Ødegaard (✉)
University of Bergen, Bergen, Norway

© The Author(s) 2018
M. Ystanes, I.Å. Strønen (eds.), *The Social Life of Economic Inequalities in Contemporary Latin America*, Approaches to Social Inequality and Difference, DOI 10.1007/978-3-319-61536-3_8

through the promotion of entrepreneurship and trade also among the poor. During the presidency of Alejandro Toledo (2001–2006), Peru signed several free trade agreements facilitating overseas, bilateral trade by eliminating trade obstacles, consolidating access to goods and services, and fostering private investments between bilateral partners. From the turn of the millennium and onwards, Peru experienced significant economic growth due to the boom of primary materials. Yet inequalities persisted, and during presidential campaigns in 2006 and 2011, Ollanta Humala built his political platform by promising to create a more equitable framework for distributing wealth from the country's natural resources. Before his presidency, Humala was thus closely affiliated with other Pink Tide leaders in Latin America, although his time in office (2011–2016) resulted in political continuity rather than change. Hence inequalities in Peru have persisted, and thousands of Peruvians still struggle to find a way out of poverty, often by relying on precarious forms of work at the margins of the formal economy.

This chapter is an attempt to analyse economic processes in Peru from the perspective of women vendors. It examines how vendors manoeuvre between varying degrees of formality/informality, and how identity markers related to gender, 'race' and class are in different ways made relevant in their everyday manoeuvres. Focusing on enactments of identities at the crossroads between improvisation and formalisation, the chapter illustrates how women's everyday economic tactics are shaped by Peru's particular socio-economic configurations under neoliberal regimes. In this regard, and considering how economic operations are socially embedded and informed by social relations and institutions of various kinds (Polanyi 1944), the chapter argues that the (in)formalisation of economic activities is informed by post-colonial legacies and existing social relations and institutions. Processes of (in)formalisation hence play out in spaces that are created through, and often contributing to reinforce, relations and categorisations connected to gender, 'race' and class. Against this backdrop, the question of neoliberal policy and in(formalisation) in the Peruvian context needs to be highlighted through an ethnography of the class, ethnic and gender relationships in which these processes are actualised. Indeed, the work of vendors, and especially the entrepreneurial *chola*, epitomises the development and effects of neoliberal politics in post-colonial Peruvian society, by actualising and reproducing class, 'race' and gender categories, stereotypes and relationships. The so-called *chola* can be seen both to resist and to convey the intersections between class, race and gender in Peruvian society, as she is ambiguously positioned and envisioned in-between racialised and class-based categories such as indigenous and mestizo, rural and urban. Living the life of the urban poor, the *chola* maintains her rural ways and relations, while making a living through trade and entrepreneurship. In many ways, the *chola* may appear as the 'perfect neoliberal citizen', as hard-working and self-made, and accommodating her own quest for social mobility to growing demands of growth, flow and consumption. Yet the entrepreneurial *chola* seeks to develop her economic strategising and tactics on her own terms. The chapter therefore demonstrates how vendors rely on relational and symbolic resources in their economic endeavoirs.

The chapter builds upon several periods of fieldwork in Peru since 1997 (with subsequent fieldworks in 2001, 2007, 2011 and 2016), when I conducted research among vendors and *contrabandistas* associated with the marketplace La Feria Altiplano[1] in the city of Arequipa. At the Feria in Arequipa, most vendors are bilingual Quechua- or Aymara- and Spanish-speakers, primarily women. The goods offered at the Feria are agricultural products, textiles and artisan crafts, pirated CDs and computer software, as well as industrial and electronic articles. Many of these goods are smuggled from Bolivia or Chile, often produced in China. The Feria was established after several years during which a group of vendors had occupied land in different areas of the city for purposes of vending. Since they initiated these unauthorised markets in the 1980s, the vendors were repeatedly fined or removed by the police. These difficulties resulted in the creation of an association of vendors and finally their acquisition of an area that they formally bought in 1999. While the association has thus acquired land titles—at least in part—and most members pay for a license, the vendors do not pay taxes, and many of them also bring undocumented merchandise from across the border, referred to as *contrabando*. Those who bring goods like this, generally self-identify as *contrabandistas* (smugglers), and proudly so. Leaders of the association take responsibility for paperwork and communication with the municipality, and these positions are often held by men. This is despite the fact that the majority of members are women, and is related to the expectation that leaders should be experienced with reading and writing.

Considering that many vendors have a background from the Andean highlands and limited economic and educational resources, their work in vending reflects the structural inequalities in Peruvian society and the intersections between class and a racialised hierarchy. For most, vending has been and continues to be a precarious means of making ends meet but, as one of my interlocutors said, 'at least it makes some coins circulate through my hands'. Others—especially *contrabandistas*—may earn more than the minimum salary, and some have managed to expand and make new investments, for instance in land, trailers or buses.

Emerging 'Cultures of Informality'

The mid-century migration boost in Peru and the land occupations that followed aroused anxiety for delinquency and social breakdown among the urban elites. In the city, migrants from the Andes were considered 'matter out of place' in the perspective of the upper and middle class, and the migrants' presence disturbed the racialised spatial dichotomies of rural-urban, indigenous-mestizo. Women vendors came to occupy a particularly ambiguous position in relation to these racialised dichotomies and stereotypes, as their ways of living disturbed dominant norms of gender-appropriate behaviour too. Not complying with the dominant norms that feminine realms should be hidden away from the eyes of strangers and that the public sphere is the domain of men (Weismantel 2001:47, Seligmann 2004), women vendors and their activities were regarded as chaotic and unhygienic—and market places as incompatible with the desire to modernise Peruvian cities. Seen from the perspective of social scientists in Peru as elsewhere in Latin America, in contrast, these informal economic ventures (including the land occupations) were seen to involve new claims for citizenship among the urban poor (Roberts 1995), and to represent a form of 'insurgent citizenship' with a potential to alter the poor's terms and conditions for citizenship (Holston 2008). Poor people's initiatives at the margins of the formal economy were thus seen as heralding a new era of contestation against the legal institutional apparatus, which has given rise to what is often referred to as 'cultures of informality' (Matos Mar 1984).

With the economic down-turn in Peru during the 1980s, informal economic ventures gained increased importance as a source of livelihood for rising numbers of urban poor. Migration to Peruvian cities continued during the 1980s, also due to the war between the guerrilla movement Sendero Luminoso and the military, as thousands of people were forced to flee from rural areas to the cities. The existing labour surplus in the cities was augmented with Fujimori's austerity measures (the so-called Fuji-shock) in the 1990s, as structural adjustment programs, privatisation and dramatic cuts in public spending further exacerbated the need for alternatives to waged labour (see also Stensrud, (Chap. 10) this volume). The economic set-back was to affect Peruvian society severely, while other Latin American countries involved in similar processes tried to soften the negative effects of adjustments through the introduction of safety nets. Among people living in the shantytowns of Peruvian cities, many, both men and women, turned to different forms of self-employment—men sometimes combining taxi-driving with short-term employment in construction, and women in different kinds of informal work and vending. Among my women interlocutors, some first started working as domestic servants, in textiles factories or as day labourers at the farms surrounding Arequipa, but later many of them turned to vending due to low payment and a strict labour regime in other forms of low-skilled work.

As indicated in the introduction, the neoliberal promotion of entrepreneurship in Peru does not exist in a vacuum, nor does women's predominance in the country's—often informal—market places. There are indeed long traditions in the Andes for barter and trade, and for women's involvement therein, so vending is not necessarily something they first learn in the city, or by participating in micro-credit arrangements. Women's involvement in vending can also be seen in light of historical traditions for women in the Southern Andes to be responsible for barter and vending, due to their traditional responsibilities for herding and commercialising the produce (Harris 2000). The promotion of entrepreneurship from the part of recent governments, often directed at women in particular, have nonetheless contributed to reinforce the tendency that women occupy precarious and low-income forms of employment. The targeting of women also reflects how women have often been seen as tools for development because of their link to issues of reproduction and domestic space (Ewig 2010:7; Ødegaard 2010). According to one of my interlocutors, vending and contraband is a 'plan for women. If a man gets involved, people will say he is doing women's work'.

Policies for the formalisation of unauthorised economic activities and use of land have been introduced alongside the promotion of entrepreneurship. The government of Fujimori established specific institutions for this purpose, such as Commission for the Formalisation of Informal Property (COFOPRI), and succeeding governments followed up with this and similar land-titling projects aiming to promote 'development', security for owners and a more effective land market. These initiatives form part of a continuing expansion of a neoliberal rationality, by facilitating the commodification of land and contributing to fortify already existing fissures along class lines, due to the high cost of formalisation and rising prices of land (Larkins 2015:156). It indicates how an increasing significance ascribed to formality and the legal (Sieder et al. 2005) is central for the liberalisation of markets worldwide, entailing mechanisms through which contrasts between 'licit' and 'illicit' are both intensified and continually blurred (Comaroff and Comaroff 2006). In Peru, policies of formalisation have been recommended by economists like de Soto (1989, 2001), who argued that formal ownership among the poor would promote development, by contributing to the integration of unauthorised economic activities into the economy at large. As noted by Scott (1998), formality is indeed part of making society legible (Scott 1998)—and may represent a prerequisite for increasing tax revenues and improved welfare services. De Soto's concern with formalisation, however, appears to be related primarily to its 'property effects', i.e. that formalisation would promote economic activities and development through the security of formal ownership. Despite the fact that formalisation may enable people to legally use and protect their resources, the terms and conditions can nonetheless create and fuel other processes that may lead to increased dispossession and marginalisation (Mitchell 2002). To think otherwise would be to overlook an important insight from economic anthropology; that the economy must be understood as instituted through societal relations and institutions of various kinds (Polanyi 1944).

In a study of Lima's contraband markets, Gandolfo (2013) describes how vendors explicitly evade formality, and resist attempts by state bureaucracies to draw them into regimes of regulation. Although the vendors' resistance carries costs and risks, she argues that they nonetheless value more highly the 'freedom and autonomy that informality affords. One of the key freedoms of informality, she notes, is to subsume profit to particular modes of sociality. By investing in market colleagues, kin, earth beings, and saints, wealthy vendors give time and money to 'reciprocal relations and forms of consumption that limit the accumulation of wealth' (ibid.: 280). As I have illustrated elsewhere (2010, 2016), this intense cultivation of social relationships at the margins of the formal carries similar importance among vendors in Arequipa. This does not necessarily mean that vendors evade formality, since actors who operate informally may also seek formalisation (see also Holston 2008). It is therefore necessary that we analyse how people may also seek to mediate between informality and the demands of formalisation. A useful approach to this end may be found in Bear's (2014a, b) emphasis that we explore ethnographically the divergent social rhythms of different institutions such as those of production, consumption, finance, social reproduction and governance. In particular, she exhorts us to explore how the divergent social rhythms of different institutions may create conflicts and uncertainty at the level of the human life-course, and how people seek to mediate between such divergent social rhythms through acts of labour. We must therefore include into our enquiries also the acts of labour that are not necessarily recognised as such, such as the issue of informal labour, in considering the social formation of capital and wealth. Bear's concern is not to problematise the boundaries of formality and informality, or the many intersections between formalised and unauthorised economic activities (Comaroff and Comaroff 2006), but to explore the acts of labour that cross-cuts such distinctions. While informal labour represents aspects of inequality that are often invisible and unaccountable to state institutions, informality is nonetheless part of social relations that significantly contribute to the accumulation of wealth in society (2014a:643). Considering how key aspects of inequality are played out as well as reproduced through different kinds of informal or unrecognised work, the following section examines how vendors draw upon key identity markers and relations in their economic tactics. It includes an exploration of how vendors deal with and mediate between official demands and other modes of sociality, and hence how economic processes are informed by existing social relations and institutions. These economic processes play out in spaces that are created through, and contributing to reinforce, relations and categorisations related to gender, 'race' and class.

The Social Embeddedness of Trade

With its location on the slopes of the Andes and as the second largest city in Peru, Arequipa is an important regional distribution point for trade between highland and coast, and a convenient location for importation and distribution of goods from Bolivia and Chile. The *contrabandistas* travel every week to bring merchandise in large quantities to the retailers at market places in Arequipa. Some *contrabandistas* also have their own market pitches, where they also run retailing businesses.

My interlocutor Rosaria (which is the pseudonym I have given her) is among the vendors who have been part of the Feria association in Arequipa since the beginning. Like many of the other vendors, she is from a community outside Puno, and came to Arequipa as a young girl. With only a couple of years of primary school, she first worked a few years as a domestic servant before she started selling sweets in the streets and later became part of the association. For a long time Rosaria lived with her family in a shack on occupied land in Arequipa's outskirts, and when her husband was laid-off from his job in 2000, she started to bring contraband from Bolivia in the hope of increasing her earnings.

Several scholars have noted how women are further marginalised and impoverished through their involvement in vending and informal work (e.g. Kabeer 2010). While informal work may indeed contribute to reproduce structural inequalities, the significance of earnings made from vending should not be underestimated. Like her mother, Rosaria's daughter Dorothea also turned to trade and contraband, after having worked a few years at a textile factory. While Dorothea used to be paid the minimum salary when working in the factories, she earns a lot more now, as a vendor. As a result, she has managed to construct a big house in one of Arequipa's shanty towns and to send her son to a private school. Indeed, Dorothea's earnings gradually resulted to be more predictable and sometimes even higher than her husband's. He used to work in construction, and although earning a monthly salary, his earnings were unpredictable since job contracts were only for three months. After a while her husband grew tired of this and decided to accompany Dorothea in business. The income earned from vending may thus represent the more steady income of a household, and upon realising this some men join their wives' businesses. At the Feria, there are also vendors who have university education, but who, due to low pay, have decided to work in vending. This situation illustrates how weak regulation of labour conditions, combined with low pay in the public sector, makes vending the better alternative for many.

While Dorothea and her mother trade in groceries, many *contrabandistas* prefer to work with clothes since the gain per unit is higher compared to other goods. Clothes are also easier to hide than many other goods. Contraband clothes are sold without tags; the *contrabandistas* remove them to make customs and fiscal authorities believe that the clothes are not meant for commercial sale. Victoria is one of my interlocutors who not only sells textiles from her own pitch at the Feria, but also travels to collect goods. Victoria's husband is a teacher, and often comes to help his wife in her business. When she is travelling, he sells from her pitch. Their daughters sometimes assist, too. Victoria is originally from the department of Puno, from a community close to Desaguadero and the border with Bolivia. During her journeys to Desaguadero and on her way back to Arequipa, she always stops to visit with relatives in the area. This gives her a good opportunity to hide the garments without being disturbed. Desaguadero is an important town for the transport and distribution of contraband, as it is located just at the delineated border between Peru and Bolivia. Desaguadero is often referred to as *tierra de nadie* (no man's land), referring to the absence of state control in areas where vending is *already* institutionalised. In and around Desaguadero, people bring their merchandise across the border without particular interference, or by paying bribes (*coyma*).

The fact that most of these enterprises are kinship-based and involve the labour input of partners, children and other kin helps vendors maintain the everyday operations of their businesses and accommodate for the risks. Vending demands long working hours and a lot of travel, so there is a division of labour among household members as to who sells from the pitch and who travels. Many vendors have learned the skills of vending from their parents or older kin, and it may be difficult to enter these businesses without such connections. The *contrabandistas* often travel together in small groups, cooperating about where to buy goods, and how to avoid getting caught. Sometimes they make joint investments in particular commodities in order to benefit from the better prices given when buying *por mayor*. Like Victoria, many *contrabandistas* have kin living in the border areas. Kin and local farmers often help the *contrabandistas*, providing information and storage for goods. The economic strategising of vendors thus draws upon socially and spatially embedded relations and identities, and reinforcing the constitution of this kind of work as defined by key inequality markers (class, 'race', gender).

While often seeking to evade formality, as suggested by Gandolfo, vendors may also attempt to strike a balance between formality and informality, in the sense that they seek to operate formally enough not to constantly get caught, and informally enough to actually earn money, as is illustrated in the case of Victoria. While Victoria sometimes goes to Lima to buy merchandise from the authorised importers operating in Gamarra, these legal clothes are more expensive. More often, when she has less capital to invest, Victoria travels to the border areas, instead, for contraband. Since transporting contraband can be difficult, she brings only a few garments at a time. To avoid confiscation at customs, she might wear the clothes (especially the bigger, heavier garments), hidden underneath her own clothes, or mixes them with other things in a big bag. She removes tags, so that customs officers do not notice that the clothes are new, but view them as personal items. From Lima, in contrast, it is possible to transport large quantities from a legal importer, with taxes paid and an RUC-number (shop registration number). Victoria's different tactics for bringing merchandise to Arequipa illustrates the considerations *contrabandistas* make regarding formality and informality and the different routes for obtaining contraband versus documented goods. Like Victoria, some *contrabandistas* prefer to bring goods legally if they have sufficient capital, but turning to contraband in cases when they are in lack, and hence combining their trade in contraband goods with documented merchandise. It shows how vendors do not necessarily resist formality, but that formality requires more capital to invest and often gives vendors a lower income compared to the trading of undocumented goods. Official demands of formalisation thus contain the potential of exacerbating inequalities.

Ambiguous Status as Work

Several scholars have observed how market women are seen as vulgar, indecent and somewhat dirty figures by the 'educated' classes, as 'matter out of place' within dominant gender ideologies, and evoking the dread of the indian, and especially of the indian woman who transgresses symbolic boundaries (Seligmann 2004; Weismantel 2001; Rivera Cusicanqui and Arnold 1996). The work of women vendors thus involves not only risk and uncertainty, but often humiliating and abusive treatment, also from public functionaries. Despite this, it seems as if public functionaries have also typically shown a certain degree of tolerance for these activities, an issue I return to.

What appears as the transgressive aspects of vendors' practices is illustrated by the representation of these women as somewhat 'men-like' and 'out of proportions', in a way that was captured in the program Paisana Jacinta, broadcasted by Latina Television. In the program, a male actor plays the role of Jacinta, depicting an indigenous woman trying to accommodate to urban ways in Lima. More than simply illustrating racial and gendered stereotypes connected to the *chola*, Paisana Jacinta embodies the social uneasiness spurred by the image of a woman who struggles to make ends meet. Now, while the presence of women vendors in urban market places is indeed considered disturbing by many, their market work is at the same time regarded as an extension of domestic and reproductive activities. Market work thus has an ambiguous status as *work*. During my first fieldwork, when I asked women in a shanty town in Arequipa about their work, many responded that they did not work since there were no jobs to get. Later I learned that the same women worked as vendors. In this manner, they seemed to consent with the view that vending is not really 'proper work'. I also learned that many women prefer to work in vending due to, among other things, the possibility to bring their children along to the market—something which is difficult in other forms of work. Market spaces are not regularised through norms or supervisors to the same extent as other workplaces, and especially small children can be looked after while working at a market pitch. Also *contrabandistas* who travel to bring goods from Bolivia or Chile often bring children along on their journeys. Indeed, vending represents an opportunity to both look after the children and earn money at the same time. These dimensions reinforce the perception of vending as not really 'proper work', despite the fact that women's vending activities often represents an important contribution to their households' income. As argued by de la Cadena (1995), perceptions of vending in the Andes are informed also by the notion that women are regarded as more indian than their male counterparts. As women sell products from the highlands and often wearing Andean clothing and braids, women's work in trade is often considered of less value than that of men. It indicates how vending is imagined and constituted through particular, key markers of inequality.

Several feminist scholars have demonstrated that the dichotomous association of women with the domestic and men with the public sphere serves as a way to mask structural features of employment, to undercommunicate and/or devalorise women's labour (Leacock 1972; Sacks 1974; Yanagisako 1987). Binaries like public/domestic and production/reproduction have thus come to be seen as a disguise for power mechanisms and cultural-specific gender ideologies. Babb (2001) has argued that vendors in the Andes do not operate within what can simply be considered a 'reproductive' sphere or by selling small-scale food products, by demonstrating how vending in the Andes may also involve mass-production. Thus criticising the widespread view of market women's labour as strictly reproductive and distributive, Babb stressed how different kinds of food processing take place in the market that would have been interpreted as productive if done in a factory. Indeed, vendors add economic (as well as cultural) value to their work in a manner that not only resists the productive/reproductive binary, but throws such binaries into a critical light, as veiling the interconnectedness of these social processes and the significant role of vendors in the national economy (Babb 2001). It illustrates how the monetary significance of vending, both for individual households and for the national economy, is skewed due to its construction as a feminine realm. As I will return to, the image of vending as a feminine realm and extension of household activities may nonetheless represent a resource in vendors' tactics and encounters with public officials.

Several unauthorised markets have continued for years without particular interference, and many *contrabandistas* have brought goods across the borders throughout their often long working careers. On occasion their goods have been confiscated, but not frequently enough to prevent them from continuing their businesses. It is of course impossible, however, to generalise regarding the official interference in vending and contraband, since such interference has varied over time, and with the kind of activity and merchandise. While there have been periods when vendors have experienced significant persecution and abuse, my impression, since my first fieldwork in 1997, is that there has also been a certain degree of toleration for vending and contraband, especially under the presidency of Fujimori. The frequency of official interference seems to have increased over the recent years though, although with significant variations across regions. During my fieldwork in 2011, interferences at marketplaces were becoming more frequent in Lima than in Arequipa and Puno, although the controls along the roads, especially before Arequipa, had become a lot stricter than before. Some public functionaries also seemed to find it difficult to intervene in these businesses, and explained their non-interference by stressing that 'there are no jobs to get anyway'. As underlined by a legal advisor I interviewed in Arequipa: 'it is difficult to do anything, because people get angry and will ask for an alternative'.

Enactments of Gendered and Racialised Identities

In recent years, Rosaria's daughter Dorothea has had her merchandise confiscated several times. On one such occasion, her husband criticised her for not being able to avoid such interference and for thus letting her goods be confiscated. As we met a few days later, Dorothea said that: 'he thinks it is easy, but it is not easy at all, it is not as if you can just take some products and then you earn'. Many vendors similarly stressed the struggle, suffering and sacrifice that vending involves, but simultaneously emphasising that they just have to go on 'with their eyes closed', in order to support their children. In this and other ways, vendors evoke a notion of motherhood in terms of suffering and sacrifice, a notion that has been discussed in literature from Latin America as central for making political claims (Goddard 2000), as they plead that vending is their only way to earn a living and feed their children. By actualising these notions, more specifically the poor and marginalised mother, vendors try to make interference more difficult for the public functionaries.

Some *contrabandistas* bring second-hand clothes into Peru by travelling to Iquique in Chile for clothes shipped from the USA, Europe or Japan. These women are called *cachineras* (referring to discarded things), and sell from the streets close to the Feria. The commercialisation of second-hand clothes is a contested issue though. In 2005, the importation and sale of second-hand clothes was prohibited by law, in what was considered a half-hearted attempt to protect the national textile industry. This commercialisation nonetheless continues, as vendors move their pitches from place to place, or place themselves hidden in the middle of other vendors who sell legally. At a huge let-out sale for second-hand clothes hidden in a parking lot, I encountered a group of vendors selling clothes from huge plastic bags to retailers from neighbouring markets. One of them explained that some women from Puno take care of the importation from Chile and that these women are the ones in charge of the whole business. 'These women can earn money from anything', she said. 'They even fight the police. If they were men, they would have been put to jail. But not with the women. They [that is, the functionaries] have more respect for women. For this reason vending is easier for women'.

This notion, that functionaries have 'more respect for women', hinges upon an idea about woman as mother. It indicates the significance of particular constructions of womanhood for how vending and interferences in vending are negotiated. This notion, deliberately associating womanhood with domestic chores and disassociating them from commercial activities and regulation, may allow women to be involved in contraband or other businesses at the margins of the formal, perhaps even giving women a relative advantage over men. Such constructions of womanhood may even work to reinforce claims to local sovereignty in practices of vending and cross-border trade. While this notion of womanhood as motherhood may, in many cases, contribute to facilitate women's involvement in vending, it is also related to the devalorisation of women's work, that women's work is not regarded as important enough for the authorities to interfere, due to a view that it is men who do the real work and women's work is seen as 'extra' (Lazar 2008). In a similar vein, Carsten (2004) has noted how most kinds of work are considered legitimate as long as it is related to household subsistence. This is not to say that women vendors are not exposed to abuse by public functionaries, but rather is to stress how constructions of womanhood may affect the ways in which official interferences are negotiated.

In encounters with fiscal, customs or police authorities, vendors may also represent themselves as 'ignorant', claiming that they did not know it was illegal, that they are humble and cannot read and write, and that the officials must understand and forgive them. When referring to what she regards as the sometimes bad ways in which vendors are treated by the customs and fiscal authorities, one vendor for instance said that 'although we are humble and do not know, they [that is, the functionaries] ought to respect us'. In this and other ways, vendors and *contrabandistas* may construct an image of themselves as humble and 'not knowing'. This does not mean that they not also criticise, mock or manipulate public functionaries though, and *contrabandistas* sometimes fight the custom officials in order to pass with their goods, or they destroy their goods by pouring petrol on so that the goods will be of no value for the officials either.

Racial categorisation too is made relevant in vendors' encounters with public functionaries. Dorothea for instance said that 'I have this look [referring to herself as a *chola*]. The customs know immediately when they see me'. Her colleague Juana suggested that she should start dyeing her hair, in order to look like a tourist. In this and other ways, appearances are made important in encounters with public functionaries—and identity markers may also be changed with such encounters in mind. Juana herself works as a *cachinera*. When she and her *cachinera* colleagues travel to bring merchandise they try to look like tourists, making sure to be nicely dressed with make-up and all, and travelling with huge, stylish suitcases— in contrast to the more common *bultos* (bundles). In this manner, some *contrabandistas* try to mimic the looks of tourists or mestiza women. It is also not uncommon that *contrabandistas* manipulate their identity papers, and some even change their surnames to more Hispanic-sounding ones, in order to avoid the prejudice that a Quechua or Aymara surname may result in. There are other *contrabandistas* though, who refuse to show their papers when being stopped by police or customs agents. As we were discussing the dangers of getting caught when bringing contraband, Juana stressed that 'you have to make an effort never to show them your documents, and never give your name'. Vendors may thus not only seek to hide their practices to avoid official interference, but also, once caught, try to make themselves 'illegible' to state institutions by refusing to provide documentation.

As illustrated in the case of the *cahineras*, vendors seek to make themselves 'visible' in very specific and deliberate ways, by making use of identity markers such as clothes, and hence drawing upon particular racialised and gendered stereotypes in their attempts to avoid interference. While some try to dress up as mestiza women, others wear the traditional many-layered skirts (*polleras*), braids and bowler-hats on their journeys, and in this manner emphasising an image of indigenous farmer-women, as a kind of strategic essentialism. For instance, when my interlocutor Justina travels to bring contraband, she always dresses in her *pollera*, and on top of her contraband goods, she places agricultural products from her land in the border village, Yapita. In this manner, public functionaries are more likely to consider her as a 'humble farmer woman'. This strategic use of identity markers can be related to the ways in which women are ascribed a particular symbolic significance in representations of the Andean, as 'uncontaminated' by colonisation, hybridisation and geographical displacement (Crain 1996). According to Crain, this image can be seen as part of a strategic essentialism in order for women to gain a voice in a post-colonial context, as well as extend their employment opportunities in urban contexts (1996:137). It reflects how projects of subjectification in this context entail a binary logic of classification, situating persons as either mestiza woman or indigenous woman, positions that may involve different claims for being 'citizen' or 'legal'. The mestiza or tourist-looking woman may more easily be allowed to pass as 'legal', while the indigenous women may be allowed to pass for simply being situated 'outside'. The *chola* in contrast, as located in-between these categories, does not fit either, and may, as illustrated in the case of Dorothea mentioned earlier, be more easily suspected to work illegally. Specific constructions of womanhood and racialised identities are thus actualised and enacted in vendors' encounters with public officials, as categories of identity are made relevant in attempts to mediate between informality and official requirements. While they may appear as 'perfect neoliberal citizens' as noted in the introduction, they simultaneously oppose and circumvent the demands of the state's neoliberal regime, by drawing on relational as well as symbolic resources. Hence, informal trade is constructed and reconstructed as a particular feminine and racialised realm. As we shall see in the next section, recent economic policies contribute to skew some of these symbolic multiplicities by intensifying mechanisms of exclusion and inclusion, and to 'un-make' women vendors as apparently 'perfect neoliberal subjects'.

THE REGIME OF FLOW AND REGULATION

During the last few years, Peruvian authorities have increased border controls, and measures have been taken to formalise commodity flows and modernise the border control system. This has partly been in response to demands from the USA, with which Peru in 2006 signed a trade promotion agreement (ratified in 2009). As part of this agreement the USA is to assist Peru in limiting exportation of narcotics, modernising the equipment and procedures of the National Police and Customs Agency, and strengthening the rule of law. These dimensions of trade agreements indicate how, as previously noted, the current liberalisation of the market worldwide is accompanied by an increasing significance ascribed to formality and the legal. In addition to strengthening and modernising checkpoints at the borders, Peruvian authorities have also placed checkpoints along the highways before entering the big cities, and, as previously noted, policies have been implemented to formalise economic activities. In addition, routines for the registration (and destruction) of confiscated goods have been introduced to reduce the problem of functionaries who take confiscated goods for themselves.

With stricter control and regulation of commodity flows at the borders and beyond, the advantages of bringing contraband from Bolivia and Chile seem to be in gradual decline. In Arequipa, many people who ran relatively large contraband businesses, from a local point of view, told me that they were downsising or leaving their businesses. One of them is Camila, a woman regarded as a grand business woman among her colleagues at the Feria. She brings leather jackets from Bolivia, which she buys for 120 *soles* and sells for about 300 *soles*. She used to earn well, bringing 300 jackets at a time, but now that the border controls have increased she brings only 20 or 30. Other *contrabandistas* have decided to stop bringing contraband altogether, and formalise their businesses. For instance, Dorothea, after repeatedly having her goods confiscated, invested in a copy machine and started selling authorised office equipment. After formalising, however, her earnings declined and she decided to invest in an informal mining project to compensate. This investment proved to be more hazardous than any of her previous ventures, however. As in Dorothea's case, many *contrabandistas* feel forced to formalise in response to increased border controls, but suffer a loss of income as a result. Formalisation may thus pose new and unforeseen challenges and dilemmas.

After Peru signed a free trade agreement with China in 2009, China was expected to replace the USA as Peru's most important bilateral partner, a prospect which might seem ever more likely now after Trump has been elected president. The agreement with China contributes to facilitate the exportation and importation of Chinese goods and has contributed to an increase of importation especially of textiles to Peru. The agreement involves reduced import taxes and specifies the possibility of refunding these taxes on a long-term basis. Some of the people I interviewed argued that the agreement would give Peruvians great opportunities to earn money through importation, and there was almost no end to their ideas for new business ventures. This optimism was especially widespread among the young and middle class in Lima, but less so in Arequipa.

Seen from the perspective of *contrabandistas* in Arequipa, the free trade agreement with China has resulted in more competition from grand-scale actors whose activities depend less on chains of local intermediaries, and importing directly (and formally) from overseas. As a result, vending activities seem to become increasingly centred around Lima, as more goods are brought in directly and legally through the capital. So, while people used to come to Arequipa—even from Lima—in order to buy contraband goods, opportunities related to cross-border trade with Bolivia and Chile are in decline. The activities of *contrabandistas* are thus increasingly restricted, as their reliance on small-scale, informal and socially embedded forms of trade is complicated by a strengthening of controls as well as increased competition.

While there is an expectation that free trade agreements will break down the limitations on trade across borders, the situation of *contrabandistas* shows that such agreements may contribute to open up some borders while increasingly restricting others, and opening up trade channels for some, but restricting them for others. Hence, while accommodating legal importation, the business opportunities offered through these agreements seem to be limited to the middle/upper-classes. Indeed, free trade agreements can be seen to produce specific sorts of 'governable spaces' (Watts 2004) where trade is allowed to happen only in specific, pre-defined ways, while excluding other forms of trade from the same spaces. In the Peruvian context, the mechanisms of inclusion and exclusion that are thus created must be understood in terms of their gendered effects, as the agreements increasingly constrain the small-scale, unskilled and more localised forms of trade dominated by women. Overseas importation demands higher financial investments and greater knowledge of national regulations and procedures of importation. Legal imports thus contrast sharply to the localised and often small-scale modes of bringing contraband from neighbouring countries, which rely firstly on social networks. The greater importance of overseas importation may therefore serve to exclude actors who lack capital and knowledge. Indeed, free trade agreements may put particular constraints on regional cross-border trade in ways that are likely to affect, particularly, women reliant on this kind of economic activity. The regulation and formalisation of trade (through, for instance, free trade agreements) may thus marginalise many women further and render their market work even more ambiguous as *work*. In this regard, Peru's signing of free trade agreements in recent years represents an accentuation of the country's insertion into global markets in a way that puts new demands on the 'perfect neoliberal citizen', and with the potential of fortifying certain forms of inequality. It indicates how economic policies and processes are moulded by and through existing social relations and institutions, and hence play out in spaces that are created through, and contributing to reinforce, relations and categorisations connected to class, gender, and 'race'.

Conclusions

Exploring how economic activities at the margins of the formal economy are socially embedded and informed by existing social relations and institutions of various kinds, this chapter has argued that policies for the promotion of entrepreneurship and formalisation cannot be considered a historically and socio-culturally neutral or isolated process. The chapter has therefore sought to provide an ethnographic exploration of the class, ethnic and gender relationships in which these economic activities are actualised. These are important aspects to take into account if we are to understand the proliferation of Peru's so-called culture of informality, and how it is constituted and affected by neoliberal reforms and ongoing policies for entrepreneurship, formalisation and regulation.

There are significant class, racialised and gendered dimensions to the ways in which vending and contraband in Peru are practised and negotiated, illustrated not only by many people's lack of other alternatives to earn an income, but also by how vendors draw upon relational and symbolic resources in their economic strategising. The chapter has therefore demonstrated how vendors seek to mediate between official demands and informal dimensions of vending by relying on social relations and particular enactments of womanhood and racialised identities. While the view of vending as an extension of domestic activities may contribute to devalorise women's work, I have illustrated how women may also seek to enact these particular constructions of womanhood in attempts to facilitate vending at the margins of the formal. By evoking a notion of womanhood as mother, and more specifically the poor mother's suffering and sacrifice, vendors plead that vending is their only way to earn a living. In this and other ways, they seek to make it more difficult for public functionaries to interfere, by actualising and enacting an image of womanhood that has long been considered central in Latin America for making political claims. Drawing on particular gendered and racialised identities and stereotypes, vendors try to avoid and circumvent official interference.

Through their economic strategising and tactics, vendors both subscribe to—and oppose—the stereotypical expectation towards the *chola* as well as the demands to the 'perfect neoliberal' citizen, but increasingly so with a risk of being criminalised, as I demonstrated in the last part of the chapter.

While women's activities in market work and contraband is ascribed an ambiguous status as *work*, there have been continual attempts in recent years to include such activities in state regimes of regulation and control. The stimulation of entrepreneurship and market liberalisation initiated by Fujimori in the 1990s has thus gradually been accompanied by measures to promote the formalisation of unauthorised businesses and border controls. Aiming to promote 'development', security for owners and a more effective land market, such measures may, however, contribute to fortify existing fissures along class, ethnic and gender lines, and result in further exclusion, even criminalisation, of vendors. With the signing of free trade agreements in recent years, we see yet an example of how market liberalisation operates through an increased significance ascribed to formality and the legal. While such agreements are contributing to facilitate Peru's access to global markets, several *contrabandistas* experience their businesses to be negatively affected, due to the strengthening of border controls and increased competition from overseas importation. By this I do not intend to romanticise entrepreneurship at the margins of the legal, but rather to demonstrate how small-scale entrepreneurs from the working classes may be affected in very different ways than grand-scale entrepreneurs. In particular, considering that vending activities in this context are actualised through relations and categorisations connected also to gender and racialisation in specific ways, the promotion of formalised, overseas importation may have particular gendered and racialising effects. It is therefore important to acknowledge, in discussing Peru's now long-standing promotion of market liberalisation, how the production of specific sort of 'governable spaces' may serve to exclude certain actors and forms of economic activities from the same spaces, and, as a result, reinforce long-standing economic and socio-cultural inequalities.

Note

1. Altiplano refers to the presence of vendors and goods from the Andean highlands.

References

Babb, Florence. 2001. Market/Places as Gendered Spaces: Market/Women's Studies over Two Decades. In *Women Traders in Cross-Cultural Perspective: Mediating Identities, Marketing Wares*, ed. L. Seligmann, 229–240. Stanford: Stanford University Press.

Bear, Laura. 2014a. Capital and Time: Uncertainty and Qualitative Measures of Inequality. *The British Journal of Sociology* 65 (4): 639–649.

———. 2014b. For Labour: Ajeet's Accident and the Ethics of Technological Fixes in Time. *Journal of the Royal Anthropological Institute* 20 (S1): 71–88.

Carsten, Janet. 2004. *After Kinship: New Departures in Anthropology*. Cambridge: Cambridge University Press.

Comaroff, Jean, and John Comaroff. 2006. *Law and Disorder in the Postcolony*. London/Chicago: The University of Chicago Press.

Crain, M. 1996. The Gendering of Ethnicity in the Ecuadorian Andes: Native Women's Self-Fashioning in the Urban Marketplace. In *Machos, Mistresses and Madonnas: Contesting the Power of the Latin American Gender Imagery*, ed. M. Melhuus and A.K. Stølen, 134–158. London: Verso.

de Soto, Hernando. 1989. *The Other Path: The Invisible Revolution in the Third World*. London: Taurus.

———. 2001. *The Mystery of Capital. Why Capitalism Triumphs in the West and Fails Everywhere Else*. London: Black Swan.

De la Cadena, Marisol. 1995. Women are More Indian: Ethnicity and Gender in a Community Near Cuzco. In *Ethnicity, Markets and Migration in the Andes: At the Crossroads of History and Anthropology*, ed. B. Larson and O. Harris, 329–348. Durham: Duke University Press.

Ewig, Christina. 2010. *Second-Wave Neoliberalism : Gender, Race, and Health Sector Reform in Peru*. University Park: The Pennsylvania State University Press.

Gandolfo, Daniella. 2013. Formless: A Day at Lima's Office of Formalisation. *Cultural Anthropology* 28 (2): 278–298.

Goddard, Victoria. 2000. The Virgin and the State: Gender and Politics in Argentina. In *Gender, Agency and Social Change: Anthropological Perspectives*, ed. Victoria Goddard, 221–249. London/New York: Routledge.

Harris, Olivia. 2000. *To Make the Earth Bear Fruit: Ethnographic Essays on Fertility, Work and Gender in Highland Bolivia*. London: Institute of Latin American Studies, University of London.

Holston, James. 2008. *Insurgent Citizenship*. Princeton/Oxfordshire: Princeton University Press.

Kabeer, Naila. 2010. *Gender and Social Protection Strategies in the Informal Economy*. London/New York/New Delhi: Routledge.

Larkins, Erika R. 2015. *The Spectacular Favela. Violence in Modern Brazil*. Oakland: University of California Press.
Lazar, Sian. 2008. *El Alto, Rebel City. Self and Citizenship in Andean Bolivia*. Durham/London: Duke University Press.
Leacock, E. 1972. Introduction. In *The Origin of the Family, the State and Private Property*, ed. F. Engels, 7–67. New York: International Publishers.
Matos Mar, José. 1984. *Desborde Popular y Crisis del Estado. El Nuevo Rostro del Perú en la Decada de 1980*. Lima: Instituto de Estudios Peruanos.
Mitchell, Timothy. 2002. *Rule of Experts: Egypt, Techno-Politics, Modernity*. Berkeley: University of California Press.
Ødegaard, Cecilie Vindal. 2010. *Mobility, Markets and Indigenous Socialities: Contemporary Migration in the Peruvian Andes*. Burlington: Ashgate Publishing.
———. 2016. Made in China. Contraband, Labor, and the Gendered Effects of 'Free-Trade', China-Peru. *Journal of Development Studies*, published online 29 June, 1–15.
Polanyi, K. [1944] 2001. *The Great Transformation: The Political and Economic Origins of Our Time*. Boston: Beacon Press.
Rivera Cusicanqui, S., and D.Y. Arnold. 1996. *Ser mujer indigena, chola y birlocha en la Bolivia postcolonial* [To Be a Woman; Indigenous, Chola and Westernised in Postcolonial Bolivia]. La Paz: Ministerio de Desarrollo Humano.
Roberts, Bryan R. 1995. *The Making of Citizens. Cities of Peasants Revisited*. London: Edward Arnold.
Rousseau, Stephanie. 2007. The Politics of Reproductive Health in Peru: Gender and Social Policy in the Global South. *Social Politics* 14 (1): 93–125.
Sacks, Karen. 1974. Engels Revisited: Women, the Organization of Production and Private Property. In *Woman, Culture and Society*, ed. M. Rosaldo and L. Lamphere, 207–222. Palo Alto: Stanford University Press.
Scott, James. 1998. *Seeing Like a State: How Certain Schemes to Improve the Human Condition Have Failed*. New Haven: Yale University Press.
Seligmann, Linda. 2004. *Peruvian Street Lives: Culture, Power, and Economy Among Market Women of Cuzco*. Urbana/Chicago: University of Illinois Press.
Sieder, Rachel, Line Schjolden, and Alan Angell, eds. 2005. *The Judicialization of Politics in Latin America*. New York/Hampshire: Palgrave Macmillan.
Watts, M.J. 2004. Resource Curse? Governmentality, Oil and Power in the Niger Delta, Nigeria. *Geopolitics* 9: 50–80.
Weismantel, Mary. 2001. *Cholas and Pishtacos: Stories of Race and Sex in the Andes*. Chicago/London: University of Chicago Press.
Yanagisako, Sylvia. 1987. Mixed Metaphors: Native and Anthropological Models of Gender and Kinship Domains. In *Gender and Kinship: Essays Toward a Unified Analysis*, ed. J. Collier and S. Yanagisako, 86–118. Palo Alto: Stanford University Press.

Open Access This chapter is licensed under the terms of the Creative Commons Attribution 4.0 International License (http://creativecommons.org/licenses/by/4.0/), which permits use, sharing, adaptation, distribution and reproduction in any medium or format, as long as you give appropriate credit to the original author(s) and the source, provide a link to the Creative Commons license and indicate if changes were made.

The images or other third party material in this chapter are included in the chapter's Creative Commons license, unless indicated otherwise in a credit line to the material. If material is not included in the chapter's Creative Commons license and your intended use is not permitted by statutory regulation or exceeds the permitted use, you will need to obtain permission directly from the copyright holder.

CHAPTER 9

Coming of Age in the Penal System: Neoliberalism, 'Mano Dura' and the Reproduction of 'Racialised' Inequality in Honduras

Lirio Gutiérrez Rivera, Iselin Åsedotter Strønen, and Margit Ystanes

INTRODUCTION

One of the ways in which colonially instituted 'racial' hierarchies are being reproduced in the Americas today, is through the penal system. The heightened levels of securitisation that accompanied the introduction of

---

Ethnographic research for this chapter was assisted by a grant from the Drugs, Security, and Democracy Program administered by the Social Science Research Council, in partnership with the Universidad de Los Andes (Colombia) and Centro de Investigación y Docencia Económicas, and in cooperation with funds provided by the Open Society Foundations.

L.G. Rivera (✉)
Universidad Nacional de Colombia, Medellín, Colombia

I.Å. Strønen
University of Bergen and the Chr. Michelsen Institute (CMI), Bergen, Norway

M. Ystanes
University of Bergen, Bergen, Norway

© The Author(s) 2018
M. Ystanes, I.Å. Strønen (eds.), *The Social Life of Economic Inequalities in Contemporary Latin America*, Approaches to Social Inequality and Difference, DOI 10.1007/978-3-319-61536-3_9

neoliberalism throughout the region, have particularly targeted 'racially othered' young males living in poor neighbourhoods. The Pink Tide did little, or nothing, to challenge this state of affairs. On the contrary, the targeting of 'racially othered,' poor, young males as criminals is a strong feature of securitisation in Brazil, Venezuela and Honduras alike, despite these countries' radically different engagements with the Pink Tide. The massive targeting of 'racially othered' poor, young, males in Latin America also has important similarities to processes of securitisation in the United States (see, e.g. Goffman 2014). In this chapter, we focus on the particular case of Honduras, yet we also draw comparisons with other countries that allow us to reflect upon the broader implications of the country's 'iron fist' approach to crime control. By doing so, we wish to emphasise how punitive control over 'surplus' populations in neoliberalised societies are informed by and contribute to the reproduction of historically constituted 'racial' and socio-economic hierarchies. As this chapter shows, the prison population in Honduras has not only dramatically increased in size, but once being inside the penitentiary system, the young prisoners end up passing important formative years in a system that has nothing to offer them in terms of rehabilitation or education. Whilst Honduras' socio-economically better off can pay their way out of the prison system by legal or illegal means, poor men are systematically discriminated against even before they enter the prison. Indeed, the punitive profiling of certain groups of citizens, the inefficiency of the judicial system and the legal design of processual and penal codes indicates that the Honduran prison system is better understood as a place of containment for 'unwanted elements' than as an instrument for the rule of law.

The official justification for pursing an 'iron fist' approach towards crime in Honduras is the escalating levels of violence in the country during the past two decades. In the early 1990s, Salomón (1994) observed that a

---

Parts of this chapter have previously been published as part of the research project *Everyday Manouvers. Military-Civilian Relations in Latin American and the Middle East*, led by professor Nefissa Naguib and financed by the Norwegian Ministry for Foreign Affairs. The original paper was titled *CMI Working Paper: Security and Remilitarization in the Name of Democracy: The Impact of Global Crime Control Policies in Honduras* (2015). Lirio Gutiérrez Rivera et al. graciously acknowledges Professor Nefissa Naguib and the Chr. Michelsen Institute (CMI), Bergen, Norway, for permission to reprint.

new type of violence was emerging that differed from the political violence in prior decades. This implied the gradual proliferation of criminal and delinquent acts such as armed robbery and theft, mostly involving male adolescents and young adults. Towards the end of the 1990s and early twenty-first century, various scholars recognised the emergence of 'new violence' in various post-conflict scenarios (Koonings and Kruijt 2004; Rotker 2002),[1] including a variety of actors such as death squads, paramilitary groups, organised crime and youth gangs. In Honduras, youth gangs and, more recently, organised crime, proliferated. The former, known as the *maras*, appeared in the 1990s. Part of the reason why this happened was changes in the conditions for social reproduction, such as the family, the educational system and the labour market. These changes were brought about by the implementation of neoliberal policies, leading to increased poverty, inequality and unemployment.[2] Today, around 60 per cent of the Honduran population live in poverty (UNDP 2014). Most of the population, particularly the youth segment, has been hit by the lack of job opportunities in the country, forcing many to immigrate mainly to the United States. In other cases, entering the illicit drug economy or joining the gangs becomes a solution to the difficulties of overcoming economic hardships and for finding a place for identity and belonging (Strocka 2006:139).

Another intersecting factor was the massive arrival of deportees from the United States with a background as active gang members in the 1990s. Shifts in the US migration policy led to the deportation of documented and undocumented migrants who had criminal records. Many of the deportees were members of two street gangs from Southern California: the *Mara Salvatrucha* and the Eighteenth Street Gang (*Dieciocho*). Shortly after returning 'home,' a place where many had never lived and which did not even exist in their childhood memories, the deportees, who were members of either one of the *maras*, reorganised and merged the gang with the existing local ones. Following these 'mergers' (there had been gangs in Honduras since the 1950s), street gangs' organisation became more complex due to increasing membership numbers, and the use of violence became more institutionalised (Salomón et al. 1999). However, even if the *maras* were framed as the main culprits for escalating violence and crime in the country, they were not the centre of the storm. Rather, organised crime was (Rodgers 2009; Jüttersonke et al. 2009; UNODC 2012). However, these networks are much more difficult to target, whilst also being tied to more powerful sectors in the country (Bosworth 2010; Shipley 2016).

Since the turn of the twenty-first century, the prison population in Honduras has been on the rise. Currently, there are 17,017 female and male inmates, out of a population of 8 million (World Prison Brief 2016). This is almost twice the number of prisoners in 2002 and three times more than in the late 1990s. In 2012, the prison population rate was at 152 of 100,000 per inhabitants. In 2014, it had risen to 194/100,000.

The Honduran government's security agenda is one of the main reasons for the increase of the inmate population. Introduced in 2002 by the administration of Ricardo Maduro (2002–2006) and continued by the subsequent administrations of president Manuel Zelaya (2006–2009), Porfirio Lobo (2010–2014) and Juan Orlando Hernández (2013–), the domestic security agenda has sought to reduce violence and crime by incarcerating not only convicted delinquents and criminals but also those who are perceived—judged by their physical appearances—to be associated with crime and gang membership. Typically, this includes clothing, tattoos and haircuts, but in practice, class- and ethno-racial identity markers is also enough to be singled out for arrest and imprisonment.

As we discuss further below, the 'iron fist' approach to crime taken by successive Honduran governments is typical of what Wacquant (2009) and others have theorised as an intrinsic part of the neoliberal state, a state that seeks to 'control' those who are structurally excluded and marginalised by the neoliberal order through an expanding punitive prison system. Thus, our purpose in this chapter is not to single out Honduras in particular for maintaining this neoliberal approach to securitisation. As other chapters show, even Brazil, which has been one of the leading forces of the Pink Tide, has done the same (see Sørbøe (Chap. 5); Ystanes (Chap. 4), this volume). Rather, we take the firm continuation of this agenda across the political spectrum as indicative of the scope of possibilities, and of imagination, of Latin American governments and the deep-seated punitive ideology and structural features in which they are embedded. At the same time, Honduras' particular geopolitical context as part of the US War on Drugs, and the increasingly authoritarian stance taken by its ruling elites, points to an increasing consolidation of 'iron fist' security politics that is undercut by a general repressive stance towards marginalised and excluded groups.

The Pink Tide in Honduras: Zelaya's Brief Interlude

Honduras was briefly considered to be in the orbit of the so-called Pink Tide during Manuel Zelaya's presidency until he was ousted by the military and conservative elites in June 2009. Zelaya, a wealthy land and ranch owner belonging to one of the regional elites of the country, had been elected for the Liberal party in 2006. Initially, he took a slightly softer approach to security politics than his main contender, Porfirio Lobo. However, this softer stance never really came into effect, arguably because he was caught up in other economic and political issues (Bosworth 2010:19).

Whilst in office, Zelaya introduced free school enrolment, increased the minimum wage, increased wages for teachers and attempted to reduce fuel costs (Gordon and Webber 2011). Moreover, he reformed the mining laws, introducing a new bill that would raise tax on foreign mining companies, passed a Reforestation Law (Ley de Reforestación) designed to protect the environment and refused to privatise the state-owned electric and telecommunications companies.

The traditional elites and the military, though not happy with these reforms, did not initially feel threatened. Eventually, however, this attitude changed, mostly due to two of Zelaya's initiatives. Firstly, in 2008, Zelaya decided to join the Bolivarian Alliance for the Peoples of Our America (ALBA) led by Venezuela, in order to address an economic downturn in the country (Gordon and Webber 2011). Secondly, in 2009 Zelaya decided to call a referendum asking the Honduran population to vote for a new Constituent National Assembly that would reform the constitution. The traditional elites and the military, as well as other conservative sectors of civil society such as the Catholic Church, immediately reacted against Zelaya. They claimed the referendum was part of a plan for Zelaya to remain in power, and that he was becoming a puppet of Venezuelan president Hugo Chávez.[3]

The military refused to comply with Zelaya's order to distribute the ballots for the referendum scheduled to take place during the presidential elections in November 2009. Zelaya then fired the head of the Armed Forces, Gen. Romeo Orlando Vásquez Velásquez. Shortly thereafter, the Minister of Defense, Ángel Orellana, resigned. The Supreme Court ruled both the referendum and Gen. Vásquez's dismissal as illegal. In Congress, Roberto Micheletti from the Liberal party and president of Congress, as well as other members of the Liberal party, turned against Zelaya. This group, the right-wing faction of the Liberal party, allied with the military high officials, conservative groups such as the Catholic Church—especially the Opus Dei—and the traditional elites to overthrow Zelaya.[4] On Sunday, June 28, Zelaya was ousted when the military arrived at Zelaya's home and sent him to Costa Rica in his pajamas. Roberto Micheletti became interim president until the new elections in November 2009. These elections were won by Porfirio 'Pepe' Lobo, who Shipley (2016:9) describes as 'a coup-supporter and member of the Honduran oligarchy.' Subsequent presidential elections in 2013 were won by Juan Orlando Hernández, who was president of Congress during Lobo's presidency. The elections were strongly criticised by international observers (Shipley 2016:12). In recent years, political violence, murder and persecution of dissent has escalated in Honduras (see Blitzer 2016; Hallinan 2009). Escalating violence and impunity has also been linked to US military funding and presence in Honduras, through the so-called War on Drugs (Grosso 2014; Shipley 2016). Honduras is now ranked as the world's most dangerous country for environmental activists (Global Witness 2017), an issue that received increasing international attention following the brutal murder of the internationally known environmental activist Berta Cáceres in 2016. In January 2017, Juan Orlando Hernández, a staunch ally of the United States, announced the he would seek re-election as president. Paradoxically, one of the main justifications for overthrowing Zelaya was concerns that he would change the constitution in order to do the same thing.

Neoliberalism in Honduras

Nearly 30 years of neoliberal reforms have not only left a wide gap between rich and poor in Honduras, but also they reinforced the racial and gender hierarchies established in the colonial period. This contemporary overlap between poverty and being 'racially othered' is, as discussed below and in the introduction to this volume, an outcome of long historical processes in the region.

The first attempts to introduce neoliberal reforms in Honduras occurred during the government of José Azcona Hoyo (1986–1990) under the supervision of USAID (Bull 2016:97). The United States had a strong military presence in Honduras during the 1980s, using Honduran territory as the base to launch its operations against the Sandinistas in Nicaragua. At the time, US ambassador John Negroponte was widely considered as 'the real power holder' in the country (Shipley 2016:5). The first structural adjustment programme was signed in 1988, whilst the government of Rafael Leonardo Callejas (1990–1994) implemented further reforms including economic liberalisation and the privatisation of state industry and public services (Bull 2016:97).

In general, neoliberal reforms favoured Central America's elites and dominant economic groups, who seized upon new opportunities in emerging private markets whilst simultaneously gaining access to global chains of production and capital with little state intervention (Robinson 2003; Bull et al. 2014; Bull 2016). However, these reforms also widened the gap between poor and rich. The privatisation of social services and economic liberalisation policies undermined both social security nets and opportunities in the labour market. The International Labour Organization (ILO) estimates that 70 per cent of new jobs over the past 15 years have been generated in the informal economy (ILO 2007:5). Furthermore, they estimate that some 75 per cent of workers in Latin America are involved in the informal economy, generating about 40 per cent of the continent's GDP (ILO 2007:5). As explanatory factors for this increasing size of the informal sectors, the organisation points to:

> High rates of rural–urban migration, structural adjustment programs of the 1980s and 1990s and/or for some from burdensome regulations and lack of recognition of the property rights and capital of informal operators. (ILO 2007:5)

The reduction of the formal job market also resulted in the expansion of criminal economy, creating a new labour market for the least qualified part of the workforce (Ziccardi 2008:9). For Portes and Hoffman, it is 'perhaps remarkable' (Portes and Hoffman 2003:70) that only a small percentage of the informal proletariat has succumbed to crime in reaction to increasing impoverishment and marginalisation over the past decades.

> Despite a relative and often absolute deterioration of their situation, the large majority of informal workers continue to toil at minimally paid domestic service, unprotected work in micro-enterprise, or by inventing some form of marginal activity. (Portes and Hoffman 2003:70)

In Honduras, neoliberal reforms in the agricultural sector also had severe ripple effects. The 1992 Decree of Modernisation and Development of the Agricultural Sector (*Ley de Modernización y de Desarrollo del Sector Agrícola*) restructured traditional forms of production and land tenure by prioritising the development of agroindustry business. *Campesinos* (peasants) were unable to produce these types of crops because, contrary to the regional elites, they did not have access to credit or technology. Unable to sustain themselves, many peasants were forced to sell their lands to the growing agroindustry and migrated to the main cities (such as San Pedro Sula or Tegucigalpa) or even abroad (mainly the United States) in search of better economic opportunities. In the cities, however, many migrants become un- and/or underemployed, which in turn added to the crisis of urban marginality that is fuelling the negative cycle of structural inequality, violence and security politics in contemporary Honduras, affecting young men in particular.

The Neoliberal Punitive State

As Garland (2002) discusses, the 1970s marked the start of a significant international shift in crime control and the criminal justice system, which implied the transformation of various institutions and technologies for social control. Rather than the belief in the rehabilitation of criminals and delinquents that predominated until the 1970s, today's contemporary societies are driven by a culture of anxiety demanding a 'tough-on-crime' approach. The result has been a considerable increase of the prison population, changes in attitudes and perceptions towards 'criminals and delinquents' and the increasing use of technology for surveillance (for instance, cameras in public areas such as shopping centres) and private forms of security. The global ascendance of neoliberal ideologies and governance have also greatly contributed to this shift. Previous explanatory frameworks focused on the assumption that crime occurs due to lack of opportunities; an approach that sought to connect individual behaviour to structural factors. However, in the neoliberal culture of crime control, the focus has shifted towards explaining crime by individual deviance (Garland 2002).

As Wacquant (2011) has argued, the neoliberal state deals with the 'destructive consequences' of economic deregulation—such as the increase of poverty, marginality and exclusion—with violence against the lower classes:

> [The neoliberal state] practices *laissez-faire et laissez passer* toward corporations and the upper class, at the level of the causes of inequality. But it is fiercely interventionist and authoritarian when it comes to dealing with the destructive consequences of economic deregulation for those at the lower end of the class and status spectrum.

Thus, in effect, the neoliberal state does not 'retreat' from the social arena. Rather, social investment and the provision of job security is replaced with punitive measures as a new form of regulation and control of those who become structurally marginalised in the neoliberal economy (Antillano et al. 2016:198). Resistance against the effects of neoliberal policies by the lower and working classes is labelled as disorderly and threatening by the dominant classes, propelling the increased use of police and imprisonment in order to prevent the 'undermin[ing] the authority of the state' (Wacquant 2011). Underlying these policies and the ideological moral framing of them is a re-articulation of the culture of poverty (Lewis 1966), placing the burden of guilt upon the poor themselves. As Garland (2002:196) notes, poverty is attributed to 'lack of effort, reckless choices, a distinctive culture, a chosen conduct.' The individualising underlying tenant of neoliberal ideology reinforces such explanatory models. This leaves the poor in a situation whereby they not only have to bear the burden of being subjected to structural marginalisation as 'surplus' populations in a deregulated, precariatised economy, but they also have to bear ideologically and culturally codified stigmas of being 'unfit' and 'undesired' citizens in a 'sink or swim' ideological social order. For those who end up, guilty or not, in the prison system, the combined burden of structural and cultural-ideological marginalisation hits them with full force; they are considered as unwanted and deviant castaways from the desired social order altogether.

Racialised Crime and Punishment

Scholars have pointed out the overrepresentation in prison of persons belonging to certain racial groups or with other markers of distinction such as the colour of their skin (Hunter 2007; Bosworth et al. 2008; De Lissavoy 2013; Golash-Boza 2015). The racialised targeting of poor men is both an aspect of neoliberal approaches to crime prevention in their US configuration (see Goffman 2014) and an outcome of particular Latin American historical trajectories. Indeed, scholars have shown that the emergence of the modern prison in Latin America in the late nineteenth century aimed at abolishing traditional forms of punishment whilst maintaining racial and class divisions established in the colonial period (Salvatore and Aguirre 1996; Aguirre 2005). Hence, blacks and indigenous groups or persons with dark skin colour, who were at the bottom of Latin American societies and perceived as 'racially' inferior, populated the modern prisons in the late nineteenth century as well.

The associations between poverty and 'racial otherness' established in colonial hierarchies are an important aspect of how this 'racialised' concept of the criminal poor has come into being. For example, Cynthia Milton (2007) shows how in eighteenth-century Ecuador policies introduced by the Spanish Crown to address poverty proscribed differential approaches depending on the 'racial' status of the poor in question. On the one hand, downwardly mobile Spanish elites could claim *pobreza de solemnidad*. The kind of assistance offered to such persons centred on maintaining their privileged position. In contrast, for persons of African or indigenous descent, poverty assistance involved various kinds of punishment; imprisonment, enclosure in a poorhouse or a home for wayward women (*recogimiento*) or forced labour. Thus, poverty was not neutral; instead, people were poor according to their class, 'race' and gender (Milton 2007:66–67). For the 'racially othered,' lower spectrums of society, then, the kinds of poverty assistance offered was difficult to distinguish from the deprivation of liberty handed out to criminals.

The long-term outcomes of such ideas and policies can be observed in contemporary Latin American societies. Despite numerous gains in identity politics and the challenging of racism on several fronts, notions of poverty and criminality remain 'racialised' (see, e.g. Ystanes (Chap. 4), this volume). It is well established that poverty discourse as well as poverty itself is gendered; women are both symbolically associated with poverty and carry the burden of poverty more often than do men (Broch-Due 1995). However, conceptualisations of the criminal poor are more strongly tied in with images of young men (Bourgois 2003; Goffman 2014; Ystanes (Chap. 4), this volume). Furthermore, the increasing 'talk of crime' (Caldeira 2000) permeating the media and the public sphere has 'naturalized some groups as dangerous' (Caldeira 2000:2) and accentuated public demands for tough-on-crime approaches. In the neoliberal configuration of crime prevention, this has led to 'racially othered,' poor men being the main targets of policing and punishment.

CRIME CONTROL POLICIES IN HONDURAS

Honduras's current hard-line security agenda, known as *mano dura* ('iron fist'), is modelled after former New York mayor Giuliani's 'broken windows' policies (Müller 2009). The new security agenda has not only perpetuated the perception of poor unemployable young male adults as 'criminals,' it has also led to severe changes in the institutions and legal frameworks dealing with crime, such as criminal codes, the police, the military and the penitentiary system.

The Honduran governments in the 1990s promoted mainly preventive policies towards violence and crime. Because most of the persons involved in crime and violence were adolescents and young adults, targeted preventive programmes were introduced in the form of awareness programmes in public schools focusing on drug use and gang memberships. Importantly, civil society organisations, youth organisations, local scholars and government officials attempted to draft a bill that directly addressed the *mara* phenomenon—Decree 141-2001 and 170-2001 known as the Law for Prevention, Rehabilitation and Reinsertion of Gang and Mara Members (*Ley para la Prevención, Rehabilitación y Reinserción Social de Personas Integrantes de Pandillas o Maras*). However, the bill was stalled in 2001, and the government opted instead for the hard-line security policies that are in force today. The new security agenda as of 2002 involves carrying out military and police raids in poor neighbourhoods (many of them controlled by gang members), the massive incarceration of 'criminals and delinquents' and changes in the criminal justice system—in particular an increase in sentences.

Although local gangs and *maras* initially had been involved in illegal activities (e.g. theft), these did not account for the rise of violence, insecurity and crime in the country. Rather, organised crime did (Rodgers 2009; Jüttersonke et al. 2009; UNODC 2012). Today, the *maras* are involved in the organised crime economy, but—to the extent that it is possible to establish comprehensive knowledge of this—hitherto mainly thought to be as associates further down in the food chain rather than as spiders in the web (Bosworth 2010:10).

However, through media representations conjuring up an imagery of gang and *mara* members as dangerous 'criminals' constituting a threat to Honduran society (Peetz 2011; Oetller et al. 2009), the government drummed up public approval for far-reaching reforms of penal and processual codes targeting the *maras* in particular. In August 2003, Congress reformed the 332 Article of the Penal Code, known as the Anti-gang Law. The new article declared gangs to be illicit associations, meaning that the sole membership of any gang was a motive for arrest and incarceration. This law works in tandem with the 2002 Law of Police and Social Co-Existence (*Ley de Policía y Convivencia Social*), which allows police to detain 'anyone suspicious or vagabonds' (Ungar and Salomón 2012:30).

However, because it was not clear, from a legal standpoint, how to define membership to a gang, police and security agents had discretionary power to arrest anyone who appeared to be a gang member. In practice, this translated into the targeting of young males between 18 and 30 who had distinct markers, including the way they dressed (baggy jeans and T-shirts, sneakers), the way they carried their bodies (buzz cuts, shaved heads) as well as the use of piercings and tattoos. Because of this generalised targeting, gang members changed the way they dressed, covered their tattoos and resorted to other strategies for evading arrests (Gutiérrez Rivera 2010). However, the blurring of symbolic markers of gang membership led to new targeting practices directed against 'criminals' and 'delinquents,' centred mostly on young males' physical appearance such as skin colour.

Gang Members' Life Trajectories

Studies of gang members' social background in Honduras indicate that they often are school dropouts from violent homes, living in neighbourhoods with low income levels, high degrees of social exclusion and scarce access to public services (Gutiérrez Rivera 2010:495). Consequently, they have limited venues for being socialised into 'normal' adulthood through a youth-to-adulthood transition passing from school and into the labour market (Fawcett 2001). This serve as 'push-factors' for 'street-corner' socialisation, which, in turn, increases the risk of becoming involved in criminal activities and the drug economy (see Strocka 2006 for an in-depth analysis of the multiple causes for gang formation in Latin America; see also Bourgois 2003 and Strønen 2014). Additionally, high levels of social distrust and the consumption of drugs and alcohol foment local social violence (Gutiérrez Rivera 2010:495). As Gutiérrez Rivera (2010:495) notes, 'gangs may thus impose local order or 'street level politics' through the use of violence, constituting a form of social structuration that undermines the existing local social fabric.' Gangs in Honduras, as in other Latin American countries, are highly territorialised. Different gangs control different territories, and gang members are with different degrees of rapport and animosity part of the local social fabric (Penglase 2010). It was exactly this territorial control and presence in marginalised neighbourhoods that the Honduran state's new security policies were aimed at breaking up, through constant raid carried out by the police and the military. As Gutiérrez Rivera (2010:497) has previously remarked:

Mano Dura and the Anti-gang Law had a strong territorial component because they aimed at controlling a certain group (gang members) and territories (marginal neighbourhoods). Police and military forces raided gang-controlled barrios looking for members hanging out on street corners and in their homes.

As noted above, the generalised targeting of 'deviant youth' through the anti-gang legislation prompts and justifies that arrests are being made at the officers' own discretion. Increases in arrests furthermore works in tandem with changes in the Processual Penal Code in 2002, which removed judges' discretionary powers of pre-trial detention (*prisión preventiva*). Previously, judges had discretionary power to decide whether to send suspect (or not) to a prison whilst waiting for the sentence. With the changes in the Processual Penal Code, everyone who was arrested was sent to prison to wait for their sentences. Furthermore, the time lapse between arrests and waiting for a sentence is considerable due to the inefficiency of the criminal justice system and Public Prosecutor's Office. Seen together, all these changes not only significantly increased the prison population, and by extension, the number of families whose lives were marked by various kinds of legal entanglements. It also led to an increase in the periods spent in prison whilst they wait for the sentence and, then, an increase in the time they spend in jail when they receive the sentence. The exception were inmates from the middle class or other inmates who could draw on considerable economic help from their family. These inmates hired lawyers and, in some cases, gave bribes to civil servants and judges in the Public Prosecutor's Office or the Criminal Courts to accelerate the trials and hearings.

As a result of these combined effects of the new security agenda, the prison population has increased significantly during the past two decades, collapsing the penitentiary system. Currently, 98 per cent of the inmate population is male (CIDH 2013).

BLEAK FUTURES

In 2014, Gutiérrez Rivera interviewed inmates in the prison in the city of Comayagua. As other prisons in Honduras, the Comayagua prison is overcrowded and self-governed by inmates. During one visit, Gutiérrez Rivera met 'William', an inmate who had been in prison for 12 years and was hoping to be released that year because of good conduct. He was not sure though. 'Only God knows', he said. William appeared to be around 32–35 years of age. When asked what he would do when released, he said: 'Oh I don't know…I haven't thought about it. I mean, I need to see if I can find a job…,' his voice trailed off. On average, an inmate spent 8–10 years in the Comayagua prison.

William's lack of certainty about the future points to important questions concerning the consequences of mass incarceration of young, poor men. What lies ahead for them when released from prison? Will they be able to rebuild their lives after spending 5, 10 or 15 years in prison? What long-term consequences will it have for Honduran society that such high numbers of already disadvantaged young men spend such a long time in prison without any possibilities for 'rehabilitation?' And how may we better understand the underlying rationale and structural underpinnings that legitimise such a punitive model?

The extended period that characterises prison life in Honduras reinforced the interruption of conventional youth-to-adulthood transitions set in motion by the neoliberal reforms. Youth unemployment rose significantly in Latin America in the 1990s (Fawcett 2001:3), and low-income youth were hit the hardest (Fawcett 2001:5). The changing structures in the labour market from the 1980s and onwards crowded out parts of the potential work force, particularly those on the bottom rungs of society. As Fawcett notes: 'for many unskilled youth of Latin America, the distance between the average schooling level and the "needs of the market" is too far. There is no job pathway, which continually rewards a student in school, and keeps the students in school' (Fawcett 2001:16). This pattern was also present in Honduras. Large numbers of youth dropped out from the school system, which, as discussed above, makes them more vulnerable to ending up in the illegal street economy. A recent report shows that 23 per cent of the inmates in Honduran prisons are illiterate. Out of the 59 per cent of the inmate population that had access to primary education prior to entering the prison, only 26 per cent had actually finished primary school (CONAPREV[5] 2011).

Several of the inmates that Gutiérrez Rivera interviewed had not completed primary school (which consists of 6 years). Even fewer inmates had enrolled in middle and secondary school. However, through ethnographic interviews, several of the inmates revealed that they would like to go back to school whilst in prison in order to have something lean on when they are released in the future. However, the only educational venue available to them is the EDUCATODOS programme, run by the

Honduran Ministry of Education and the US development programme USAID. Despite being partially state-run, EDUCATODOS is not offered free of charge. Rather, parts of the programme are privatised and incur costs for the students. For example, USAID owns the copyright of the books and learning material, and all inmates enrolled by the programme have to buy their own copies. For many of the poor inmates, coming from poor households, this is a cost beyond their reach. Because of the high prices of the learning material, many inmates gave up on the idea of finishing school through the EDUCATODOS programme. 'Carlos', an inmate who had finished primary school, was eager to finish secondary school whilst serving his sentence. However, upon hearing that EDUCATODOS demanded payment for the books, he dropped the idea of enrolling.

> I was going to organise a group because many of us [inmates] want to finish school. But I don't have money, we don't have money, not enough money to pay for the material. The little money I earn here is not enough. Nothing is free in prison, I have to pay for my bed, my space, food, everything. My family can't help either. They can't come here [to visit at the prison] because they live in Tegucigalpa and that means time and money, and they can't send me money either.

The other possibility for an inmate was to learn a skill from another inmates, such as carpentry, electric installation work or cooking. The Institute of Special Services for Prevention (Dirección General de Servicios Especiales Preventivos), part of the Ministry of Security, ran a programme for inmates who wanted to learn a skill in some of the prisons in Honduras; but the Comayagua prison was not one of them. Some inmates nevertheless organised the teaching of skill amongst themselves; however, this was highly subjected to the level of trust and tranquillity amongst prisoners. Neither was it of much worth to be 'self-taught' in prison when they had to search for work in a highly competitive labour market. As 'Manuel', an inmate who was scheduled to be released in four months, worded it:

> I would like a job…in carpentry. I learned that here [in the prison]. [Other inmates] taught me…but you know, I don't know… I pray I can find a job. But I don't really if, you know, if anyone will hire me.

The limited access to education or professional training accentuated inmates' levels of uncertainty regarding their lives when released from prison. On the other hand, the long-term sentences served inside the prison wall contributed to strengthening their networks with other arrestees and convicted prisoners, as well as socialising them even further into the harsh rules of 'street corner society'—even within closed prison walls.

The Self-Governed Prison

As most prisons in Latin America, lack of funds and manpower have turned the Comayagua prison into self-governed prison (Darke and Karam 2016). The hierarchical prison order is governed by the *Presidente* or president of the inmates, followed by the vice president and the *Jefe de Bartolinas* or the boss of the blocks. All inmates start from below and are expected to comply with this self-governing regime which has established a 'prison order' (See Gutiérrez Rivera 2017). The president delegates other inmates to oversee prison life and the prison economy, which includes selling food, handicrafts, medicine, as well as illicit activities such as selling drugs and arms. As Carlos alluded to in the quote above, everything in the prison costs money: food, medicines, somewhere to sleep, protection and so on. The prison economy is an enclosed free-market sphere in the extreme; everything is commoditised, and the consequences of not being able to pay are harsh. The internal rule of law is maintained by violence and brutality, and the incumbent 'president' has to constantly demonstrate his willingness to subdue others by force in order to not be subjected to a coup or a mutiny.

This prison order is not unique for Honduras. Antillano et al. (2016) has carefully documented similar conditions in the prisons in Venezuela. Starting in the 1990s, Venezuelan prisons have increasingly been characterised by the retreat of state order and the ascendance of a complex self-governed prison hierarchy that is thriving on an illegal economy within and beyond prison walls. Venezuela's prison population rose significantly in the 1980s and 1990s in line with increasing marginalisation and inequality under subsequent neoliberal regimes (see Strønen (Chap. 7), this volume). However, as Antillano et al. (2016) note, the current penal system in 'Bolivarian' Venezuela contradicts conventional wisdoms of a correlation between reduced socio-economic inequality and a milder punitive approach to crime and delinquency. Whilst Venezuela's prison population dipped significantly in the beginning of the twenty-first century—a period characterised by expansive pro-poor social policies and a political discourse emphasising structural explanatory models for crime—the prison population has been on a steady rise for the past near ten years (Antillano et al. 2016:200).

In contrast to the neoliberal period—when the rise of the incarcerated population coincided with the increase in poverty, exclusion and inequality—during Chavismo the relation seems to be inverse: a substantial improvement social indicators for the poor goes hand by hand with an increase in the penal population. (Antillano et al. 2016:201)

Antillano et al. (2016:2001) explain this apparent paradox through underlining the lopsided effects of social policies in the face of structural inequalities. Post-industrial societies, and not least rent-based countries such as Venezuela, continue to produce 'surplus' populations that 'remain excluded and marginalized and that are resistant to strategies of social inclusion' (p. 201).

Gledhill (2013) has also pointed out contradictions in the Brazilian state's security politics under the Lula and Rousseff administrations. As also noted in several of the chapters in this volume (Ystanes (Chap. 4), Sørbøe (Chap. 5), Costa (Chap. 3) and Lavros Pinta (Chap. 6)), these governments rolled out a series of reforms that effectively reduced poverty and inequality levels in the country. Yet so, security policies implemented in the major cities during their tenure were also characterised by the targeting of poor communities—and young men in particular. Above all, this included the increased police and military presence in impoverished communities and a 'war' against gangs involved in drug trafficking. Focusing in particular on policies rolled out in Salvador do Bahia aimed at detracting young men from entering into the consumption and trafficking of drugs, Gledhill writes that:

> The danger of this focus is that it singles out particular communities as the source to delinquency and violence for the whole city, transforming their social problems stemming from poverty, the lack of clarity in land- and property rights, and the deficient infrastructure and life conditions, into the problems that threatens the security of all residents of the city. Such a "securitisation" of social problems runs the risk of brushing all the residents in these communities over the same comb. (Gledhill 2013:30, authors' translation from Spanish)

These comparative observations alert us to the structural underpinnings as well as cultural framing of '*mano dura*' policies, regardless of political inclination right or left. Whilst Brazil, Honduras and Venezuela followed significantly different political trajectories during the Pink Tide époque, all three countries are carrying the legacy of long-term structural inequalities and marginalisation that has produced a 'surplus' population of primarily young, poor, coloured and unskilled male. In a de-proletarised economy, combined with the ascendance of a cross-border drug and crime economy across the Latin American continent, many of these young men end up in the penal system. Simultaneously, rising levels of violence and the pan-continental rise of the '*mano dura*' approach consolidate public and political demands for taking a punitive, rather than rehabilitory stance, towards (real or perceived) criminal elements.

Final Reflections

The US sociologist Alice Goffman speaks of two different trajectories that take persons from childhood to adulthood; one goes via the education system, the other goes via the penal system. As many young men in the neighbourhood she worked entered their late teens or early 20s, 'the penal system has largely replaced the educational system as the key setting of young adulthood' (Goffman 2014:107). In the United States, it is mostly black men living in poor, segregated neighbourhoods that end up reaching adulthood via the penal system. This process reinforces 'racialised' socio-economic inequalities that the full granting of civil rights to African Americans was meant to eliminate. While other teenagers are freshmen or seniors in high school, the young men and boys Goffman worked with were defendants and inmates, spending time in courtrooms rather than classrooms, attending sentencing hearings and probation meetings rather than proms and graduations. As she notes:

> As the criminal justice system has come to occupy a central place in their lives and by extension those of their partners and families, it has become a principal base around which they construct a meaningful social world. It is through their dealings with the police, the courts, the parole board, and the prisons that young men and those close to them work out who they are and who they are to each other. (Goffman 2014:107)

Of course, there are numerous differences between the Honduran and the US legal system, and the inmate-governed prisons in the former cannot meaningfully be compared to the highly securitised US prisons. Nevertheless, Goffman's work points to some important comparative parallels. The prison system itself serves as a centrifugal site for the socialisation of group membership cut off from 'official society.' Just as in the United States, inmates in Honduras are stuck in the punitive system during their most formative years, making it extremely difficult to rebuild their lives once they get out even if they should so wish. Moreover, just as the young, black men in Goffman's case, the Honduran prison population belongs to those groups in society that were crowded out from the educational system and the labour market in the first place. In sum, all of these features underline how structural processes, legal systems and punitive ideologies are conditioning the individual life trajectories and opportunities of the prison population.

By stressing this point, it is not our intention to underestimate the seriousness of crime and violence in the Latin America continent or to deprive criminal actors of a will and agency of their own. However, we contend that it is paramount to take a critical look at the historical trajectories, local/international political agendas and underlying racial and social profiling that propels and justifies hard-line security agendas. As Gledhill notes, 'it is necessary to look beyond the smoke screen created by the securitisation of poverty in order to capture social realities and power relations' (Gledhill 2013:53, authors' translation from Spanish), and ultimately, be able to create public policies that lead to permanent transformations. As this chapter has sought to address, the current 'iron fist' approach to crime in Honduras is taking place within a dense history of structural marginalisation, fuelled by the effects of the neoliberal era and its continuation up until today. Moreover, since the coup in 2009, these policies are taking place in the context of an escalating political proclivity to subdue unwanted social groups. Additionally, the US War on Drugs has contributed to a further violent and militarised persecution of real or perceived criminal elements, whilst the underlying factors and processes fuelling the drug economy are largely left unchallenged. Ultimately, this has resulted in a dramatic increase in the targeted incarceration of young, poor and dark-skinned men with few prospects for becoming inserted into an 'ordinary life' when they eventually are released from prison. This bodes for a perpetuation of, rather than a solution to, Honduras' security situation, which, in turn, will continue to reproduce the country's historically informed legacy of entrenched inequalities.

Notes

1. Koonings and Kruijt aptly point out that the 'new violence' means that 'a variety of social actors pursue a variety of objectives on the basis of coercive strategies and methods' (2004:8). This new form of violence is not directed towards the state, that is, to overthrow the status quo. Rather, it is a

'democratisation' of violence (Koonings and Kruijt 2004; Rotker 2002) that can target anyone.
2. On the other hand, these neoliberal policies also entailed modernising the state institutions opening up for more citizen participation. For instance, human rights groups become more organised. The Honduran governments also attempted to increase youth participation through the creation of the National Institute of Youth (*Instituto Nacional de Juventud*) and the National Forum for Youth (*Foro Nacional de Juventud*).
3. The traditional elites and the military believed Zelaya wanted to change the constitution to allow re-election for a second term, which is prohibited in the current constitution. Ironically, Honduras's current president, Juan Orlando Hernández from the National Party, is also seeking to change the constitution to allow re-election. However, contrary to Zelaya, the traditional elites and the military have backed him. On 26 April 2015, the National Congress approved the re-election of the Honduran president.
4. There are also strong indicators of US complicity in the coup, see Beeton and Chun Tang (2016).
5. Comité Nacional de Prevención Contra La Tortura, Tratos Crueles Inhumanos o Degradantes,

References

Aguirre, Carlos. 2005. *The Criminals of Lima and Their Worlds: The Prison Experience (1850–1935)*. Durham: Duke University Press.

Antillano, Andrés, et al. 2016. The Venezuelan Prison: From Neoliberalism to the Bolivarian Revolution. *Crime Law and Social Change* 65: 195–211.

Beeton, Dan and Ming Chun Tang. 2016 Hillary's Role in Honduran Coup Sunk US Relations With Latin America to a New Low. *Counterpunch*, June 1. Available at http://www.counterpunch.org/2016/06/01/hillarys-role-in-honduran-coup-sunk-us-relations-with-latin-america-to-a-new-low/. Accessed 18 Apr 2017.

Blitzer, Jonathan. 2016. Should the U.S. Still Be Sending Military Aid to Honduras? *The New Yorker*, August 17. Available at http://www.newyorker.com/news/news-desk/should-the-u-s-still-be-sending-military-aid-to-honduras. Accessed 17 Apr 2017.

Bosworth, James. 2010. *Honduras: Organized Crime Gaining Amid Political Crisis*. Woodrow Wilson Center for International Scholars. Available at https://www.wilsoncenter.org/sites/default/files/Bosworth.FIN.pdf. Accessed 18 Apr 2017.

Bosworth, Mary, B. Bowling, and M. Lee. 2008. Globalization, Ethnicity and Racism: An Introduction. *Theoretical Criminology* 12 (3): 263–273.

Bourgois, Phillipe. 2003. *In Search of Respect. Selling Crack in El Barrio*. 2nd ed. Cambridge: Cambrigde University Press.
Broch-Due, Vigdis. 1995. *Poverty Paradoxes: The Economy of Engendered Needs. Occasional Papers, The Nordic Africa Institute*. Uppsala: Nordiska Afrikainstiuttet.
Bull, Benedicte. 2016. Governance in the Aftermath of Neoliberalism: Aid, Elites and State Capacity in Central America. *Forum for Development Studies* 43 (1): 89–111.
Bull, Benedicte, F. Castellacci, and Y. Kasahara. 2014. *Business Groups and Transnational Capitalism in Central America. Economic and Political Strategies*. Houndmills/Basingstoke/Hampshire: Palgrave Macmillan.
Caldeira, Teresa P.R. 2000. *City of Walls. Crime, Segregation, and Citizenship in Sao Paulo*. Berkeley: University of California Press.
CIDH. 2013. *Informe sobre la situación de las personas privadas de libertad en Honduras*. Documento 6 (18 de marzo), Organización de los Estados Americanos, Comisión Interamericana de Derechos Humanos. Available at https://www.oas.org/es/cidh/ppl/docs/pdf/HONDURAS-PPL-2013ESP.pdf. Accessed 18 Apr 2017.
CONAPREV. 2011. *Diagnóstico del Sistema Pentienciario en Honduras*. Comité Nacional de Prevención Contra la Tortura, Tratos Crueles, Inhumanos o Degradantes, Tegucigalpa, Honduras.
Darke, Sacha, and Maria Lucía Karam. 2016. Latin American Prisons. In *Handbook on Prisons*, ed. Y. Jewkes, J. Bennet, and Ben Crewe, 2nd ed., 460–474. Abingdon: Routledge.
De Lissavoy, Noah. 2013. Conceptualizing the Carceral Turn: Neoliberalism, Racism, and Violation. *Critical Sociology* 39 (5): 739–755.
Fawcett, Caroline. 2001. *Latin American Youth in Transition: A Policy Paper on Youth Unemployment in Latin America and the Caribbean*. Sustainable Development Department, Social Development Division, Labor Markets Policy Briefs Series, Inter-American Development Bank.
Garland, David. 2002. *The Culture of Control: Crime and Social Order in Contemporary Society*. Chicago: University of Chicago Press.
Gledhill, John. 2013. La mala administración de la seguridad pública. *Revista de Antropología Social* 22: 25–57.
Global Witness. 2017. *Honduras. The Deadliest Place to Defend the Planet*. London: Global Witness.
Goffman, Alice. 2014. *On the Run: Fugitive Life in an American City*. New York: Picador.
Golash-Boza, Tanya. 2015. *Deported. Immigrant Policing, Disposable Labor, and Global Capitalism*. New York/London: New York University Press.
Gordon, Todd, and J.R. Webber. 2011. Canada and the Honduran Coup. *Bulletin of Latin American Research* 30 (3): 328–342.

Grosso, Joseph. 2014. The Honduras Drug War. *Counterpunch*, June 27. Available at http://www.counterpunch.org/2014/06/27/the-honduras-drug-war/. Accessed 17 Apr 2017.

Gutiérrez Rivera, Lirio. 2010. Discipline and Punish? Youth Gangs' Response to 'Zero Tolerance' Policies in Honduras. *Bulletin of Latin American Research* 29 (4): 492–504.

———. 2017. The World of the 'Rondines': Trust, Waiting and Time in a Latin American Prison. In *Carceral Mobilities: Interrogating Movement in Incarceration*, ed. Jennifer Turner and Kimberley Peters, 178–190. Abingdon: Routledge.

Hallinan, Conn. 2009. Honduran Coup: The U.S. Connection. *Foreign Policy in Focus*, August 5. Available at http://fpif.org/honduran_coup_the_us_connection/. Accessed 18 Apr 2017.

Hunter, Margaret. 2007. The Persistent Problem of Colorism: Skin Tone, Status, and Inequality. *Sociology Compass* 1 (1): 237–254.

ILO, International Labour Office. 2007. *The Informal Economy*. International Labour Office (ILO). Available at http://www.ilo.org/wcmsp5/groups/public/---ed_norm/--relconf/documents/meetingdocument/wcms_gb_298_esp_4_en.pdf. Accessed 20 Dec 2013.

Jüttersonke, Oliver, R. Muggah, and D. Rodgers. 2009. Gangs, Urban Violence, and Security Interventions in Central America. *Security Dialogue* 40 (4–5): 373–397.

Koonings, Kees, and Kruijt Dirk. 2004. Armed Actors, Organized Violence, and State Failure in Latin America: A Survey of Issues and Arguments. In *Armed Actors. Organized Violence and State Failure in Latin America*, ed. Kees Koonings and Dirk Kruijt, 5–15. London: Zed Books.

Larkins, Erika M. Robb. 2015. *The Spectacular Favela: Violence in Modern Brazil*. Oakland: University of California Press.

Lewis, Oscar. 1966. *La Vida: A Puerto Rican Family in the Culture of Poverty*. San Juan/New York: Random House.

Milton, Cynthia E. 2007. *The Many Meanings of Poverty. Colonialism, Social Compacts, and Assistance in Eighteenth-Century Ecuador*. Stanford: Stanford University Press.

Müller, Markus-Michael. 2009. Wenn Null Toleranz und Zebrochene Fensterscheiben auf Reisen gehen: Globalisierung und die Restrukturierung des historichen Zentrums in Mexiko Stadt. *Kriminologisches Journal* 41 (2): 82–99.

Oetller, Anika, Sebastian Huhn, and Peter Peetz. 2009. Contemporary Discourses on Violence in Central American Newspapers. *International Communication Gazette* 71 (4): 243–261.

Peetz, Peter. 2011. *Maras, Medien, Militär. Gesellschaftlicher Diskurs und staatliche Politik gegenüber Jugendbanden in Honduras*. Münster: LIT Verlag.

Penglase, Ben. 2010. The Owner of the Hill: Masculinity and Drug-trafficking in Rio de Janeiro, Brazil. *The Journal of Latin American and Caribbean Anthropology* 15 (2): 317–337.

Portes, Alejandro, and Kelly Hoffman. 2003. Latin American Class Structures: Their Composition and Change During the Neoliberal Era. *Latin American Research Review* 38 (1): 41–82.

Robinson, William I. 2003. *Transnational Conflicts. Central America, Social Change, and Globalization.* London: Verso.

Rodgers, Dennis. 2009. Slum Wars of the 21st Century: Gangs, Mano Dura and the New Urban Geography of Conflict in Central America. *Development and Change* 40 (5): 949–976.

Rotker, Susana, ed. 2002. *Citizens of Fear: Urban Violence in Latin America.* New Brunswick: Rutgers University Press.

Salomón, Leticia. 1994. *La Violencia en Honduras, 1980–1993.* Tegucigalpa: CEDOH (Centro de Documentación de Honduras).

Salomón, Leticia, Julieta Castellanos, and Mirna Flores. 1999. *La delincuencia juvenil: Los menores infractores en Honduras.* Tegucigalpa: CEDOH (Centro de Documentación de Honduras).

Salvatore, Ricardo, and Carlos Aguirre. 1996. The Birth of the Penitentiary in Latin America: Toward an Interpretative Social History of Prisons. In *The Birth of the Penitentiary in Latin America. Essays on Criminology, Prison Reform, and Social Control, 1830–1940*, ed. R. Salvatore and C. Aguirre, 1–22. Austin: University of Texas Press.

Shipley, Taylor. 2016. *"Not a Single Crack Where the Light Can Come In." Civil-military Relations in Contemporary Honduras*, CMI Working Paper 2016(1). Bergen: Chr. Michelsen Institute.

Stepan, N.L. 1991. *The Hour of Eugenics'. Race, Gender, and Nation in Latin America.* Ithaca/London: Cornell University Press.

Strocka, Cordula. 2006. Youth Gangs in Latin America. *SAIS Review of International Affairs* 26 (2): 133–146.

Strønen, Iselin. 2014. *The Revolutionary Petro-state. Change, Continuity, and Popular Politics in Venezuela.* PhD Dissertation, The University of Bergen.

UNDP. 2014. *Human Development Report 2014. Sustaining Human Progress: Reducing Vulnerabilities and Building Resilience.* New York: United Nations Development Programme.

Ungar, Mark, and Leticia Salomón. 2012. Community Policing in Honduras: Local Impacts of a National Program. *Policing and Society* 22 (1): 28–42.

UNODC. 2012. *Transnational Organized Crime in Central America and the Caribbean. A Threat Assessment.* Vienna: United Nations Office on Drugs and Crime.

Wacquant, Loïc. 2009. *Punishing the Poor: The Neoliberal Government of Social Insecurity.* Durham: Duke University Press.

———. 2011. The Punitive Regulation of Poverty in the Neoliberal Age. *Open Democracy*. Available at https://www.opendemocracy.net/5050/loïc-wacquant/punitive-regulation-of-poverty-in-neoliberal-age. Accessed 24 Mar 2017.

World Prison Brief. 2016. *Honduras*. World Prison Brief. Available at http://www.prisonstudies.org/country/honduras. Accessed 30 Mar 2017.

Ziccardi, Alicia. 2008. Pobreza y exclusión social en las ciudades del siglo XXI. In *Procesos de Urbanización de la Pobreza y Nuevas Formas de Exclusión Social*, ed. A. Ziccardi. Bogotá: Siglo del Hombre Editores and CLACSO-CROP.

Open Access This chapter is licensed under the terms of the Creative Commons Attribution 4.0 International License (http://creativecommons.org/licenses/by/4.0/), which permits use, sharing, adaptation, distribution and reproduction in any medium or format, as long as you give appropriate credit to the original author(s) and the source, provide a link to the Creative Commons license and indicate if changes were made.

The images or other third party material in this chapter are included in the chapter's Creative Commons license, unless indicated otherwise in a credit line to the material. If material is not included in the chapter's Creative Commons license and your intended use is not permitted by statutory regulation or exceeds the permitted use, you will need to obtain permission directly from the copyright holder.

PART IV

Land, the Eternal Legacy of Inequality

CHAPTER 10

Settlers and Squatters: The Production of Social Inequalities in the Peruvian Desert

Astrid B. Stensrud

INTRODUCTION

The Majes Irrigation Project (MIP) in southern Peru has transformed 15,800 hectares of previously unoccupied desert into fertile and productive land. MIP was constructed shortly after the land reform in the 1970s, in a time when progress and equality were on the political agenda. The first settler farmers, who arrived in 1983, are celebrated as strong pioneering men that started from zero and made progress through hard work. One of the goals in MIP, as it developed in the 1980s and 1990s, was to transform farmers into entrepreneurs that would compete on the global market. More than 30 years later, and after the most radical and quickest programme of neoliberal structural adjustment in Latin America, many of the first settlers have lost their farms or are struggling with debt. In the same period, Majes and its main urban centre Villa El Pedregal, has evolved into a hub of business and work and has become known as 'a place of opportunities' (*un lugar de oportunidades*) with a booming economy. During the last decade, thousands of people have migrated from the poor rural highlands in search of work or informal business in Majes, and these new migrants settle in the desert surrounding the irrigated areas.

A.B. Stensrud (✉)
University of Oslo, Oslo, Norway

© The Author(s) 2018
M. Ystanes, I.Å. Strønen (eds.), *The Social Life of Economic Inequalities in Contemporary Latin America*, Approaches to Social Inequality and Difference, DOI 10.1007/978-3-319-61536-3_10

The inhabitants of Majes come from different places, with various cultural, educational and economic backgrounds, and this diversity is emphasized interchangeably as a problem or strength.

In this chapter, I will discuss how Majes has emerged as 'a place of opportunities' through relations of capital and labour, in which inequality is also (re-)produced.[1] The analysis is inspired by Bear et al. (2015), who express an interest in 'how inequality emerges from heterogeneous processes through which people, labour, sentiments, plants, animals, and lifeways are converted into resources for various projects of production'. I argue that economic inequalities, which are embedded in differences based on conceptions of race and gender, have increased during the past three decades of neoliberalism in Peru, where working conditions have worsened and informality, precarity and uncertainty prevail. I refer to neoliberalism as a set of policies and practices inspired by a political ideology according to which human well-being can best be advanced by liberating individual entrepreneurial freedoms and skills within an institutional framework that secures private property rights, free markets and free trade (Harvey 2005). The neoliberal paradigm relies on individuals who are induced to self-manage according to market principles of discipline, efficiency and competiveness (Ong 2006). However, for most workers and farmers, the neoliberal 'freedoms' have implied increased vulnerability and uncertainty. I will therefore explore how families experience debt and loss, yet continue struggling to get ahead in a precarious informal economy.

In Latin America, including Peru, working conditions for the poor have *always* been precarious (Millar 2014). The analytical concepts have changed, however; the term citizenship had largely replaced class as a means of analysing the political struggles of the poor in Latin America at the beginning of this century (Roberts 2004). I argue that the inequalities in Majes are manifest in structures of gender, ideas of race and culture and emergent class relationships, understood as bundles of 'unstable, uneven, contradictory and antagonistic relational interdependences' (Kalb 2015:14). However, these class formations, which are emerging from the unequal conversions of humans into resources, are not always complete, consistent or coherent (Bear et al. 2015). I will show how inequality is embedded in the intersections of class, gender and race and argue that these differences did not diminish with the so-called Pink Tide that Ollanta Humala (2011–2016) barely flirted with (see Introduction (Chap. 1) of this volume, just as they did not disappear with the left-wing reforms in the 1970s.

The Diversity of Majes: Ambivalent Racism

The population of Majes consists of people from all over Peru. The majority of the recent migrants come from the impoverished rural Andean highlands: mostly from the south, but also from central Peru. The southern and central highlands constitute the main areas of what has been called 'deep Peru' (*Perú profundo*). The expression 'deep Peru' was first used by the Peruvian historian Basadre who in 1943 distinguished between 'two Perus': the state (*país legal*, or legal country) and the nation composed by its people (*país profundo*, or deep country). While Basadre referred to all sectors of the population, and not only indigenous culture, later usages of the phrase have changed and now it has come to mean 'the historical roots of Indianness as a component of Peru's sense of nationhood' (Mayer 1992:192). In his report from a massacre in the south-central highlands in 1983, during the war between the guerrillas and the armed forces, the Peruvian author Mario Vargas Llosa used the phrase to describe a country divided in space and time. One part was the official Peru and the other profound, consisting of the indigenous population: an 'Indian Peru' that was economically depressed, 'miserable' and 'primitive' (Mayer 1992:193). In an article in *New York Times*, Vargas Llosa described the village where the massacre happened: 'At these altitudes, the land is poor, the isolation is almost absolute, and the customs are archaic' (Vargas Llosa 1983). More than three decades have passed, but the phrase 'deep Peru' is still used in Majes and the rest of (mostly coastal and urban) Peru to describe the indigenous character of people in the Andean highlands, and racist connotations are still prevalent.

However, since most people have family and connections to the indigenous Andes, racist attitudes are highly ambivalent. When talking to people in Majes—whether they were municipal workers, state engineers, farmers or businesspeople—many complained to me that the people here 'have no [local] cultural identity', because 'they come from all places and they all come with their own culture'. Some went on to explain that there is 'a struggle of cultures', 'a clash of cultures' or 'a crossing of cultures and races'. A more positive comment was that 'we drink from all the cultural sources'. In his book on the local history of Majes, Edgar Zamalloa writes: 'the population of Majes is made up of men of all the bloods [*sangres*], coming from all parts of deep Peru, who have come and/or have brought or are introducing dances and customs from their different places of origin' (Zamalloa 2013:347). Zamalloa is also the author of the Majes hymn,

Himno de Majes, which has provided the phrase that was chosen the official slogan of the district municipality of Majes: *Con la fuerza de todas las sangres*, 'With the force of all the bloods'. Coming from the highland region of Apurímac, Zamalloa was inspired by his compatriot José María Arguedas, the anthropologist who authored the novel *Todas las sangres* ('All the bloods'), a title that refers to the cultural diversity of Peru. From the colonial era, differences in culture and class have been—and are still—racialised in Peru, and this is reflected in the (often used) plural form of blood.

Nevertheless, ethnic and racialised categories are intrinsically linked to social class and place, which in practice means that a person from a Quechua-speaking rural community who moves to the city, acquires formal education, learns Spanish and adopts an urban lifestyle is no longer considered to be 'indigenous' but *mestizo* (van den Berghe and Primov 1977). Class and education is translated into economic and social capital and can make a person to be considered 'socially white', given the geographical construction of race, where the coastal line is 'white' and the highlands are indigenous (de la Cadena 2000). In other words, racialised categories are fluid and can be changed through social and geographical mobility. These categories can also vary with gender, however, as women are often considered to be more 'Indian' (de la Cadena 1991). In Majes, this is mostly reflected in clothing and language, as women from the highlands often dress in traditional skirts and hats and sometimes talk in Quechua or Aymara among each other at the marketplace, while men tend to dress in urban clothes and only speak in Spanish.

The precarity and uncertainties that have followed neoliberal deregulations affect everyone, yet in different degrees: those who have historically been discriminated against based on their ethnicity and/or gender, and who always have had less access to resources and social capital, are also those who suffer most from the new kinds of precarity in labour and farming. In today's Majes, inequalities are manifest in access to water, land and capital and also in the ability to plan a future, which is a privilege that financial security allows.

'Peasant, the Landlord Will No Longer Eat Your Poverty': Agrarian Reform

In 1971, the military left-wing government of Juan Velasco Alvarado (1968–1975) started the execution of MIP: the Condoroma Dam was built 4158 meters above sea level, from which water is released downriver and led into a system of 101 kilometres of tunnels and canals through Colca Valley. In Majes, the water is led into a network of irrigation canals crisscrossing the arid pampa at 1000 m.a.s.l., where a stable and warm climate all year round secures good conditions for agriculture. MIP aimed to create economic growth based on agricultural and industrial production, and to foster development for the whole region. After the water arrived to the pampa of Majes in the end of 1982, the first settlers (*colonos*) started to work on their land. In the first group, there were 592 *colonos* who had been selected by draw according to the different categories they belonged to: smallholding farmers, landless peasants, agricultural workers and professionals—mostly agronomists, but also doctors, lawyers and engineers (Zamalloa 2013). One engineer who had worked there for 30 years, called the Majes project a *populismo culto*, which can mean a 'cultured', 'learned' or 'educated' populism, because of these different categories. Therefore, he said, here we have all kinds of people; the irrigation project was not only for the poor, but also for people of all professions, and from all parts of the country. By calling it *culto*, he alluded to the general praise of formal education in Peru, which elevates people in the hierarchies of class and race. In MIP, all settlers got an equal start: each got the opportunity to buy 5 hectares of land, which was considered a basic family unit, with a subsidised loan from the state-owned Agrarian Bank (Zamalloa 2013). Today there are 2600 farms in the irrigated areas of Majes.

MIP was implemented soon after the 1969 agrarian reform and became part of Velasco's endeavour to bring Peru out of feudalism and poverty and into an era of equality and progress. Before 1969, 3.9 per cent of the population controlled 56 per cent of the land, most of it in the form of large holdings (Seligmann 1995). In 1968, Velasco's 'Revolutionary Government of the Armed Forces' (*Gobierno Revolucionario de las Fuerzas Armadas*) started to nationalise the land, water, industry and banks. By using the power of popular mobilisation, the plan was to defeat the oligarchy, to reduce the power of the landowning elites and increase economic productivity. Cant (2012) shows how posters were used in mobilising the peasants: 'Slogans such as "Land without masters" and "We are free, the revolution is giving us land" put forth an emancipatory vision of a "new Peru", articulating the government's aspirations towards a more equal and integrated society' (Cant 2012:3). In his speech to introduce the agrarian reform on the Day of the Peasant, 24 June 1969, Velasco talked about forging a better nation that would be the owner of its own destiny, with justice and freedom. He famously concluded by saying: 'Peasant, the landlord will no longer eat your poverty!' (Velasco 1969). Between 1969 and 1974, 175,000 families received 4.5 million hectares of land (Cant 2012:4). In less than a decade, the land reform succeeded in ending the dominant power of the *hacendados* and introducing a system of cooperative farms (Collier 1978). The Velasco regime believed that they could uproot racial discrimination by destroying the power of the landed oligarchy, but they were unable to achieve economic equality and a respect for ethnic differences at the same time (Seligmann 1995). Velasco officially replaced the ethnic and racial term *indio* (Indian) by the class-related term *campesino* (peasant), but peasants are still discriminated against in today's Peru.

However, the new agrarian cooperatives, which were largely managed by technocrats and bureaucrats, encountered huge problems. State control led to corruption, clientelistic relationships and internal conflicts (Hunefeldt 1997). Lack of planning, training and technical support for the farmers were some of the reasons that the reform mainly failed (Rénique 1991). The shortcomings of the reform, in addition to rural poverty and expectations of a better life in the cities, led to a massive increase in migration from the highlands to the urban coast. A major part of the current population in Majes come from the regions of Puno, Cusco and Apurimac, where the agrarian reform had profound effects on socio-economic relations. In the Colca Valley, however, the peasants were never dominated by the haciendas (Guillet 1992), yet many have migrated to Majes because of poverty and lack of opportunities, and more recently due to climate change, experienced as seasonal instability and water scarcity (Stensrud 2015).

LA LEY DEL CHINITO: THE NEOLIBERAL TURN

> Well, now we have the law of *el chinito* [Alberto Fujimori][2]: the law of supply and demand [...], so the market manages itself. When the production is high – boom! – [the price] falls. [...] So then there is an atrocious loss for the farmer.

The farmer who told me about the 'law of the *chinito*' arrived in Majes in 1983. Since then, he has built a dairy farm with 20 cows, and has been combining the cultivation of alfalfa fodder with various other crops. As many other farmers in Majes, he describes the production of food as a lottery, because one never knows if one will win or lose until it is time to sell the products. Therefore, he has kept the dairy production as a secure base:

although milk does not pay well, it is a safe income. Dairy farming has been the main economic activity in Majes since the start, but it is dominated by the monopsony of the Gloria Group that buys the milk from the farmers.

The turn towards neoliberal economic policies started with General Morales Bermúdez (1975–1980), who replaced Velasco in a coup d'état, and was continued under President Belaúnde Terry (1980–1985). In his first presidency, Alan García (1985–1990) tried to reverse the liberalization process through what was termed a 'heterodox' economic policy. García ambitiously proposed social reform for the poor majority, without wanting to alienate the business elites. The result was a deep economic and social crisis, with soaring inflation, devaluation, rising unemployment, shortages of staples and malnutrition (Klarén 2000). In 1990, Alberto Fujimori, a populist with no affiliation to any traditional political party or to the white oligarchy, was elected president. He quickly established an extreme variant of the structural adjustment that was advocated by the 'Washington consensus' and the World Bank (Gonzales de Olarte 1993). The so-called Fuji shock consisted in radical austerity measures: higher interest rates and taxes and a slashing of price subsidies and social spending. The shock was followed by deregulation of markets, massive privatisation and incentives for international investment (Klarén 2000; Crabtree 2002). In 1991, President Fujimori issued a 'labour flexibilisation' decree, which significantly altered the laws regulating job security and the right to organise (Klarén 2000). Since then, the majority of workers in Peru are informally employed and thus deprived of benefits and protection. Simultaneously, a strong ideology of entrepreneurship as the way out of poverty and towards progress has been fostered (see also Ødegaard, Chap. 8 in this book).

In agrarian policy, the neoliberal restructuring in the 1990s entailed a total reversal of the agrarian reform. All forms of subsidies to farmers were cancelled, and the last vestiges of protectionist agrarian laws were removed, allowing unlimited private property (Mayer 2009). The 1995 Land Law (*Ley de Tierras*) promoted the titling of individual land ownership, abolished the previous upper limits on personal landholding and allowed the state to sell land currently in public ownership. The new law opened the way to the capitalisation of agriculture by enabling titleholders to raise mortgages (Crabtree 2002). This deregulation had long-term consequences, and in Majes it has led to a dramatic increase in the price of land. Peasants from the highlands can no longer afford to buy land and are reduced to rural proletarians working for landowners and the large-scale agribusiness that was welcomed in Majes in the 1990s. In 1998, a land property of 1288 hectares called Pampa Baja, where new irrigation infrastructure just had been installed, was sold to a private company. Today, the Pampa Baja Group has employed 2000 workers and produces fruit for export.[3] Fujimori's structural adjustment also affected farmers' ability to plan cultivation of food and future incomes. Among his first moves was to scrap price controls, allowing these to be set by market forces. He also closed down the institution that controlled food imports and eliminated the Agrarian Bank as a source of subsidised credit to producers (Crabtree 2002). Private lenders charge very high interest rates when they lend money to small-scale farmers due to the high risk involved.

The election of Alejandro Toledo as president in 2001 was seen as a return to democracy after Fujimori's authoritarian rule. Nevertheless, in spite of promises about ending privatisation and creating employment, he continued on the neoliberal road and so did Alan García in his second presidency (2006–2011). Toledo started the work on a Free Trade Agreement with the USA, and when García signed the agreement in 2007, he declared that this was a great day for democracy, social justice and freedom. Earlier that year, however, García had made social protests and strikes illegal, accusing the opponents of private investment and free trade—labour unions and indigenous movements—for obstructing progress due to old ideologies, laziness and inertia (García Pérez 2007).

During the presidential election campaigns in 2006 and 2011, Ollanta Humala, who became leader of the Nationalist party (*Partido Nacionalista Peruano*) in 2005, promised to fight against privatisation and imperialism, decrease the gap between rich and poor and work for 'social inclusion'. Humala, who is son of a Quechua-speaking communist lawyer and has great admiration for Velasco, got massive support, especially among indigenous peasants and working poor in the central and southern highlands. This support was a clear expression of popular anti-neoliberal sentiments, and Humala's candidature is associated with the 'Pink Tide' in South America. However, after winning the election in 2011, he did not keep his promise of a 'great transformation'. He appointed neoliberal technocrats from the previous administration and maintained the neoliberal policies favouring private investment (Poole and Rénique 2012). When Majes-Siguas II, the second phase of the irrigation project, was inaugurated in 2014, Humala promised that water would never be privatised. Yet, he allowed the private consortium Angostura-Siguas to get the concession for Majes-Siguas II. Farmers in MIP are afraid that the consortium will increase the water tariffs in order to recover its investments, and that this concession will benefit large agribusiness corporations and not small- and medium-scale farmers. In the presidential elections of 2016, the left-wing candidate Veronica Mendoza got huge support from people in the highlands who had also voted for Humala. She did not enter the second round, however, which was fought between Keiko Fujimori, the daughter of Fujimori, and Pedro Pablo Kuczynski, a white man with extensive experience from banking and mining industry, who was minister of energy and mining under Belaúnde and minister of economy and finance under Toledo. Hence, the election of Kuczynski is seen as a victory for continued neoliberalism in Peru.

'People Suffer Here Also': Children of Settlers

The very first settler arrived in Majes in October 1982, two months before the water came, and he has seen many of his fellow farmers lose their land: 'Of the first group of settlers, now there is only half left'. When I interviewed him about agriculture in Majes, he talked about the volatile prices of the free market and the farmers' dependency of the intermediary merchants:

> The prices always fall, when everyone sow potatoes, the prices fall [...] In 2009, there was a good harvest of ají paprika; then the price fell from 2,80 USD per kilo to 0,80 cents. The same happened with the onions [...] There is more risk now than 30 years ago; now there is free market. Earlier we had stable prices, but Fujimori made free market. [...] The financial institutions that give loans take a lot of interests; 18 per cent and until 30 per cent! Some get indebted because the intermediaries don't pay the products that they have bought and taken away. (17 February 2014)

Among the farmers in Majes, Velasco is remembered as a hero, both for ending the power of the landowning oligarchy and for starting the construction of MIP. Fujimori, on the other hand, is given much of the blame for everything that went wrong because of the 'free market'.

José is the son of one of the settlers who lost his land because of debt.[4] José's grandparents were very poor when they lived in his home village; they only had a tiny piece of land and a couple of cows, and they mostly worked as labourers on the land of others. Their nine children went to Arequipa city very young to work and go to school. When the Majes project opened, all the siblings registered and four brothers got farms:

José's father and three uncles. They were all dreaming about coming here and changing their lives; 'to have another way of being'. The brothers were always united and worked together, they told me. Instead of hiring help like others did, they helped each other. However, José's father had bad luck and was not able to pay his loan to the bank. The debt accumulated and he was forced to sell the farm. José's three uncles still have their farms, and sometimes José works with his cousins in the fields; he helps to rent machinery, to buy seeds and to sell the harvest. To make a living, José has worked in all kinds of jobs in different public offices, mainly as a driver or assistant, on temporary contracts. Steady employment is hard to find, and many people try to start businesses of their own. José and his wife bought a mini-bus on credit with the intention of making money in the transport business. When they finally got permission to work on one of the bus routes in Majes, however, they soon realised that the income was not enough to pay the debt and have a profitable business. They ended up selling the car.

As the daughter of a farmer who came with the third group of settlers and later got into debt, Martina has first-hand experience of the tensions and sufferings that debt creates. 'People suffer here also. Not everyone has access to credits and capital to work, they have debts', she said. She came from Colca Valley as a ten-year-old in 1990, when her parents settled into the new farm, and she learned early the value of hard work. Her father was not only a farmer but also a merchant who sold groceries from a market stall in Villa El Pedregal. When his potato harvest failed three times in a row and the prices fell, he got caught up in debt. He is still carrying these debts until today. 'The interests are very high; you pay off and you pay off, but you never finish paying the debt', Martina said. When she was 17 or 18 years old, her father gathered his eight children to tell them that they should not expect any inheritance, but should take the opportunity to study. 'This stayed in my mind, and therefore I never expected anything from my parents', Martina told me.

Today, she is the owner of a market stall in Villa El Pedregal where she sells juice and sandwiches and also CDs and DVDs with popular Peruvian music. Martina started her business ten years ago, without any bank loans and credits, and it has grown little by little. She observes how all farmers and merchants work with credits nowadays; the merchants even take out credits from two or three banks. 'It is terrible to enter into debt', she said, remembering how she used to help her dad in his business and how she took part in his constant worries: 'it is stressful!'

As I had been living in Colca Valley, I told Martina that people there think that the people in Majes are rich. She agreed, since she had experienced the same attitudes in Colca: 'Yes, there they think that we have money. I see how they look at me: "she got money, therefore she is aloof and does not talk to us" … and I'm there all shy! They don't know that we also suffer. I live off my work!'.

Apparently, the fact that Martina lives in Majes with its booming economy, and that she works in her own business, make people in her home village assume that she believes herself to be 'better' than them. She certainly has climbed economically and socially according to the dominant hierarchy of class and race: she is no longer a peasant living in the highlands, but a businesswoman who lives near the coast. Within the marketplace in Majes, however, her small fruit juice stall, where she works long days and where her children do their homework after school, is one of the least profitable businesses compared to the meat and grocery vendors or the large-scale merchants (Photo 10.1).

In an upcoming expansion of the irrigation project—Majes-Siguas II—38,500 new hectares of land in the adjacent desert of Siguas will be

Photo 10.1 'New Hope' (*Nueva Esperanza*) is the name of one the marketplaces in Villa El Pedregal and the name of the association of vendors and merchants (*asociación de comerciantes*) who work there (Photo by the author)

irrigated. However, the land will be sold in large units of 200, 500 and 1000 hectares and not in five-hectare family units as in the first phase of MIP. Hence, there will not be any opportunities for the children of farmers to buy land, and people fear the dominance of large-scale agribusiness. Martina, however, was carefully optimistic about her children's opportunities in the future:

> We will grow here. As there is industrialisation all over, it will be the same here. In Siguas there will be companies like DANPER and Pampa Baja, and we will be employed in those companies. That is why I want my children to study and become professionals and technicians (*profesionales y técnicos*), so that they will not be only [unskilled] labourers (*peones*).

Most people still think that education is important for social mobility, although it is no guarantee to get formal and steady employment, which has become scarcer since the 1990s. Education as a means of ending poverty, social exclusion and 'underdevelopment' was for a long time a national project embraced by all social classes in Peru (Degregori 2008). Until the mid-twentieth century, there was a strong belief in the power of education to improve the 'Indians' racially, and the hegemonic acceptance of legitimate social hierarchies based on levels of formal education has prevailed until today (De la Cadena 2000). However, as part of neoliberal reform, state support to public education has decreased since the end of the 1970s (Degregori 2008), and the state's strategy for ending poverty and achieving development has gradually shifted its focus from education to the importance of entrepreneurship (see also Ødegaard, Chap. 8 in this book). Individuals are encouraged by state institutions and NGOs to start their own micro-enterprise in order to get ahead in life. In most of the life stories that I heard in Majes, men and women expressed great pride in being self-made. In the later years, however, the competition to get jobs, a successful business and a place to live have increased. The farmers' children not only compete against each other but also against the new migrants that come in search of a livelihood and a future.

'WE SHOULD MAKE AN EFFORT': SQUATTERS IN THE DESERT

Today, the majority of the population no longer consists of farmers: new people move in every day in search of work, business and land. According to the census of 2005, there were 35,334 inhabitants in Majes, while in 2014 the municipality considered the number of inhabitants to be somewhere between 100,000 and 120,000. The engineers who planned MIP originally designed urban centres and infrastructure for 40,000 inhabitants. Today's population is spreading out in the surrounding desert, where there is no infrastructure for the provision of water and electricity. The majority make a living as land labourers or factory workers or work in mechanical workshops or in the service sector. Many are self-employed as taxi drivers or food-and-drink vendors in the streets, in the marketplace or in small restaurants.

These migrants are not only searching for work but also a piece of land to build a house of their own. Earlier, the state distributed land lots at subsidised prices, but today many of these lots are sold expensively. Alternatively, those without money can 'invade' a piece of empty land and claim ownership. If a person can prove that she/he has built a house (many use straw mats, which is the cheapest material) and has lived on a lot for a certain amount of time—this is called 'possession' (*posesión*)—she/he can apply for the right to buy the land and get a formal title deed. In March 2014, the sub-director of the Municipal Office of Formalisation said that they had 20,000 case files in the office. Many of these have already paid their properties, and some have contracts, while others have yet to present documentation to support their case. In order to formalise ownership, obtain title deeds and eventually get access to water pipes, electricity, roads and other infrastructure, it is common to organise in neighbourhood associations. Meanwhile, people buy potable water from trucks that come once a week, or they boil water from the irrigation canals. Many of the recently arrived migrants join squatter groups, called 'invasion groups' (*grupos de invasión*), to occupy desert land collectively in and around Ciudad Majes. This practice has led to a lot of problems, however, since some of the leaders of these squatter groups have become land traffickers. The situation was often described as chaotic and corrupt, with many illegal transactions, conflicts and violence.

One of the women that live in the desert is Lucía, who was 38 years old in 2014. She was born into an Aymara-speaking peasant family in the highlands of Puno, and as a seven-year-old, she was sent to an aunt in Arequipa city. Lucía started working as a servant in the house of a middle-class family, but she did not know how much she earned because her aunt took the money. During the next ten years, she went back and forth between Arequipa and Puno, and then to the coastal city Tacna. She worked as a domestic servant for several families and experienced different degrees of exploitation. When she was 14 years old, an elderly man working at the marketplace in Tacna taught her how to read and write. At the age of 19 she got pregnant with a man who was also from Puno. They married and moved to Villa El Pedregal. He would not allow her to work, however, and she had to stay home in their rented room, taking care of their four children. After six years, she convinced her husband that she had the right to an education, and she studied hairdressing. She also started to work as a shop assistant. After 14 years of marriage, she left him.

Lucía dreamt about having her own grocery shop, and she joined an association of vendors who collectively invaded a piece of empty land. The goal was to obtain ownership to the land and to start their own marketplace, in which all participants would have a shop of their own. Although the leaders told them that the land was empty, they soon found out that another group had already invaded it, and that they were the second invaders. Still, the leaders gave all of them a kiosk of a few square meters to have a place to work and make their business. There were 600 stalls, and as some vendors brought their partners, children or cousins for support, they were more than a thousand people in total. They all paid their fees to the association, built kiosks and defended their place. The first invaders attacked them with homemade bombs, exploding bottles, and Lucía was very scared. She wanted to escape, but the others wouldn't let her go: 'You just have to endure', they told her, 'we do this to have a place to work'. And since she already had paid 200 soles,[5] she stayed. Some vendors started selling groceries there. Everyone had to attend the meetings, do collective work and pay the fees for the lawyer and other expenses. The leaders handled everything, and 'we were the stupid ones who followed them'. She stayed for two years before she left. Two months later, she heard that the police had evicted the ones that stayed. Everything was destroyed and the vendors had lost all their supplies.

Although Lucía studied hairdressing, she did not have the courage to exercise it at first. When she at last started working in a hair salon and received payment for her first haircuts, she finally gained self-confidence. She rented a chair in a salon, and she got regular clients. But when she had a baby with her second husband, the others complained that the baby disturbed their work. Therefore, shortly before I met her, she decided to rent a locale where she would run her own hair salon. She got a credit loan from a bank to buy equipment, and she planned to pay it back in two years. 'Everything that I have, I have achieved it by myself', she said, and continued: 'I don't know what awaits me ahead ..., but everything has a solution'.

In 2013, she married her second husband, Alfredo, who is also from Puno and works as a night watchman, in addition to occasionally driving a pirate taxi. His first wife stayed in their house in one of the new neighbourhoods in the desert, and Alfredo moved in with Lucía in a rented room in Villa El Pedregal. They soon decided to build a house of their own on a land lot in the desert that Lucía had acquired when the state was handing out subsidized lots and that she had been paying little by little. They built the house together, one room at a time, and today they live there with their son and Lucía's children from her first marriage. There are no roads, water pipes or electricity in the area. Once a week, a truck brings water, which they store in plastic containers. At night, they light candles so that the children can do their homework for school.

When a squatter group tried to invade the area, the people living there decided to organise in a neighbourhood association, and Alfredo was elected leader. The purpose is to defend their land and to obtain access to electricity and water. They also wish to have a marketplace and a primary school. They have meetings once a month on Sunday mornings, since most of the neighbourhood's residents are agricultural workers and Sunday is their only day off. However, only a few of the property owners actually live there because of the lacking infrastructure. Alfredo tried to convince more people to build their houses, in order to put pressure on the municipality. He was constantly knocking on doors in the municipality in order to obtain electricity and water. Lucía supported him: 'we should make an effort; if one doesn't insist, nothing happens'.

Like Martina, Lucía had gained economic and social mobility by her own work and effort, in spite of her lack of formal education and the other hindrances that life had offered her. Instead of becoming a peasant, a domestic worker or a subdued housewife, she had made an effort to gain skills, work experience and finally her own business. In this sense, she—just like Martina—embodies the entrepreneurial and neoliberal ideal that the government envisions: that people can come out of poverty through individual entrepreneurship. Neither Martina nor Lucía wore traditional clothing from their home places but dressed and talked Spanish like urban mestizo women. Both had moved from their rural communities as small children and had lived most part of their lives in cities and/or in MIP. However, for every business that succeeds, there are many that fail. Martina and Lucía were very aware of the danger of working with credit and entering into debt, especially in a precarious economy where the competition from other vendors and micro-businesses are increasing every day.

Emerging Inequalities: 'Race', Class and Gender

After 30 years of neoliberal policies, the processes of differentiation in Majes are becoming evident. With the broad availability of expensive credit loans, and production based on uncertain anticipations of the fluctuating product prices, a few farmers have prospered and expanded their farms, while others have drowned in debt. The second generation of the first farmers who settled in MIP often work on temporary contracts in export-oriented agribusiness factories, in the service sector, transport, construction sites, or in state and municipal institutions. As job security is practically non-existent and the informal economy is growing, many young people try their luck as micro-entrepreneurs. Most of the new migrants, who come from all over the country, but mostly from the southern highlands, work as land labourers (*peones*) on a day-to-day basis. Each morning, they go very early to a place behind the main market in Villa El Pedregal, where the farmers come and take the workers they need to their farms. They are usually paid 50 soles a day or 60–70 soles if it is specialised work. Hence, there are days when they earn money and days when they don't (Photo 10.2). Many of the new migrants also make a livelihood by selling food on the streets, but they are regularly removed by the municipal agents who do not tolerate vendors without a municipal license. As the population grows, the social inequalities and structures of prejudice, stigmatisation and discrimination that predominate in Peru are also reinforced in Majes.

Jorge is one of the few first settlers who have been economically successful. He has tripled the size of his farm where he cultivates grapes and avocados for export. As most of the successful farmers, however, he did not have a background as a poor peasant from the highlands. He was originally from the coastal city of Tacna and was educated as an agronomist, and had thus the social and cultural capital that provide an advantage in the Peruvian social and racial hierarchy based on geography and education. Moreover, he and other farmers with similar interests got organised, and he is today the elected president of the Avocado Association. In an interview, he talked about the people coming to Majes in search of work, who he hires as day labourers on his farm: 'The people who live in the high parts where there is no work, where there is hunger; the 'deep Peru' as we call it, where the government does not come; those people come here, and the next day they have work, because here there is a lot of work'. With this statement, he not only confirmed the stereotypical and stigmatised image

Photo 10.2 Day labourers (*peones*) harvesting potatoes on the land of a settler farmer (*colono*) (Photo by the author)

that people on the coast have of the highlands, but he also implied that these people are lucky to get work as land labourers.

It was often pointed out to me that 'the majority' of the population in Majes were people from Puno (*puneños*). In Villa El Pedregal, most of the merchants and market vendors are *puneños*, and the women are especially easy to recognise because of their characteristic skirts and bowler hats. The leader of the 'Association of Residents from Puno' roughly estimated that there are approximately 50,000 *puneños* in Majes because of the job opportunities. He said that the majority of the population in most Peruvian cities are from Puno: 'we have always been characterized by our presence', he said. He continued: 'The *puneños* stick out (*son sobresalientes*), mostly because of the force of labour that they put in: you will never find a worker from Puno who is lazy; *el puneño* is always a hard worker (*de chamba*)'. People from Puno, as in the rest of the Andes, are proud of being good workers; to be able to work hard is a virtue. However, success in economic activities, and more importantly, a visible display of material wealth, is not always appreciated by others. The *puneños* have brought their customs from Puno, and every year they celebrate the Virgin of Candelaria with famous splendour and colourful dances (see also Stensrud 2016). I heard others comment that it 'looks more like a display of riches and of the ones with most money than a devotion of the Virgin'. In other contexts, I heard comments that reflected the racist attitudes against people from the highlands, such as 'be careful with the *puneños*'. One informant told me: 'the *puneños* are all over: they get many children, like rabbits. They multiply and need space'.

Since the creation of the municipal administration in 1983, the mayors of Majes have been keen to create and promote symbolic events, objects and performances—monuments, a coat of arms, a flag, songs and poems—that show the uniqueness of Majes and that simultaneously evoke patriotic feelings in the local population, feelings that should unite a diversified population (Zamalloa 2013; Stensrud 2016). These objects—as well as the dominant narratives about the creation of MIP—emphasize and promote a *mestizo* identity: neither indigenous nor Spanish (or white elite), but a mix that has become the new generic racial category of Peruvian national identity. The narratives are, however, highly gendered: the settlers who are praised for their hard work and sacrifice in speeches, poems, songs and monuments are represented as male *mestizo* pioneers and brave frontier men. Zamalloa's *Himno de Majes*, which was declared the official hymn of the district in 2003, says: 'Great men are your strength, ranchers and farmers, who are cultivating the furrow of progress…'. At the entrance of Villa El Pedregal you are met by the impressive statue of General Velasco, who is considered the founder of MIP. In Villa El Pedregal, the monument of the settler, *el Monumento al Colono*, which is a statue of a farmer holding a milk can, has a central place. Women, on the other hand, are included in the Cow Monument, *Monumento a la Vaca*: a statue of a cow being handmilked by a milkmaid. Women are mainly celebrated on Mothers' Day—in their capacity as mothers, wives, caretakers and nurturers—and in beauty contests, where the winner is given the title 'Queen of Majes'. Some people commented that the queen always is a 'daughter of a settler, someone of economic resources', and never a girl from the highlands. Hard-working businesswomen, like Martina and Lucía, are, however, seldom celebrated in public events.

Conclusion

Majes is portrayed as the land of milk and honey, a place of hope and progress that is bustling with opportunities of jobs and business. On the one hand, there is a desire and pressure to transform farmers into businessmen, yet on the other hand, there are processes of dispossession, proletarisation and precariasation going on, and social inequality is increasing. In 1983, all the settlers started with equal five-hectare farms in a project to create economic growth and 'progress', through the domestication of desert, water, seeds, animals and human labour. Thirty years later, a few have prospered and bought new land, while many have been forced to sell their farms. The majority keep working, hoping to make profit and praying that the prices will not fall. Today, it is not the *hacendados* that 'eat' the farmers' poverty, but the banks and the agro-corporations. Among the second generation, that is, the children of settlers, there are differences between those who have completed higher education to become engineers or other professionals and those who work in factories, construction, transport and the service sector. Many have started their own micro-enterprises: mechanical workshops, beauty salons, restaurants or grocery shops. Most of the recently arrived migrants are day-to-day land labourers, taxi drivers and vendors in markets and streets, with or without formal licenses. Formal employment is scarce, working conditions have worsened since the deregulations in the 1990s, and informality, precarity and uncertainty prevail.

Farmers and working poor are being transformed into precarious entrepreneurs, highland peasants are transformed into land labourers, and unsuccessful entrepreneurs are transformed into street vendors or factory workers on insecure contracts. The ideal citizen of Majes is a male *mestizo* farmer with an entrepreneurial spirit who has gained economic success through hard work and the taking of risks. Migrants are portrayed as coming from abject poverty and as they are used to a miserable condition, they should be content with finding work as day-to-day labourers. Women are publicly celebrated as mothers and housewives, while their reality as hard-working farmers, labourers and entrepreneurs is often disregarded. These inequalities did not disappear with the land reform, or with Toledo's promises of 'more work' or with Humala's 'social inclusion'. In fact, social inequalities will never disappear with top-down state reforms. On the one hand, political pressure from grass roots social movements is needed to obtain large-scale changes of economic structures. On the other hand, as inequalities, and the cultural attitudes that support them, are reinforced in daily life, they can only be altered through small-scale changes in everyday attitudes and practices.

Notes

1. The research for this chapter has been funded by the European Research Council (grant no. 295843) and the Research Council of Norway (grant no. 222783). The analysis in this chapter is based on 13 months of ethnographic fieldwork in Colca and Majes in 2011, 2013 and 2014, and also informed by research in Cusco in the period 2001–2008.
2. Fujimori is son of Japanese immigrants and is colloquially called 'el Chino' by most Peruvians, who tend to call any person with a physical 'Asian' appearance *chino/a*, just as they have other nicknames that are informed by racialised stereotypes: indigenous *cholos*, dark-skinned *negros*, white *gringos*.
3. http://www.pampabaja.com/eng/main.php. Website accessed 6 September 2016.
4. All personal names have been anonymised.
5. In 2013 and 2014, 1 Peruvian Nuevo Sol PEN = 0,35 USD. PEN is referred to as *sol* in colloquial language and one sol = 100 centavos.

References

Bear, Laura, Karen Ho, Anna Tsing, and Sylvia Yanagisako. 2015. 'Gens: A Feminist Manifesto for the Study of Capitalism', Fieldsights—Theorising the Contemporary. *Cultural Anthropology Online*, March 30

Cant, Anna. 2012. 'Land for Those Who Work It': A Visual Analysis of Agrarian Reform Posters in Velasco's Peru. *Journal of Latin American Studies* 44: 1–37.

Collier, David. 1978. *Barriadas y élites: de Odría a Velasco*. Lima: IEP.

Crabtree, John. 2002. The Impact of Neo-liberal Economics on Peruvian Peasant Agriculture in the 1990s. *The Journal of Peasant Studies* 29 (3–4): 131–161.

Degregori, Carlos I. 2008. Educación: La soga se rompe por el hilo más débil. *LASA Forum* 39 (3): 26–29.

De la Cadena, Marisol. 1991. 'Las mujeres son más indias': Etnicidad y género en una comunidad del Cusco. *Revista Andina* 9 (1): 7–29.

———. 2000. *Indigenous Mestizos: The Politics of Race and Culture in Cuzco, 1919–1991*. Durham: Duke University Press.

García Pérez, Alan. 2007. El síndrome del perro del hortelano. *El Comercio*, 28 October

Gonzales de Olarte, Efrain. 1993. Economic Stabilization and Structural Adjustment Under Fujimori. *Journal of Interamerican Studies and World Affairs* 35 (2): 51–80.

Guillet, David. 1992. *Covering Ground: Communal Water Management and the State in the Peruvian Andes*. Ann Arbor: University of Michigan Press.

Harvey, David. 2005. *A Brief History of Neoliberalism*. Oxford: Oxford University Press.

Hunefeldt, Christine. 1997. The Rural Landscape and Changing Political Awareness. Enterprises, Agrarian Producers, and Peasant Communities, 1969–1994. Ch. 4. In *The Peruvian Labyrinth: Polity, Society, Economy*, ed. Maxwell A. Cameron and Philip Mauceri, 107–133. University Park: The Pennsylvania State University Press.

Kalb, Don. 2015. Introduction: Class and the New Anthropological Holism. In *Anthropologies of Class. Power, Practice and Inequality*, ed. James G. Carrier and Don Kalb. Cambridge: Cambridge University Press.

Klarén, Peter F. 2000. *Peru: Society and Nationhood in the Andes*. New York: Oxford University Press.

Mayer, Enrique. 1992. Peru in Deep Trouble: Mario Vargas Llosa's 'Inquest in the Andes' Reexamined. In *Rereading Cultural Anthropology*, ed. George E. Marcus, 181–219. Durham/London: Duke University Press.

———. 2009. *Ugly Stories of the Peruvian Agrarian Reform*. Durham: Duke University Press.

Millar, Kathleen M. 2014. The Precarious Present: Wageless Labour and Disrupted Life in Rio de Janeiro, Brazil. *Cultural Anthropology* 29 (1): 32–53.

Ong, Aihwa. 2006. *Neoliberalism as Exception: Mutations in Citizenship and Sovereignty*. Durham: Duke University Press.

Poole, Deborah, and Gerardo Rénique. 2012. Peru: Humala Takes Off His Gloves. *NACLA Report on the Americas*, Spring Issue. http://nacla.org/news/2012/5/17/peru-humala-takes-his-gloves. Accessed 8 Mar 2016.

Rénique, José Luís. 1991. *Los sueños de la sierra. Cusco en el siglo XX*. Lima: CEPES.

Roberts, Bryan R. 2004. From Marginality to Social Exclusion: From Laissez Faire to Pervasive Engagement, in 'From the Marginality of the 1960s to the 'New Poverty' of Today'. *Latin American Research Review* 39 (1): 195–197.

Seligmann, Linda J. 1995. *Between Reform and Revolution. Political Struggles in the Peruvian Andes, 1969–1991*. Stanford: Stanford University Press.

Stensrud, Astrid B. 2015. Raining in the Andes: Disrupted Seasonal and Hydrological Cycles. Chapter 3. In *Waterworlds: Anthropology in Fluid Environments*, ed. Kirsten Hastrup and Frida Hastrup, 75–92. New York: Berghahn Books.

———. 2016. 'We Are All Strangers Here:' Transforming Land and Making Identity in a Desert Boomtown. In *Identity Destabilised: Living in an Overheated World*, ed. T.H. Eriksen and E. Schober, 59–76. London: Pluto Press.

van den Berghe, Pierre L., and George Primov. 1977. *Inequality in the Peruvian Andes: Class and Ethnicity in Cuzco*. Columbia: University of Missouri Press.

Vargas Llosa, Mario. 1983. Inquest in the Andes. *The New York Times*, 31 July, translated by Edith Grossman. http://www.nytimes.com/1983/07/31/magazine/inquest-in-the-andes.html?pagewanted=all. Accessed 7 Mar 2017.

Velasco Alvarado, Juan. 1969. Mensaje a la nación del presidente de la república del Perú, General Juan Velasco Alvarado sobre la reforma agraria, (Lima, 24 de junio de 1969). *Estudios Internacionales de la Universidad de Chile* 3 (11): 393–402. doi:10.5354/0719-3769.1969.18948.

Zamalloa, Ing. Edgar Bravo. 2013. *Reseña Histórica del Distrito de Majes*. Lima: Corporación Grafical

Open Access This chapter is licensed under the terms of the Creative Commons Attribution 4.0 International License (http://creativecommons.org/licenses/by/4.0/), which permits use, sharing, adaptation, distribution and reproduction in any medium or format, as long as you give appropriate credit to the original author(s) and the source, provide a link to the Creative Commons license and indicate if changes were made.

The images or other third party material in this chapter are included in the chapter's Creative Commons license, unless indicated otherwise in a credit line to the material. If material is not included in the chapter's Creative Commons license and your intended use is not permitted by statutory regulation or exceeds the permitted use, you will need to obtain permission directly from the copyright holder.

CHAPTER 11

Latin American Inequalities and Reparations

Marvin T. Brown

Whatever our social differences and unequal relationships with each other, we all share a common humanity. We have the same basic six emotions—surprise, fear, disgust, anger, happiness, and sadness (Ekman and Friesen 2003). We all have a primal consciousness of ourselves as living beings (Damasio 2010). We all live on the same planet. We begin our life breathing in the air of the biosphere and our life ends when the breathing stops. We are all contemporaries. We all acquire a story that gives us a place in the world. When inequalities emerge as a result of violations of this common humanity, the only adequate response is to work at restoring everyone's place in the world and at repairing distorted relationships.

Let's remember that inequality, by definition, is a relational term. One cannot be unequal alone. To understand inequality is to understand relationships. This means that one cannot understand Latin America inequalities without understanding the relationships between Latin American and the continents of Africa, Europe, and North America. The reverse is also true: you cannot understand Africa, Europe, or North America without understanding Latin America. Or, to be more concrete: Just as you cannot understand Haiti without understanding France, you cannot understand

M.T. Brown (✉)
University of San Francisco, San Francisco, CA, USA

© The Author(s) 2018
M. Ystanes, I.Å. Strønen (eds.), *The Social Life of Economic Inequalities in Contemporary Latin America*, Approaches to Social Inequality and Difference, DOI 10.1007/978-3-319-61536-3_11

France without understanding Haiti. If that is true, and I assume it is, then the ocean that connects these continents—the Atlantic—can be seen as the original context of Latin American inequalities. The triangular trade among Europe, Africa, and the Americas created this context, and as long as we ignore it, we will never fully grasp the background of our current situation, as well as what is necessary to change it.

As Europeans immigrated to the Americas, of course, unequal relations were transferred to American soil. The appropriation of American land by Euro-Americans was only limited by the lack of labour, a problem they solved by first enslaving native populations and later importing millions of enslaved Africans. Their wealth and their honour—wealth was honour—depended on the enslavement and stigmatizing of others. On the surface, their honour was based on their wealth. Under the surface, their wealth was based on the exploitation of others. We all know this, but many of us also share an economic narrative that omits this truth—the truth about capitalism and slavery.

CAPITALISM AND SLAVERY

The exploitation of labour and the appropriation of land began in Latin America almost two centuries before the publication of Adam Smith's *The Wealth of Nations* in 1776. Many economists today, especially neoliberals who think within Smith's framework, rarely connect capitalism with slavery. And with good reason! Of the many contradictions we witness between fact and fiction, none are more telling than the contradiction between the small-town image commonly used to represent the essence of free enterprise and the real context of early capitalism—the Atlantic trade between Europe, Africa, and the Americas. Here is the fiction:

> It is not from the benevolence of the butcher, the brewer, or the baker, that we expect our dinner, but from their regard to their own self-interest. We address ourselves, not to their humanity but to their self-love, and never talk to them of our own necessities but of their advantages. (Smith 1994, 15)

Such an image is not so difficult to imagine. Small shop owners provide different goods to each other, and the best way of doing this is for each to be guided by his or her self-interest, since in this intimate setting, it is certainly in one's self-interest to provide a good product at a good price. How nice that when we do what is best for us, it is best for everyone else.

The reality of commerce when Adam Smith was composing *The Wealth of Nations* was something else. The centre of this trade was not the town square, but the Atlantic Ocean, which Europeans used for the trafficking of millions of enslaved Africans to the Americas, who worked the land to produce products for Europeans. To complete the triangle, the Europeans sent other products, such as credit and guns, to Africa to buy more enslaved Africans. The "success" of early capitalism, in other words, depended not on individuals acting in their self-interest but rather a global system of buying and selling human beings as though they were no different than cattle.

Robin Blackburn estimates that of the 21 million Africans enslaved between 1700 and 1850, 9 million slaves were delivered to the Americas, 5 million were lost during the passage, and another 11 million were enslaved in Africa (Blackburn 1998). The numbers are astonishing. In fact, more Africans than Europeans lived in the Americas during the seventeenth and early eighteenth century.

> Indeed, in every year from about the mid-sixteenth century to 1831, more Africans than Europeans quite likely came to the Americas, and not until the second wage of mass migration began in the 1880s did the sum of net European immigration start to match and then excel the cumulative influx from Africa.... In terms of immigration alone, then, America was an extension of Africa rather than Europe until late in the nineteenth century. (Bailey 1990, 377)

True, one finds slavery in earlier historical periods, but Atlantic-based slavery was unique. For the first time, slavery was an integral part of the global economy. Yes, the Romans and Greeks had many slaves, but people were enslaved mostly due to conquest. As Blackburn writes: "One might say that many Roman slaves were sold because they had been captured, while many African slaves entering the Atlantic trade had been captured so that they might be sold" (Blackburn 1998, 11).

In the commercial world of the Atlantic, slavery was an economic institution. As Klein and Vinson say in their book on African slavery in Latin America, "It was without question American labour market conditions that most influenced the growth of the Atlantic slave trade" (2007, 18). This conclusion has been carefully documented in Eric Williams' book, *Capitalism and Slavery*. He traces the history of the plantations in the British West Indies from first using indigenous slaves and then indentured servants brought from Europe. As the plantations grew and needed more labour, and as indentured servants heard of the high rate of deaths on the plantations and refused to volunteer to move to the Caribbean, there rose the need for another source of labour, and African slaves were chosen. The motive for enslaving Africans, Williams writes, "was economic, not racial; it had to do not with the colour of the laborer, but the cheapness of the labor" (Williams 1994, 19). Only later, as whites became afraid of slave rebellions, did they begin to see Africans as racially inferior. As Williams says. "Slavery was not born of racism; rather, racism was the consequence of slavery" (7).

Although Williams' work has not been included in the canon of contemporary economics, recent scholarship has confirmed what has become known as the Williams thesis; namely, slavery was essentially economic. Blackburn, for example, supports this thesis by describing how the sugar plantations in the West Indies were not just institutions of agriculture but also commercial institutions:

> The plantation evidently belonged to the world of manufacture as much as to that of commercial agriculture. The plantation crops, especially sugar and indigo, required elaborate processing, and both permitted and required the intensive exploitation of labour …. On the productive side, the plantation required the coordinated and meticulously timed activities of between 10 and 300 workers. Specialist slaves, working long hours but receiving some small privileges, came to work in the responsible positions in the sugar works, as planters discovered that this was cheaper than hiring specialized employees. (Blackburn 1998, 333–334)

Plantations, in other words, were part and parcel of capitalism. They are actually great examples of how the division of labour increased productivity (much better than Smith's example of the pin factory). Plantations, of course, entailed not only the exploitation of forced labour, but also the appropriation of land for commercial use. The plantations turned a living biotic community into a machine for producing commodities.

If mainstream economists had recognized the plantations as a major source of wealth creation in early capitalism, we might have had many more conversations about how the inequalities in capitalistic economies have their origin in the enslavement of people rather than some sort of "invisible hand." Such inequalities—inequalities that are the result of violations of our common humanity—raise questions about reparations. What should we do to bring some sort of commonality to relationships that are so radically out-of-balance? I think this question can direct us toward what we need to talk about not only in terms of repairing the past but also in terms of securing a future. Conversations about reparations in Latin America, of course, belong to the larger narratives about land reform.

Land Reform in Latin America

In the occupation and domination of Latin America, the Spanish and Portuguese granted large tracks of land to former Conquistadors and other favourites of the Crown as a reward for their efforts in gaining control over the Americas. In contrast to the policy of the United States, where indigenous people were removed from their homeland and finally forced to live on "reservations," the policy in Latin America—*encomienda*—was much closer to old world feudalism: indigenous people remained on the land and paid tribute to the "owner." This created a massive population of landless people and a small powerful elite. Policies of land reform were attempts to improve these unequal conditions.

Most Latin American governments engaged in some form of land reform in the twentieth century. Mexico led the way in the early decades and others followed, especially in the 1950s and 1960s. The reasons were multiple, but perhaps the one that received the most support from the United States was the idea that land reform would prevent revolutions like the one in Cuba. The Alliance for Progress (1961) organized by the Organization of American States persuaded most governments to engage in some kind of land reform. With globalization and the advent of neoliberalism in the 1980s, progress in land reform was brought to a standstill (Teubal 2009). With the beginning of the twenty-first century, a majority of Latin American countries shifted to more leftist and populist governments—known as the Pink Tide—and although they improved the welfare of many people, they did not engage in a significant redistribution of land. Although land reform may not occupy Latin American politics now as much as it has in the past, it has led to the development of different principles than those of neoliberalism about the meaning of land and the rights of collectives.

Two Principles of Land Reform

For most countries in Latin America, land is interpreted as having a social function. The French Jurist, Léon Duguit, first articulated this idea in 1919 (Ankersen and Ruppert 2006). He reasoned that since the purpose of the state was to provide for certain social needs, the state had an obligation to ensure that land was being used productively—that it was fulfilling its social function. This view of land, of course, differs from the liberal assumption voiced by John Locke that land belongs to its owner and the state's primary obligation is to protect the owner's right to control his/her property. As Ankersen and Ruppert point out, by the middle of the twentieth century, most Latin American countries had incorporated the Social Function Doctrine in their constitutions (99). This doctrine gave the state the right to confiscate lands that were not serving any social function and distribute it to landless people who would use it. In Brazil, the organized squatter movement—the *Movimento dos Trabalhadores Rurais Sem Terra*, or MST—used the Social Function Doctrine to justify their occupation of large landholdings. In the past 30 years, MST has assisted over 350 thousand landless families to take unused land (Stedile 2002). Another group, the Workers Homeless Movement—Movimento dos Trabalhadores Sem Teto (MTST)—has carried out similar strategies as MST to fight for housing in urban areas. Both groups have focused on creating a place for landless and homeless people.

While the Social Function Doctrine has supported land reform, it has also had an unintended consequence. Landowners have cut down forests to make sure their land fulfils a social function through ranching. In response, governments are adding to the land's social function an ecological function. Land, in other words, is seen as belonging to both social and ecological systems.

Along with seeing land as having a social and ecological function, Latin American governments have also acknowledged the rights of collectives as well as individuals. In fact, the recognition of collective rights has now been affirmed by the United Nations. In the UN Declaration on the Rights of Indigenous Peoples in 2007, Article 26 states: "Indigenous peoples have the right to the lands, territories and resources which they have traditionally owned, occupied or otherwise used or acquired."[1] As with the notion of the social function of land, the rights of indigenous peoples have not always been respected. Also, this principle is quite different from a neoliberal view that only individuals have rights. Bettina Ng'weno's proposal that we think in terms of the rights to a territory highlights the difference between individual and collective control (Ng'weno 2007, 84). Individuals do not own territories, territories belong to groups, and the acknowledgement of collective rights gives them territorial rights.

The idea of reparations has not played a major role in most decisions about land reform, but the two principles of the social function of land and of collective rights provide a useful context for understanding current conversations about reparations.

Conversations About Reparations

Reparations differ somewhat from the task of redistributing land. Reparations involve not only compensating those who deserve it but also changing the relationships among the different parties. At the very least, those who benefited have to acknowledge that their gain depended on others' expense. But it goes deeper. It involves both sides in a process of reflection about how to live together. This means that we can see reparations not only as a process of making payments on past debts but also of transforming social relationships.

In 2001, the United Nations "World Conference against Racism, Racial Discrimination, Xenophobia and other Forms of Intolerance" called for the recognition of "the Black Holocausts (Slave trade/Slavery and Colonization) as Crimes Against Humanity" (Marable and Mullings 2001). On the issue of slavery and colonial responsibility, the NGO written document at this conference was direct and unequivocal:

> We demand that the United States, Canada, and those European and Arab nations that participated in and benefited from the Trans Atlantic Slave Trade, the Trans-Sahara Slave Trade, the Trans-Indian Ocean Slave Trade, Slavery and the Colonization of Africa ... [as well as] ... the United Nations ... shall ... Ensure that ... all nations, groups and their members who are the victims of crimes against humanity based on race, colour, caste, descent, ethnicity or indigenous or national origin are provided reparations ... [including] ... Restitution ... encompassing the unconditional return of land ... Monetary compensation that will repair the victims, including Africa, Africans and African descendants, by closing the economic gap created by these crimes...[2]

This is a serious challenge. We now turn to two countries—Brazil and Haiti—that have taken up the question of reparations. In Brazil, the descendants of what are called Quilombo communities—communities founded by escaped slaves—are petitioning for the return of their ancestors' land. In Haiti, people are demanding compensation for the billions of dollars they paid France since gaining their independence in 1804. As we shall see, both stories demonstrate an intriguing link between freedom and land. First, the story of the Quilombo movement in Brazil.

Quilombo Communities

The term "Quilombo" refers to communities of runaway slaves in the sixteenth century. Such communities, of various numbers, dotted the Brazilian countryside in the seventeenth century. The most famous, Palmares, in Northern Brazil, grew to more than 15,000 inhabitants before the Portuguese destroyed it in 1694. Palmares survivors are only one of many such communities that continue to exist today. Almost 100 years after the abolition of slavery, in 1986, Benedita da Silva, a member of Congress, convinced the body of lawmakers to pass legislation that recognized the right of the Quilombo communities to a legal title to their ancestors' land. Rogue Plantas has suggested that carrying out this policy could be the world's largest slavery reparation programme (Plantas 2014).

In 2003, the government officially defined a Quilombo community as a "self-identified, ethno-racial group with their own historical trajectory, a specific relationship to the land, and the presumption of a black ancestry connected to forms of resistance to historical oppression" (Farfán-Santos 2016).

The government policy was to grant land title to Afro-Brazilian communities that could demonstrate they were a Quilombo community—their memory and experience could match the government's definition. In her book on the Quilombo communities, Elizabeth Farfán-Santos describes many of the difficulties black communities had in bridging the gap between their everyday experiences of struggling to make a living in extremely adverse conditions and this official description (2016). Also, the process of being recognized as a Quilombo community took years of moving through the government's bureaucracy. These difficulties were largely due to treating Afro-Brazilian communities as ethnic minorities.

As ethnic minorities, the Quilombo communities enjoyed the same collective rights as Brazil's indigenous groups. They have a right to their own culture and ways of living. At the same time, as Farfán-Santos points out, treating Quilombo communities as ethnic groups also has its drawbacks: it failed to recognize the social structures of anti-black violence and inequality. As she says:

> Cultural recognition grants black and indigenous communities the right to difference, even self-identification, without necessarily changing the unequal structural distribution of rights. (Farfán-Santos 2016, 45)

Here we see a separation of land rights and social rights, when in fact they are closely related. Perhaps omitting the question of social relations accounts for the fact that of the more than 2400 communities that identified as Quilombo communities, less than 220 have received land titles (Thomas 2016). Still, we should not discount the meaning of a land title for those communities that now enjoy the right to their land.

> Securing the right to land, although not the end of a larger battle, symbolizes more than just a property title; it signifies the recognition of a life that is intimately, emotionally, and physically intertwined with the land, without which quilombolas would be left without a home but, more importantly, without a sense of life security and belonging. (Farfán-Santos 2016, 145)

So the securing of a land title could be seen as the first step toward changing social relations. The prospect for further progress, however, has dimmed considerably since the current Temer government has closed the National Institute for Colonization and Agrarian Reform (INCRA), which was responsible for reviewing applications from Quilombo communities. The government placed its titling function under the Ministry of Education, headed by a party leader opposed to recognizing Quilombo rights (Bledsoe 2016). Still, the claim for reparations has been recognized and in time it may once again receive consideration.

If reparations simply meant payment for a debt, one could imagine the Quilombo descendants asking for money instead of land. If land is merely a commodity, as neoliberals assume, then one could use the land market to settle on the payment. We totally miss the point, however, when we take this stance. For the Quilombo communities, land is their habitat—a living place. As Farfán-Santos points out:

Thus quilombolas desire the freedom and legal right to work in the mangroves, plant manioc, and live from the forest; however, they want to do these things within a secure space where they can build a future for their children without the constant fear that it might be taken away. (Farfán-Santos 2016, 50)

These desires match the doctrines of the social and ecological functions of land and even expand them by recognizing that having a title to land can provide a secure place. The failure of the current Brazilian government to respond to the demands for land titles is a form of reneging on these principles. How significant are these principles? One can see them as expressions of a deeper truth—the close connection between the right to freedom and the right to land. To explore this connection we turn to the story of Haiti.

The Story of Haiti

A number of events are central to the story of how the French colony of St. Domingue became Haiti—the first and only successful worker's revolution in the Americas. Spain granted France a portion of the island of Hispaniola in 1697, which became the major Caribbean supplier of sugar. In the 1780s, St. Domingue accounted for 30 per cent of the world's total sugar production (Klein and Vinson 2007). The colony's mountainous regions were just as fruitful as a source for coffee as the northern plains were for sugar. In stark contrast to our image of Haiti today, during its colonial period, it was extremely productive for the white planters.

Whites, however, were a very small minority of the total population. At the end of the eighteenth century, blacks outnumbered whites 10 to 1. Joan Dayan quotes the figures of Moreau de Saint-Mery, who gives the numbers of 40,000 whites, 28,000 free coloureds, and 452,000 slaves (Dayan 1998, 146). The whites included the descendants of "buccaneers, filibusters, and nobles," as well as European settlers and American Creoles. The free coloureds included slaves who had bought their freedom, slaves who were freed by their owners, and runaway slaves. The almost 500,000 blacks were primarily from Bight of Benin and West Central Africa, with smaller populations from such places as Senegambia and Sierra Leone (Manning 2009).

Following the French Revolution, the French in Paris debated what rights should be granted to the different groups in the French colonies. The white plantation owners sought the recognition of their rights, but not that of the free coloureds and of course not the slaves. That, after all, was the model provided by the United States' revolt against the British. In Haiti, however, the slaves also revolted against their masters and eventually against the French. Perhaps the most dramatic event was the meeting in 1791 organized by Dutty Boukman, a voodoo priest.

> From the number of slaves involved and the coordination that took place, the August 20 meeting must have been just one of the many such gatherings and only the final session of what was a well-planned movement with a close tie to the secret African cults. On the first night a large number of the island's best sugar plantations were put to the torch and in the next several days the island's richest plantation region, the Northern Plain was destroyed. (Klein and Vinson 2007, 186)

In 1802, Boukman was killed and Toussaint Louverture emerged as the leader of the rebel slaves. Louverture brought together disparate forces—the Spanish forces on the island and pro-royalist Frenchmen—and tried to revive the plantation sugar economy but was not successful in persuading the freed workers to leave the land they had occupied during the revolution and return to the plantation as wage earners. Without workers, of course, the economy was at a standstill. The French government plotted to replace Louverture and reinstitute slavery. Louverture was taken to France. A new revolutionary leader, Jean-Jacques Dessalines, organized an army of ex-slaves to fight against the French and forced them to leave the island. Haiti became an independent republic in January 1804.

The Haitian successful revolutionary war reverberated throughout the Americas and Europe. There is evidence that the German philosopher, Hegel, had the Haitian revolution in mind when he wrote his famous piece of master and slave relationships in *The Phenomenology of Spirit* (Buck-Morss 2009). At the time, the United States viewed a free nation of blacks as a threat to its prosperity, which was largely dependent on the labour of its enslaved population. It stopped trading with Haiti after their revolution and did not recognize it as a nation until 1863, following Abraham Lincoln's Emancipation Proclamation that freed the enslaved people of the United States (Wesley 1917).

For the Haitians, however, freedom was not only about the relationships between master and slave but also about the relationship with the land. The Constitution of 1805, declared that "no white, whatever his nation, could set foot on the territory of Haiti as master or owner of property" (Dayan 1998, 24). For Dessalines, it seems that freeing the Haitian land from foreign ownership was part and parcel of freeing the Haitian people from slavery. No better evidence of the importance of land for Haitians than the following lines from their national anthem:

> For Haiti in the name of the Ancestors
> We must toil, we must sow
> It is in the soil, that all our strength seats
> It is it that feeds us
> Let us toil the soil, let us toil the soil
> Joyfully, may the land be fertile
> Mow, water, men like women
> Must we come to live only by our arms' strength.³

At the same time, we should not underestimate how offensive white people must have found Dessalines' position that they could not own land in Haiti. The French plantation owners, in any case, did not ask for compensation for losing their slaves, but for losing the income from the appropriation of Haitian land. In 1825, with gunboats in the Haiti harbour, the French required compensation for the land in exchange for recognition of Haiti as a sovereign republic. The French demanded 150 million francs, which was reduced to 90 million in 1838, comparable to $40 billion as of 2010. The amount was calculated on the estimated value of the revenues generated by the plantations in 1789, which was determined by taking the Haitian exports in 1823 of 30 million francs over ten years (300 million francs) at 50 per cent profit, which came to 150 million francs (Dupuy 2015). Behind the math, of course, was the political intent to bury Haiti in debt. The response of the French government seems to have been that if whites could not own land, at least they could keep the Haitians so poor they could not prosper from it. The debt was twice what France received from the United States for the Louisiana Purchase, which was ten times the land mass. Haiti made regular payments on the debt plus interest for close to 60 years until 1883 (Popkin 2012). To finally pay off the French, Haiti borrowed from US banks, and only in 1947 were they out from under burdensome loan payments. So Haiti remains poor after paying France and the United States millions of dollars on a loan to compensate French slaveholders for losing their land.

The massive debt was not the only burden Western nations—especially the United States—placed on the people of Haiti. The United States refused to recognize or trade with Haiti until 1863. In 1915, the United States occupied Haiti and stayed until 1934. During that time, they collected taxes, controlled customs, and ran many government institutions. Also, the US occupation facilitated the transfer of millions of hectares of land from the Haitian people to foreign companies. As Dupuy points out, from the time of the revolution to the US occupation, Haitians had refused to leave the lands they had acquired to become dependent on plantation wages. Even though they remained poor during this period, they were not desperate. Not unlike the enclosure movements of the sixteenth and seventeenth centuries in Europe that produced the first population dependent on wages for survival, the US occupation brought about what Dupuy called the "proletarianisation of the peasants" (Dupuy 2015). More recently, this process has been accelerated by the World Bank and other international financial institutions to make Haiti a source for cheap labour in the global market.

> In short, though ostensibly designed to alleviate poverty by stimulating sustainable economic growth, the policies of the Bank and the other IFIs in fact maintained Haiti's position in the international division of labor as a supplier of cheap labor for foreign capital (96).

These neoliberal policies have taken their toll not only on the Haitian people but also on the land. Once land is nothing but a commodity, it no longer functions as a place for security—it has lost its social function.

As Philippe Girard points out in his book on Haiti, blaming foreign powers for Haiti's problems leaves out its own mistakes and failures, especially the failures of governance and the cycles of violence (Girard 2010). Still, its indebtedness to Western powers for most of its history has certainly played a significant role. In 2003, Haiti demanded reparations, in the form of debt restitution, which was calculated around $21.7 billion. Although the French parliament did declare that the slave trade was a crime against humanity in 2001, they rejected the lawsuit (Lves 2013).

If we compare the stories of the Quilombo communities' demand for reparation and Haiti's call for restitution, they are both about land and recognition, but they are also quite different. The Quilombo communities want title to land, which would give them security in living their own lives. This would improve their situation, but it would not necessarily bring about a more balanced relationship between Afro-Brazilians and White-Brazilians. That would be a second step. Haiti, on the other hand, has not asked for a restoration of its land. It seems to have discarded the early Haitian principle that whites would never again own Haitian land. What if they had demanded that their land be restored so they could achieve food sovereignty—so they could provide for themselves? That might have been a first step toward a more balanced relationship between Haitians and the International community?

Remember the principle I proposed earlier: If you cannot understand Haiti without understanding France, then you cannot understand France without understanding Haiti? The refusal to make restitution for Haiti's debt seems to violate this principle. So, what would one have to assume to agree with France's refusal to make restitution? The following assumptions come to mind:

- Past actions do not affect future possibilities
- We can divorce our future from the future of others
- Haiti is not part of our global community
- Haiti does not exist

These are my assumptions, of course, but they seem to follow from the refusal to engage in a conversation about reparations. They not only contradict the principle that inequality is always a relationship among different parties—one cannot be unequal alone—but they also fail to recognize the common humanity that the French and Haitian people share. What would happen if we begin the conversation about reparations on the basis for our common humanity instead of our social differences? If we begin with the recognition that we all belong to the earth, then land would not be defined primarily as someone's private property, but as a habitat for human and non-human communities. One terminology that would allow us to think together from such the perspective of a common humanity would be to speak of land as a commons.

Land as a Commons

Although the idea of land as a commons is not directly linked to the Brazilian notions of the social and ecological functions of land, it is also not that far afield. It is certainly much closer than the neoliberal idea that land is nothing but a commodity. Land as a commons is also close to the views of many Native American and African cultures.

Land was treated as a commons even in Europe before the enclosure movements at the beginning of the modern period. This all changed with the rise of our modern commercial society, and it has changed even more with the rise of modern cities. In cities today, the value of land depends not only on its use but also on its location.

Through analysis of how land values change in cities, the early twentieth-century economist, Henry George, developed a creative link between the more traditional view of land as a commons and the modern view of land as location. He begins with the idea that land is a source of wealth.

> Wealth, then, may be defined as natural products that have been secured, moved, combined, separated, or in other ways modified by human exertion to fit them for the gratification of human desires. (George 2010, 42)

The term "natural products" refers to land in the ordinary sense as the ground we walk on. George's definition may seem rather limited today, when we speak of many different kinds of wealth, but let's stay with his focus on the production and distribution of natural products. From this perspective, we can easily notice not only that land can be cultivated to produce goods for use and exchange, but also that land itself acquires value as property. The owners of land, in other words, not only receive rent from the land's productivity but also from its increased value as property. This increase in value depends largely on the land's location, and as that location increases in value so does the wealth of the owners. At the same time, those who do not own land see their expenses rise. As this trend continues, so does the inequality between those who own land and those who do not. George draws the following conclusion: "The great cause of inequality in the distribution of wealth is inequality in the ownership of land" (2010, 163).

Let's compare two empty lots in Rio: one in a favela and the other in an affluent neighbourhood. If both were assigned their market value, the two lots would have very different prices. Could there be any other reason for this difference than their different locations? I don't think so. It was not the owner, in other words, that caused the higher value of the lot in the affluent neighbourhood, but rather the city's social structures. Since social conditions caused this difference, George argues that the extra rent received from selling the lot in the affluent neighbourhood should be returned to society, probably through taxes (see Costa in this volume for a discussion of the Brazilian tax system).

> If rent were taken by the state in taxes, then land would really be common property—no matter in whose name or in what parcels it was held. Every member of the community would participate in the advantages of ownership. (George 2010, 224)

This seems to make sense. As members of a city, we could all enjoy the benefits of the increased value of city properties. Our collective rights would entail rights to share in the city's growth and prosperity. Such a view of a city would certainly oppose the liberal view of private property, but it would not necessarily eliminate the ownership of property. It would simply change its meaning.

The Meaning of Ownership

In a credit-based market economy, owning property is important. As the Peruvian economist Hernando de Soto has pointed out, people may have assets, but if they do not have a legal title to them, these assets will not count as "property" (De Soto 2000). De Soto has tried to get governments in South America to give property titles to people living in buildings they have built on the edges of cities so they could use them as collateral for obtaining credit, as well as other benefits. Such a title, however, is not based on possession, but rather on the law.

> The crucial point to understand is that property is not a physical thing that can be photographed or mapped. Property is not a primary quality of assets but the legal expression of an economically meaningful consensus about assets. Law is the instrument that fixes and realizes capital. In the West, the law is less concerned with representing the physical reality of buildings or real estate than with providing a process or rules that will allow society to extract potential surplus value from those assets. Property is not the assets themselves but a consensus between people as to how those assets should be held, used, and exchanged. (De Soto 2000, 157)

If we agree with de Soto, then belonging to a civic community—a community of law—is the first step toward owning property. Possession by itself, in other words, is not enough. Legal title is also necessary. This explains the Quilombo movements drive for acquiring a legal title of land they already occupy. Still, we need to remember that property is a legal creation. Land is not. Law is something like a map, which is never the same as the territory. The territory belongs to all inhabitants. This is George's view of land as a commons:

> The equal right of all people to the use of land is as clear as their equal right to breathe the air—a right proclaimed by the very fact of their existence. (George 2010, 187)

Treating land as a commons does not mean, for George, that we try to give each person his or her share of land, but rather that each person should have a share of the land's wealth. So let owners own their property, but when the land value increases because of social trends, that increase in value should be shared. A person's right to property, in other words, exists within, and is limited by, the collective rights of all city members to share in the prosperity of their city. The city, in other words, should be treated as a territory. We belong to it and it belongs to all of us.

When the Europeans crossed the Atlantic, they approached the "new" land as something they could own and treat as they wanted, much like they believed that they could own people and treat them as they wanted. Neoliberalism has similar assumptions. We know they were wrong on both counts, and we now live with the consequences of these mistakes. The question is whether reparations can correct them.

Inequality and Reparations

We need to remember that inequality has two sides: some receive less than they deserve and some receive more than they deserve. As long as we focus only on those who deserve more—on the poor—we have limited our options. Henry George reminds us that when people receive more than they deserve—unearned income—they should not be able to keep it. It should be returned to the community that created the increase. In a city, the increase and decrease in land values—real estate—depends mostly on the city's policies on granting titles, establishing taxes, police protection, and so on. Given the role of white privilege in determining such policies, one can understand that cities today not only reflect inequality among citizens but also perpetuate it.

Reparation requires more than increasing the welfare of the poor and homeless. It also requires the repair of human relationships. What this repair will entail remains to be seen. It will depend on who becomes involved in the struggles for justice and equality. What we do know is that the story of economics that we have inherited from Adam Smith prevents us from even recognizing the inequality created and maintained by capitalism. Smithian economics blocks out from view the violations of our common humanity that are the basis of its success. If we want to move our societies toward equality, we will need to first acknowledge our common humanity and from that perspective work on policies that will create more just social relations.

Acknowledgements I wish to express my appreciation to Margit Ystanes for inviting me to the workshop "Rethinking Inequalities in Latin America" (Bergen, March 5–6, 2015) and for her assistance in writing this chapter.

Notes

1. https://www.humanrights.gov.au/publications/un-declaration-rights-indigenous-peoples-1.
2. http://www.africanfilmny.org/2014/a-report-on-the-world-conference-against-racism-racial-discrimination-xenophobia-and-related-intolerance-2/.
3. http://www.hougansydney.com/haiti-national-anthem.php.

References

Ankersen, Thomas T., and Thomas Ruppert. 2006. Tierra y Libertad: The Social Function Doctrine and Land Reform in Latin America. *Tulane Environmental Law Journal* 19: 69. Available at: http://scholarship.law.ufl.edu/facultypub/277

Bailey, Ronald. 1990. The Slave(ry) Trade and the Development of Capitalism in the United States: The Textile Industry in New England. *Social Science History* 14 (3): 373–414.

Blackburn, Robin. 1998. *The Making of New World Slavery: From the Baroque to the Modern, 1492–1800*. London/New York: Verso.

Bledsoe, Adam. 2016. *The Racist and Sexist Nature of Brazil's New Government*. Available: http://www.counterpunch.org/2016/06/20/the-racist-and-sexist-nature-of-brazils-new-government/print/

Buck-Morss, Susan. 2009. *Hegel, Haiti, and Universal History*. Pittsburgh: University of Pittsburgh Press.

Damasio, Antonio. 2010. *Self Comes to Mind: Constructing the Conscious Brain*. New York: Pantheon Books.

Dayan, Joan. 1998. *Haiti, History, and the Gods*. Berkeley/Los Angeles/London: University of California Press.

De Soto, Hernando. 2000. *The Mystery of Capital: Why Capitalism Triumphs in the West and Fails Everywhere Else*. New York: Basic Books.

Dupuy, Alex. 2015. *Haiti: From Revolutionary Slaves to Powerless Citizens: Essays on the Politics and Economics of Underdevelopment, 1804–2013*. London/New York: Routledge.

Ekman, Paul, and Wallace V. Friesen. 2003. *Unmasking The Face: A Guide to Recognizing Emotions from Facial Expressions*. Cambridge, MA: Malor Books.

Farfán-Santos, Elizabeth. 2016. *Black Bodies, Black Rights: The Politics of Quilombolismo in Contemporary Brazil.* Austin: University of Texas Press. Kindle edition.

George, Henry. 2010. *Progress and Poverty: Why There Are Recessions and Poverty Amid Plenty—And What to Do About It!* Ed. B. Drake. New York: Robert Schalkenbach Foundation

Girard, Philippe. 2010. *Haiti: The Tumultuous History—From the Pearl of the Caribbean to Broken Nation.* New York: Palgrave Macmillan.

Klein Herbert, S., and Ben Vinson III. 2007. *African Slavery in Latin America and the Caribbean.* 2nd ed. New York: Oxford University Press.

Lves, Kim. 2013. *HAITI: Independence Debt, Reparations for Slavery and Colonialism, and International "Aid" Global Research.* Available at: http://www.globalresearch.ca/haiti-independence-debt-reparations-for-slavery-and-colonialism-and-international-aid/5334619

Manning, Patrick. 2009. *The African Diaspora: A History Through Culture.* New York: Columbia University Press.

Marable, Manning, and Leith Mullings. 2001. World Conference Against Racism— Durban, South Africa. In *Let Nobody Turn Us Around: An African American Anthology*, 2nd ed. Lanham/Boulder/New York/Oxford: Rowman & Littlefield Publishers, Inc

Ng'weno, Bettina. 2007. *Turf Wars: Territory and Citizenship in the Contemporary State.* Stanford: Stanford University Press.

Plantas, Rogue. 2014. Brazil's "Quilombo" Movement May Be the World's Largest Slavery Reparation Program, *LATINO VOICES*, August.

Popkin, Jeremy D. 2012. *A Concise History of the Haitian Revolution.* Malden: Wiley-Blackwell.

Smith, Adam. 1994. *The Wealth of Nations.* Ed. Edwin Cannan. New York: Random House, Inc., Modern Library Edition.

Stedile, Joao Pedro. 2002. Landless Battalions: The Sem Terra Movement in Brazil. *New Left Review*, 15, May June.

Teubal, Miguel. 2009. Agrarian Reform and Social Movements in the Age of Globalization: Latin America at the Dawn of the Twenty-first Century. Trans. M.O. Brena. *Latin American Perspectives*, 36(167), No. 4.

Thomas, Anthony. 2016. *Brazil's "Quilombo", The Largest Slave Movement Relentlessly Fighting for Reparations.* Urban Intellectuals. Available at: http://urbanintellectuals.com/2016/07/30/brazils-quilombo-largest-slave-movement-relentlessly-fighting-reparations/#ixzz4PcixL0Hd

Wesley, Charles H. 1917. The Struggle for the Recognition of Haiti and Liberia as Independent Republics. *The Journal of Negro History* 2(4): 369–383..

Williams, Eric. 1994. *Capitalism & Slavery.* Chapel Hill/London: The University of North Carolina Press.

Websites

http://www.africanfilmny.org/2014/a-report-on-the-world-conference-against-racism-racial-discrimination-xenophobia-and-related-intolerance-2/
http://www.hougansydney.com/haiti-national-anthem.php
https://www.humanrights.gov.au/publications/un-declaration-rights-indigenous-peoples-1

Open Access This chapter is licensed under the terms of the Creative Commons Attribution 4.0 International License (http://creativecommons.org/licenses/by/4.0/), which permits use, sharing, adaptation, distribution and reproduction in any medium or format, as long as you give appropriate credit to the original author(s) and the source, provide a link to the Creative Commons license and indicate if changes were made.

The images or other third party material in this chapter are included in the chapter's Creative Commons license, unless indicated otherwise in a credit line to the material. If material is not included in the chapter's Creative Commons license and your intended use is not permitted by statutory regulation or exceeds the permitted use, you will need to obtain permission directly from the copyright holder.

PART V

Postscript

CHAPTER 12

Postscript

Sian Lazar

The chapters in this volume assess the state of inequalities in Latin America today, in the context of the interplay between recent attempts by the Pink Tide (PT) regimes to tackle inequality and the deep divisions within Latin American societies since colonisation. Together, they show how inequalities intersect, as income inequality and class interact with gendered and racialised inequalities, and are expressed in spatial distinctions and associations of some communities or categories of persons with crime and violence. These 'entangled inequalities' (Costa, Chap. 3, this volume) are complex to analyse, not least because the ethnographic approach taken by most of the contributors seeks to explain how these intersections play out in the relation between experience ('lifeworld') and structural economic conditions, which of course change over time.

One of the orienting questions is an evaluation of how PT regimes dealt with poverty and inequality. They are of course not the same thing, but the signs are quite good on both fronts, as Pedro Mendes Loureiro argues in his survey piece, and Sergio Costa and Iselin Åsedotter Strønen for Brazil and Venezuela, respectively. Significant strides were made, to the point that analysts now debate not whether these regimes achieved reductions in poverty and inequality, but to what extent can those reductions be

S. Lazar (✉)
University of Cambridge, Cambridge, UK

© The Author(s) 2018
M. Ystanes, I.Å. Strønen (eds.), *The Social Life of Economic Inequalities in Contemporary Latin America*, Approaches to Social Inequality and Difference, DOI 10.1007/978-3-319-61536-3_12

attributed to state policy, rather than (just) to economic growth, and the related problem of how sustainable they are likely to be in the longer term. The jury is still out, but as the editors say in their introduction, the outlook is sobering.

For Mendes Loureiro, state actions were effective and influential, and he points especially to the rise in living standards due to Conditional Cash Transfers (CCTs) and rising minimum wages. The latter is related to increased formalisation of the economy, but is also thought to have a knock-on effect on employment in the informal sector. Neither of these policies are especially anti-neoliberal, but nor should they be dismissed too lightly. For Mendes Loureiro, PT governments used a positive international scenario—high commodity prices—to finance social goals, and as such they made some important gains in the fight against inequality. Sergio Costa agrees at least partially, and he gives some impressive numbers for Brazil, showing increases in employment, formal employment and social policy expenditure, along with reductions in poverty rates and a decline in the GINI inequality coefficient over the years of the Lula-Rousseff regimes of the PT. However, he suggests that the consensus for Brazil at least is that this was due more to economic processes rather than social policy.

If correct, this is a problem because it makes reductions in inequality highly vulnerable to changes in economic and political conditions. As is well known, the downturn in the commodity super cycle from about 2011 onwards left PT governments with less income to spend on social programmes. In the absence of policies for actual wealth redistribution, that inevitably had consequences for tackling inequalities. With high incomes from healthy commodity prices, governments had been able to spend more on social programmes—principally CCTs, but also housing, infrastructure and other welfare projects. However, that expenditure is vulnerable to shifting governmental priorities, reduced budgets and erosion of value through inflation. Costa argues that increased state spending is not the same as redistribution of wealth, and that different fiscal policies would have had a greater redistributive effect, and hence a more dramatic and longer-term effect on reducing inequality.

Specifically, he discusses taxation reform. Latin American tax regimes are highly regressive, because they focus on taxation of consumption; if taxes on higher incomes and on capital and financial profits were set at more European levels, Brazil's GINI coefficient could reduce by about 20%, we are told. This is shocking. Outside of Scandinavia, European taxation levels are hardly radically redistributive. Yet even in quite low taxation regimes such as the UK, the GINI coefficient changes significantly after taxation: in 2013, it was quite close to Brazilian levels before taxation, at 0.527, while after, it was 0.358[1]. Nonetheless, even mildly progressive legislation was not politically possible in Brazil, even under a PT regime. Across the region, governments have found themselves constricted in what they can do to confront inequality, even if they wanted to: Evo Morales, for example, struggled against well-funded and well-organised resistance from lowland elites until he signalled that he would set aside plans for land reform in the eastern region of Bolivia. Celina Sørbø argues that the successful impeachment process against Dilma Rousseff was a conservative counter-reaction to the challenge to entrenched inequalities represented by the PT regimes in Brazil. In Venezuela, that opposition was articulated through nastily racist discourses, as Iselin Åsedotter Strønen documents.

This hints at one of the most important reasons for the limits within which PT and other regimes had to operate, namely the deeply embedded divisions within society, which are conceptualised in this collection as intersecting inequalities, or 'entangled inequalities' in Costa's words. All of the contributions one way or another outline the complex social life of these entangled inequalities, as class divisions between poor and wealthy intersect with topographical divisions of urban space, gender inequalities, violence, generation and race. The chapters on Rio show how the division between the *morro* (hill) and the *asfalto* (street) justifies differential access to and militarisation of urban space. As Margit Ystanes points out, the association of the *morro* with the *favela* and with drugs is matched by an association of the state with whiteness and violence, envisaged as protecting the wealthy (white) areas of the *asfalto* from the dangerous dark *favela* residents. In state discourse, this is resignified as 'accelerated development' for the sake of the 2014 FIFA World Cup and the 2016 Olympics. She argues that this in fact reversed some of the gains of PT social policy—as state expenditure on a specific version of urban space for the mega-events diverted funds from public services. For the poor, that meant resentment, but also fear, prompted by the highly militarised nature of this 'development'.

That said, the topographical distribution of wealth and poverty in Rio is not quite as straightforward as a *morro-asfalto* distinction, as Michele de Lavra Pinto shows in her study of attitudes to the most famous CCT programme in the region, the *Bolsa Familia*. Although the poorest live higher up the hill, the *favela* displays complex class differentiation internally, nowadays very much associated with car ownership and other forms of consumption. Here, we see some of the strides made by the PT governments, as people have a sense of coming out of poverty and aspiring to a more middle-class lifestyle.

Nonetheless, topographies and urban spaces are inflected with understandings of violence, crime and the appropriate state response to such social problems. The *favela* is seen as dangerous, and therefore it is acceptable for the police to sweep in, engage in gunfights with local gangs and plant the Brazilian flag in a highly symbolic act of conquest of this space understood as dark, violent and criminal. The criminals they find—and sometimes kill—are poor, dark-skinned, young and male. Honduras is a little different, and Lirio Gutiérrez Rivera et al. outline how the development of *mano dura* (iron fist) security policies has affected young men from poor neighbourhoods, many of whom now spend 7–15 years of their lives in prison. While men from wealthier families can pay for their court trials to proceed without delays, poorer men must spend months or years in jail waiting for their sentence; and youths are picked up by police on cues such as their clothing, tattoos or skin colour. This is social policy as penalisation of young, dark-skinned men, and although its full effects are yet unknown, the signs are deeply worrying. Gutiérrez Rivera et al. argue that the prisoners cannot transition from youths to adults, precisely because the penal regime is so punitive. They have no access to educational programmes or other forms of rehabilitation. According to the general public, perhaps they do not deserve such treatment. But what will happen when they complete their sentence? What will be the outcome of this punitive turn, which has targeted a whole generation of men?

The entanglement of class inequality with inequalities of gender, topography and race has a long history, as the editors of this volume point out in their introduction. Marvin Brown describes the region's deep colonial history of invasion and slavery, and the effects of that on landholding and territory. That history of conquest underlies most of the inequalities discussed in this volume, but emerges in complex ways. In Venezuela, it has contemporary expression in a discourse of civilisation versus savagery from the opposition to the Chávez and Maduro regimes. Iselin Åsedotter Strønen documents a real schism between the 'Americanised' upper classes, who see themselves as modern, global and civilised, and subaltern struggles for alternative political conceptualisations of the relation between market, state and society. For the upper classes, the poor are barefooted lumpen hordes; and this disdain was frequently expressed in racialised insults directed at Chávez, whom they attacked as 'monkey'. Subaltern political agency was delegitimised by these discourses that saw chavistas as duped masses, resentful of the civilised wealthy and seeking power and resources that they had no right to.

But oppression or exploitation modelled on colonial (or capitalist) relations is not inevitable; rather, it is the result of political will and specific choices. Astrid Stensrud describes a project of land reform begun in Southern Peru in the 1970s, following the progressive military regime of Velasco Alvarado. The Majes irrigation project has attracted immigrants from the highland region of Puno, leading to ethnicised tensions between mestizo Peruvians from the coast and Aymara-Quechua Peruvians from the highlands. This is exacerbated by the ways that the distribution of the irrigated land has changed over the years. At first, in the early 1980s, land was sold to families in 5 hectare plots; in the upcoming expansion, the plots available for sale will be 200, 500 and 1000 hectares (current price per 5 hectare is 400 000 US dollars). It is clear that the prospects for the children of the first generation of immigrants do not lie in farming their own land; rather, they can only be wage labourers, at best educated technicians, at worst day labourers. They compete with new immigrants from the highlands, who have contributed to remarkable population growth in the area over the last few decades.

Policy decisions about how to regulate the economy are also central to Cecilie Vindal Ødegaard's chapter, which shows how changes in free trade agreements affect informal vendors in Arequipa, Peru. A trade promotion agreement signed by Peru with the USA in 2006, and ratified in 2009, has meant that Peruvian authorities have attempted to formalise economic activities via checkpoints and control over commodity flows at the borders. The 2009 trade agreement between Peru and China put small-scale vendors in competition with large-scale actors who can now import Chinese goods legally through Lima. The vendors in Arequipa who used to move goods between Bolivia, Chile and Peru are therefore subject to increased competition and border checks, which have led them to reduce the amounts of stock they bring across, and diversify their investment strategies, including into more risky ventures. This has a gendered effect as the small-scale vendors are in the majority women, in contrast to the large business owners benefitting from reduced controls on Chinese imports. The trade agreements are economic arrangements negotiated at very high levels of government; but for all this, they are by no means inevitable.

Politicians could have decided to negotiate free trade agreements differently, or to continue the allocation of irrigated land in Majes in small family plots. They could have developed alternative security policies in Honduras to address increases in urban crime, or a more progressive taxation regime in Brazil. They could have decided to make Rio ready for the recent mega-events in ways that took into account the views of the *favela* inhabitants. Inequalities of class, race and gender are deeply entrenched and historically embedded, but their emergence in and through state policy is the result of political decisions.

The inequalities are, then, both inevitable and not, both structural and the outcome of particular decision-making processes. And so, in the face of this, how do the subaltern subjects respond? All of the chapters in this volume answer that question to some extent, demonstrating one of the advantages of an ethnographic approach that seeks to document lifeworlds in the context of structural economic conditions. We see how people live their lives, as entrepreneurs in 'neoliberal' modes, or as educated professionals, as in the chapters by Cecilie Vindal Ødegaard (Chap. 8), Astrid Stensrud (Chap. 10) and Michele de Lavra Pinto (Chap. 6). People borrow money to set up a business, buy land or buy a car to travel between two jobs; they cross borders with smuggled goods hidden under their own clothes, and dress as either tourists or poor farmer women to disguise their lucrative endeavours. They encourage their children to go to school and university, to become engineers and technicians rather than day labourers. They negotiate the entangled inequalities in which they find themselves, and make the best of it.

They also resist. Margit Ystanes describes the development of subaltern counterpublics through citizen media projects from the *favelas* that denounce police violence and forced evictions in social media. Iselin Åsedotter Strønen argues that popular mobilisation under Chávez created a 'Bolivarian political space' comprised of popular appropriation of the state's pro-poor political alignment. Pedro Mendes Loureiro highlights the neo-corporatist incorporation of social movements by PT governments, giving the example of Argentina under the Kirchners. There, the *piquetero* organisations so prominent in the anti-neoliberal uprisings of the turn of the century were 'absorbed' into the state as channels for the distribution of some social policy programmes. Why not? he asks. For the government, when money is available from increased export revenue, 'why attempt a larger overhaul of macroeconomic policies if there had been growth and this would require confronting powerful interests?' (Mendes Loureiro). The social movements took pragmatic decisions to cooperate: why seek to be any more radical if neo-corporatism has delivered wage gains? The interesting aspect of this will be to see what happens now, after the election of the right-wing Mauricio Macri in late 2015. The signs from the first two years of his government are that the social movements, including the *piqueteros*, are reluctant to give up the gains of the Kirchner years.

As I write this postscript in April 2017, the PT is ebbing. With the exception of Ecuador, where Lenin Moreno recently won the presidential election, the more radical ALBA[2] states look vulnerable. Economic and political troubles in Venezuela become more acute every day, and tensions are also rising in Bolivia, as Evo Morales seeks to extend his presidential reign beyond constitutional provisions. The Right gained power electorally or by parliamentary coup in 2015–2016 in Argentina, Brazil and Peru. We are facing a new wave of neoliberal or rightist regimes across the region, and consequently we are facing the reaction of those who suffer the effects of such regimes. The true test of the PT will be whether progress on fighting inequality has meant a shift in terms of debate, such that some economic and social policies—for example, repeal of CCTs—are simply not politically possible, because subaltern subjects will not allow them. In Argentina, social movements that were re-empowered during the Kirchner years are repeatedly filling the streets to protest budget cuts and the authorities' refusal to negotiate salary increases in line with inflation. On 6 April 2017, Argentina's main union federation, the CGT,[3] held its first full-blown strike as a unified body in more than 10 years. Latin America has a long history of entrenched inequalities, but it also has a long history of resistance to inequality, both collective and individual. The balance of power between oppression and resistance has characterised economic and political life for centuries, and seems likely to do so for years to come.

Notes

1. OECD. Stat http://stats.oecd.org/index.aspx?queryid=66670; retrieved 4 April 2017.
2. Bolivarian Alliance of the Americas; the main ALBA countries are Venezuela, Bolivia, Ecuador and Cuba.
3. Confederación General del Trabajo; General Confederation of Labour, the body that coordinates most of the traditional trade unions in the country.

Open Access This chapter is licensed under the terms of the Creative Commons Attribution 4.0 International License (http://creativecommons.org/licenses/by/4.0/), which permits use, sharing, adaptation, distribution and reproduction in any medium or format, as long as you give appropriate credit to the original author(s) and the source, provide a link to the Creative Commons license and indicate if changes were made.

The images or other third party material in this chapter are included in the chapter's Creative Commons license, unless indicated otherwise in a credit line to the material. If material is not included in the chapter's Creative Commons license and your intended use is not permitted by statutory regulation or exceeds the permitted use, you will need to obtain permission directly from the copyright holder.

Index[1]

A

Activism, 84, 86, 87, 95, 99
Activism-as-journalism, 29, 84–88
Affirmative action, 60, 75, 108, 121
Alternative media, 85, 96, 98
Argentina, 12, 15, 17, 19, 22, 25, 26, 35, 36, 40, 47, 65, 159, 280, 281
Atlantic, 254, 255, 269
  trade, 254, 255
Austerity politics, 4, 99

B

Barrios, 158, 160, 162, 163, 217
Bolívar, Simón, 165
Bolivarian/ism, 24, 28, 153–156, 159–163, 168, 173, 174, 177, 220
Bolivia, 15, 19, 22, 24, 25, 42, 47, 48, 185, 189, 190, 192, 198, 199, 277, 279, 281, 281n2
Bolsa Familia programme (BFP), 5, 25, 70, 71, 100, 120, 129, 130, 132–135, 138, 139, 143–145
Borders, 14, 23, 59, 110, 185, 190, 191, 193, 196–199, 201, 279, 280
Brazil, 5, 7, 8, 12, 16, 17, 22, 25, 26, 29, 36, 42, 46, 59, 76n4, 83, 84, 86, 87, 93, 98–100, 107–109, 111–113, 119–123, 206, 208, 221, 258, 260, 275–277, 280, 281

C

Capital accumulation, 18, 39
Capitalism
  class, 18, 155
  critique of, 14
  effects of, 18
  gender, 234
  inequality, 8, 21, 38, 232
  neoliberalism, 19, 161, 162

---

[1] Note: Page numbers followed by "n" refers notes.

Caracas, 28, 158, 160, 162, 165, 169, 172, 178n6
Caracazo, el, 16, 158, 162, 163, 167, 168
Cardoso, Fernando Henrique, 16, 71, 131
Catholic, 10, 111, 209, 210
CEPAL, 12, 40, 66
Chávez, Hugo, 4, 16, 21, 22, 25, 28, 153, 155, 156, 158–164, 168–170, 172–175, 177, 178, 178n1, 178n5, 209, 278–280
Chile, 16–18, 22, 35, 185, 189, 192, 194, 195, 198, 199, 279
China, 18, 113, 185, 198, 199, 279
Citizenship, 11, 61, 63, 74, 107, 109, 111, 115, 118–121, 123, 232
Class
  conflict, 49, 121, 167, 169
  inequality, 3, 49, 75, 83, 154, 157, 246–248, 278, 280
  poverty, 157, 178n3
  race, 3, 7, 65, 73, 153, 164–167, 169, 177, 184, 189, 191, 200, 214, 232, 235, 241, 246, 278
  struggle, 18, 19, 38, 108, 122
Coletivo Papo Reto (the Straight Talk Collective), 81–83, 85–87, 95, 98, 99
Colonialism
  class, 153, 213, 234
  gender, 28, 210
  inequality, 9–11, 63, 89, 153–178
  race, 9
  racisim, 11, 28, 63, 89, 153, 205, 210, 214
  violence, 89
Commodities, 4, 8, 21, 36, 38–40, 42, 49, 50, 67, 68, 191, 197, 198, 256, 261, 265, 266, 276, 279
Commodities export, 36, 39, 40, 49, 50
Conditional cash transfer (CCT) programme, 36–38, 42, 45, 47, 49, 50, 99, 130, 143, 276, 277, 281
Consumption, 8, 21, 26, 69, 75n3, 98, 120, 121, 174, 185, 188, 216, 221, 276, 278
Corruption, 15, 36, 107, 118, 119, 155, 157, 178n2, 178n3, 236
Coup, 16, 17, 25, 36, 65, 146n2, 159, 160, 163, 170, 210, 220, 223, 224n4, 237, 281
Crimes, 27, 82, 113, 117, 120, 172, 206–208, 211–216, 220, 222, 223, 259, 265, 275, 278, 280
Cuba, 9, 10, 171, 257, 281n2

D
Debt crisis, 38
Debts, 13, 18, 121, 157, 231, 232, 239, 240, 245, 246, 259, 261, 264–266
Deindustrialization, 38, 68, 75n2
Dependency, 12, 239
  theory, 11–13
Developmentalism, 12, 13, 174, 177
Division of labour, 191, 256, 265
Drug trafficking, 27, 82, 85, 89–91, 110, 111, 221
Dutch disease, 39, 40

E
Economic growth, 15, 18, 42, 65, 66, 68, 72, 73, 83, 100, 184, 235, 249, 265, 276
Economic redistribution, 119
Ecuador, 15, 19, 22, 25, 214, 281, 281n2
Entrepreneurial governance, 113, 118
Ethnicity, 3, 7, 60, 65, 153, 234, 259
Europe, 9, 11, 69, 194, 253–256, 263, 265, 266
Exchange rates, 40, 76n3
Exploitation, 20, 141, 167, 243, 254, 256, 279

F

Facebook, 81–83, 85, 96, 98, 99
Favela
  vs. "the asphalt", 91, 100, 139
  community, 85, 94
  Complexo do Alemão, 92, 95, 98
  Pavão Pavãozinho, 134, 138, 141–145, 146n1
  Rocinha, 27, 28, 101n3, 108–111, 113–120, 122, 123
  Vila Autódromo, 92, 93, 96–98
FIFA World Cup 2014, 26, 29n1, 81, 83–86, 89, 108, 113, 140, 277
Forced removals, 84, 87, 96, 110
Formal economy, 21, 27, 28, 91, 117, 184, 186, 200, 211, 232, 246
Free trade, 11, 16, 17, 22, 232, 238
  agreements, 184, 198, 199, 201, 279, 280
Friedman, Milton, 16, 17, 130, 146n2
Fujimori, Alberto, 183, 186, 187, 194, 201, 237–239, 250n2

G

GDP, 39, 45, 66, 69, 71, 73, 75n2, 211
Gender, 3, 8, 20, 21, 28, 60, 63, 65–68, 71, 73, 75, 153, 169, 183–201, 210, 214, 232, 234, 246–248, 275, 277–280
Gentrification, 84, 91–93, 140
Gini coefficient, 41, 66, 68–71, 276, 277
Gini index, 41, 59
Globo Media Group, 87, 99
Growth
  economic, 15, 18, 42, 65, 66, 68, 83, 100, 184, 235, 249, 265, 276
  rates, 18, 36, 38, 40, 43, 45, 49, 51n2, 73
Guatemala, 20, 22

H

Haiti, 253, 254, 260, 262–266
  revolution, 262, 263, 265
Hegemony, 23, 168, 173, 177
Hierarchies
  racial, 11, 153, 205, 246
  social, 20, 65, 242
Honduras, 4, 5, 22, 26, 29, 205–224, 278, 280
Humala, Ollanta, 22, 184, 232, 238, 239, 249

I

Ideologies
  leftist, 22, 156, 257
  racial, 164, 166
Import Substitution Industrialization (ISI), 11, 14
Incomes, 8, 18, 36, 41, 42, 59, 61, 64, 66, 67, 69–71, 73, 75, 75–76n3, 76n4, 114, 115, 120, 122, 130, 133–139, 141, 143–145, 146n13, 187, 190, 191, 193, 198, 200, 216, 218, 237, 238, 240, 264, 269, 275, 276
Inequalities
  economic, 26–29, 100, 119, 232
  entangled, 4, 59–75, 275, 277, 278, 280
  entrenched, 29, 84, 108, 111, 119, 172, 223, 277, 280, 281
  horizontal, 62
  intersectional, 62, 65, 75
  layered, 63
  persistent, 62–64, 86, 101
  power, 61, 62, 65, 70, 74, 83
  racial, 63, 66, 71, 75, 89, 205, 275
  reduction, 60, 66, 67, 70, 74, 75, 83, 109, 275, 276
  regimes, 28, 63, 64, 220, 275, 276

Inequalities (*cont.*)
  social, 59–62, 65, 70, 231–249
  socio-economic, 15, 25, 61, 62, 89, 163, 220, 222
Informal labour, 188, 189
Informal vendors, 21, 279
Infrastructure projects, 28, 92, 93, 115, 116, 139, 276
Iron fist, 206, 208, 214, 223, 278

L
Labour, 11, 14, 17, 20, 24, 28, 35, 38, 41–43, 45, 47, 49, 50, 66, 67, 73, 93, 110, 158, 186–191, 193, 207, 211, 216, 218, 219, 223, 232, 234, 238, 239, 242, 243, 246, 247, 249, 254–256, 263, 265, 279
  movement, 18
Lands
  access to, 5, 21, 61, 83, 84, 92–94, 99, 234, 277
  as commons, 29, 266–269
  landless, 111, 235, 257, 258
  as location, 267
  meaning of, 257, 261, 268
  ownership, 187, 201, 209, 234, 237, 243, 244, 257, 258, 267–269
  as property, 112, 170, 221, 237, 238, 243, 245, 258, 267–269
  reforms, 159, 231, 234, 236, 237, 249, 257–259, 277, 279
  social function, 112, 258, 259, 265
  value of, 28, 29, 266, 267, 269
Landscapes
  social, 28, 96, 123, 166
  urban, 29, 84, 88, 100, 120
Legacy, of sporting mega-events, 86
Liberalization, 183, 237
Lost decade, 15

Lula da Silva, Luiz Inácio, 66, 92, 100, 108, 112, 132, 139, 146n3
Lulismo, 112, 120, 121

M
Market, 6, 8, 13–16, 21, 27, 28, 35, 37, 38, 41–45, 50, 52n5, 66, 67, 87, 93, 112, 117, 119, 122, 176, 183–201, 207, 211, 216, 218, 219, 223, 231, 232, 236–240, 246, 247, 249, 255, 261, 265, 267, 268, 278
  capitalism, 176
Mass media, 86, 88, 99–101
Mestizaje, 164
Mestizo, 60, 64, 72, 164, 184, 234, 245, 248, 249, 279
Migration, 186, 207, 211, 236, 255
Militarisation, 4, 5, 26, 83, 84, 94, 277
Military, 17, 84, 88, 93, 94, 111, 146n2, 158, 166, 186, 209, 210, 215–217, 221, 224n3, 234, 279
Military police, 26, 81, 82, 85, 90, 94
Minimum wage, 20, 37, 41–43, 45, 49, 50, 65, 68, 70, 72, 73, 75, 76n3, 99, 108, 114, 120, 209, 276
Modernity, 12, 75n1, 153
Morales, Evo, 22, 42, 277, 281
Morar Carioca, 113

N
Neo-corporativism, 49, 50, 281
Neo-extractivism, 37–40, 49, 50
Neoliberal/ism
  class, 18, 43, 49, 50, 212, 213
  dictatorship, 17
  economic reforms, 15, 122, 200, 210, 211, 218, 242
  elites, 14, 18, 23, 175, 211

inequality, 18, 19, 28, 41, 49, 94, 154, 158, 183, 207, 280, 281
International Monetary Fund (IMF), 157, 158
policies, 4, 15, 16, 18, 28, 94, 158, 184, 207, 213, 224n2, 238, 246, 265
poverty, 18, 25, 41, 49, 207, 212, 213, 221
social movements, 18
state, 42, 43, 208, 212, 213
Washington Consensus, 14, 237
World Bank, 38, 45

O
OECD, 69
Oil, 8, 25, 68, 155–157, 159, 160, 166, 170, 175
Olympic Games 2016, 26, 81, 83–85, 88, 89, 92, 99, 100, 107, 108, 113, 140, 277
Organized labour, 51n4

P
Pacification, 26–28, 90, 91, 94–96, 100, 116–118
Paraguay, 22, 25, 26, 65
Peasants
  gender, 63, 246
  land reforms, 159, 236, 249
  markets, 244, 249
  poverty, 234–236, 245, 249, 265
Penalty system, 205–224
Penitentiary system, 206, 215, 217
Peru, 187, 189, 190, 194, 197–201, 231–237, 239, 242, 246, 279, 281
Pink Tide, 4–8, 16, 21–29, 35, 60, 65, 66, 69, 74, 83, 84, 92, 99, 100, 107, 130, 144, 145, 154, 156, 176, 178, 184, 206, 208–210, 221, 232, 238, 257, 275
Pinochet, Augusto, 16, 17

Police, 26, 27, 47, 82, 86, 87, 90, 91, 93–95, 100, 110, 111, 115–120, 122, 123, 185, 195–197, 213, 215–217, 221, 222, 244, 269, 278, 280
Populism, 178n5, 235
Populist, 22, 167, 237, 257
Poverty
  inequality, 15, 17, 25, 35, 41, 45, 65–68, 71, 83, 84, 89, 94, 109, 119, 130, 141, 145, 157, 184, 221, 275
  neoliberalism, 24
  race, 153, 184
Prisons
  class, 213
  gender, 214, 278
  reforms, 218
  violence, 17, 206, 220, 223, 278
Privatisation, 14, 15, 26, 43, 68, 117, 122, 211
Program of Accelerated Growth (PAC), 113–115, 118, 119, 122, 123, 139
Public spheres, 85–88, 99, 111, 169, 193, 214

Q
Quilombo communities, 27, 260–262, 265
Quotas at federal universities, 70–72

R
Race, 234
  class, 3, 7, 73, 166, 169, 184, 189, 191, 200, 214, 232, 235, 241, 246, 280
  colonialism, 9
  gender, 3, 8, 60, 63, 65, 67, 68, 73, 75, 169, 184, 189, 191, 200, 214, 232, 246, 280

Race (cont.)
  indigenous, 20, 62, 163, 184, 214, 234, 255
  inequality, 9–11, 60, 68, 73, 191, 232, 246–248, 278, 280
  neoliberalism, 184, 200, 232
  racism, 20, 164
Racism, 20, 63, 72, 75, 85, 89, 95, 164, 177, 214, 233, 234, 256, 259
Redistribution, 5, 8, 24, 63, 67, 68, 70, 72, 73, 109, 115, 130, 154, 177, 257, 276
Reparations, 5, 29, 253–269
Right-wing
  economic policies, 4
  politics, 4, 23, 26
Rio de Janeiro, 4, 5, 25, 62, 81, 107, 129–146
Rousseff, Dilma
  impeachment, 68, 74, 99, 102n5, 133, 277

S
São Conrado, 107–110, 116, 122, 123
Securitization, 221, 223
Slavery
  enslavement, 254, 256
  slaves, 9, 11, 27, 89, 255, 256, 260, 262, 263
Social media, 29, 83, 85, 86, 94–96, 99, 101, 101n3, 120, 280
Social movements, 5, 18, 23, 37, 38, 44, 46–49, 51n4, 87, 89, 94, 111, 160, 249, 280, 281
Social structures, 28, 63–65, 261, 267
Social welfare, 23, 25, 122, 135, 140, 153, 159
Sporting mega-events, 5, 83, 86

State
  colonial, 10, 11, 60, 89, 169, 234
  intervention, 68–73, 91
  power, 38, 39, 42–45
  reforms, 249
  violence, 82, 83
Street protests, 85
Structural adjustment policies, 13
Subaltern counterpublic, 84, 86, 94–99, 280

T
Tax system, 8, 69, 70, 74, 267
Temer, Michel, 26, 68, 71, 72, 74, 75, 99, 122, 145, 261
Twitter, 85, 98

U
Unemployment, 15, 18, 19, 25, 35, 41, 66, 121, 133, 207, 218, 237
Unidades de Polícia Pacificadora (UPPs), 90
United States of America (USA), 13, 17, 18, 22, 97, 169, 194, 197, 198, 206, 207, 210, 212, 213, 219, 222, 224n4, 238, 254, 255, 257, 259, 262–265, 279
Urban
  development, 5, 84, 88–91, 100, 107
  informality, 42, 109
Utopias, 23

V
Venezuela, 7, 8, 12, 16, 19, 22, 24, 25, 29, 35, 42, 153, 206, 209, 220, 221, 275, 277, 278, 281, 281n2

Violence, 17, 19, 27, 47, 81–101, 113, 116, 122, 123, 144, 158, 162, 163, 167, 175, 206–208, 210, 212, 215, 216, 220–223, 223–224n1, 243, 261, 265, 275, 277, 278, 280

W

War on Drugs, 208, 210, 223
Welfare programmes, 25
  in Brazil, 130–133
Whatsapp, 85, 96, 98
Women
  inequality, 193, 249
  labour, 73, 187, 193, 214, 280
  race, 62, 73, 184, 214
  struggle, 192
Workers Party Brazil (Partido dos Trabalhadores)
  PT administration, 68, 70, 71, 74
  PT government, 121, 122, 276, 278, 280
World Bank, 38, 45, 59, 69, 137, 237, 265

Z

Zelaya, Manuel, 22, 25, 36, 208, 209

The manufacturer's authorised representative in the EU is Springer Nature Customer Service Centre GmbH, Europaplatz 3, 69115 Heidelberg, Germany. If you have any concerns regarding our products, please contact ProductSafety@springernature.com

Printed and bound by CPI Group (UK) Ltd, Croydon, CR0 4YY
23/03/2026
02076667-0007